# *A Treasured Inheritance*

# A Treasured Inheritance

## 600 YEARS OF OXFORD COLLEGE SILVER

HELEN M. CLIFFORD

ASHMOLEAN MUSEUM, OXFORD

2004

## A Treasured Inheritance at the Ashmolean Museum, Oxford

16th June–19th September 2004

Copyright © Ashmolean Museum, University of Oxford 2004

Helen Clifford has asserted her moral right to be identified as the author of this work

British Library Cataloguing in Publication Data

A catalogue record for this book is available from the British Library

ISBN 1 85444 195 7

Catalogue designed by Rhian Lonergan-White
Typeset in Garamond and Cochin

Printed and bound in the United Kingdom by Cambridge University Press, 2004

# *The* Ashmolean

Cover: **5** Standing Salt, silver parcel-gilt and painted, crystal lid, *c.*1400–50. All Souls.

Frontispiece: **142** University Chest, or the 'Chest of the Five Keys', iron-bound wood, 17th century. Corpus Christi. On loan to the Ashmolean Museum.

Facing title page: A servitor, from R. Ackermann, *History of the University of Oxford: its Colleges, Halls and Public Buildings*, 1814.

Back cover: **25** Paten, silver-gilt, London 1527–8, given by Sir Thomas Pope to Trinity.

# CONTENTS

Numbers in bold in the text and captions
refer to the Catalogue on pp. 136–151.

# ACKNOWLEDGEMENTS

This project began with Timothy Wilson's inspired idea to look at the rich vein of documentation in the Oxford colleges connected with their silver, a largely untapped primary source of information. Funding from the Leverhulme Trust turned the idea into reality, and I was fortunate to be invited to take the project on. I thank the staff in the Department of Western Art at the Ashmolean for their warm welcome. I spent my days between looking at silver with butlers in butteries, and with college archivists tracking centuries of housekeeping records. I am warmly grateful to Balliol, New College, and Hertford, for providing me with SCR Fellowships, helping me see life from the inside out, as well as from the outside in.

Turning the academic project into an exhibition has been possible through the generosity of the sponsors named in the Director's preface. I am particularly indebted to Brian Wilson, an ex-Pembroke man who was the first to offer sponsorship and shared with me his extensive research on his college's silver, and his enthusiasm for commissioning new silver. The Whiteley Trust's timely generosity secured the staging of the exhibition and publication of this book and I thank the executors of the late Mrs Corinne Whiteley and especially Michael Gettleson, to whom English silver studies owe so much.

From the Ashmolean I would like to thank Timothy Wilson, Sarah Brown, Graeme Campbell, Rhian Lonergan-White, Geraldine Glynn, Clare Farrah, Chezzy Brownen, Katherine Dallas and Sabrina Shim; David Gowers and the Photography team; conservators Mark Norman, Elisabeth Gardner, Stephanie Ward, and Karen Wilson; Declan McCarthy in Publications, and particularly Julie Summers, Exhibitions Officer. Our expert advisers Michael Burden, Marian Campbell, John Culme, Clive Ellory, Philippa Glanville, and Timothy Schroder have provided inspiration and guidance. Timothy Schroder, Brian Wilson, and Timothy Wilson commented on drafts of the catalogue; and Sarah-Louise Wilkinson provided much assistance of all sorts. Mistakes are entirely my responsibility. I would also like to thank the silversmiths Rod Kelly, Jenny Edge, and Peter Musson.

From the colleges there are many to thank, from All Souls, N.A.R. Potter and T.W. Seaman; from Balliol, Andrew Graham, John Jones, Jasper Griffin, Penny Bulloch, and Alan Tadiello; from Brasenose, W.G. Richards, Elizabeth Boardman, and Alan Bennett; from Christ Church, Judith Curthoys, Edward Evans, Oliver O'Donovan, Millins Palaywi, and Janet McMullin; from Corpus Christi, Clive Ellory, Colin Holmes, Julian Reid; from Exeter, E.M. Bennet and John Maddicott, Mrs Topliffe, and Susan Marshall; from Green, Sir J. Hanson, Oliver Impey, and Gerald Chambers; from Hertford, Toby Barnard and Kenny Lewis; from Jesus, Peter J. Clarke, David Rees, Sara Cobbold, and Ellis Evans; from Keble, Mrs Sarosi and Janet Betts; from Lady Margaret Hall, Julie Courtenay and Allan Doig; from Lincoln, Tim Knowles, Rachel King, Mrs Piddock, Andrew Mussell, Alice Gosling, and Kevin Egleston; from Magdalen, Tony Smith, Jane Cottis, Terry Newport and Ted Donohoe; from Merton, Richard McCabe and John Gloag; from New College, Michael Burden, Caroline Dalton and Nigel Halsey; from Nuffield, Mr Porter and Mrs Vallis; from Oriel Mike Stephens, Yvonne Scott, and Elizabeth Boardman; from Pembroke, Dan Prentice, Brian Wilson, and Ellena Pike; from Queen's, John Kaye, Linda Irving-Bell, and Mr Heath; from St Anne's, R.S. Saunders and Sarah Oakley; from St Catherine's, Mr Bennett; from St Cross, John Tobin, Derek Roe, and Sarah Dickson; from St Edmund Hall, Geoffrey Bourne-Taylor and R. Crampton; from St Hilda's, Ms Clewlow and Mr Needle; from St John's, M.G.A. Vale, Gordon Baker, Paul Craig, and Michael Riordaen; from St Peter's, Clendon Daukes; from Trinity, C. Hopkins and David Mills; from University College, Robin Darwell-Smith, Christine Ritchie, and Elizabeth Crawford; from Wadham, Stephen Tucker and M.P. Sauvage; from Wolfson, Stuart McKerrow; and from Worcester, J.H. Parker and Emma Pennington.

Thanks also to Ann Ashby, Simon Bailey, Ann Hansen, John Lange, Peter, and Judy Payne, and Sarah Boada-Momtahan. Too many other people have helped to be named here; they know who they are and have my gratitude.

Helen Clifford

# PREFACE

For centuries before the British Museum was dreamt of, the University of Oxford, its libraries and its colleges, some dating back to the thirteenth century, represented institutional permanence in England; and the collections accumulated and preserved in Oxford colleges since the Middle Ages are an important part of the nation's cultural inheritance. The Ashmolean Museum's own collections have a pedigree unrivalled in the United Kingdom, dating back to the arrival of Elias Ashmole's collections in Oxford in 1683, and before that to 'Tradescant's Ark', the great Cabinet of Natural and Artificial Curiosities assembled in Lambeth in the first half of the seventeenth century by the Tradescants, father and son, Royal gardeners and avid collectors both. Oxford colleges fiercely preserve their independence and the ownership of the collections that have been built up by gift over the centuries, but it is part of the mission of the modern Ashmolean to be the showcase of the University as a whole, and to provide public access to works of art which have in the past been accessible only to insiders and privileged visitors. Not since 1928 has a comprehensive exhibition of silver from Oxford colleges been mounted, though an exhibition of plate from Cambridge colleges was last held in our sister institution the Fitzwilliam in 1975.

The silver held in the colleges is a wonderful historical survival and includes a substantial proportion of the greatest works of the goldsmith's art from the Middle Ages onwards that survive in England; as a whole there are few cities in Europe that have comparable holdings. This has been preserved because it has been regarded as integrally connected with the history and institutional identity of colleges, as it still is. It is part of the ritual that binds present-day Oxford colleges to their past, as when historic medieval and later goldsmith's work is put on high tables at college ceremonies. Furthermore, the tradition of commissioning new works of art in silver is alive, and several colleges have been enabled by the generosity of old members to commission works by some of the leading silversmiths of recent times. This close and continuing connection to institutional life and identity means that the silver is accompanied by an extraordinary wealth of archival documentation, reflecting every aspect of the 'life' of a piece of silver - its commissioning, its value, its modification to meet changes of fashion or eating habits or religion, its care, and attitudes to it. The college archives, indeed, accurately document many of the aspects of the study of silver which have been of greatest interest to recent silver scholars, notably in the pioneering work of Philippa Glanville.

It was therefore the documentary evidence for Oxford silver in relationship to surviving pieces, more than the connoisseurial study of makers and marks, that formed the basis of the research project conceived by Timothy Wilson, Keeper of Western Art. The Leverhulme Foundation's generous and enthusiastic support enabled us to take on Helen Clifford, a scholar with extensive archival as well as silver expertise, and uniquely well equipped to tackle the subject, as a research fellow from 1993 to 1995. The present exhibition is not only a spectacular accumulation of works of art and a demonstration of the best of the art of working precious metal in England and further afield from the fourteenth century to the twenty-first; it is also the result of powerfully innovative research.

The exhibition and this book have been made possible by many kind supporters: the executors of the late Mrs Corinne Whiteley, Mr and Mrs Brian Wilson, Christie's, Darbys, Mallams, the University's Van Houten Fund, the bequest of B.D.H. Miller, the Lord Faringdon Charitable Trust, the Paul Mellon Centre for Studies in British Art, the Silver Society, the South Square Trust, Mr and Mrs J.A. Pye's Charitable Settlement, Mr and Mrs Simon Davidson, Mr and Mrs Oliver Makower, Payne and Son, and benefactors who prefer to remain anonymous. We greatly appreciate the support of the colleges, which have without exception agreed to support the exhibition with loans, sometimes of objects that are in regular use. The Visitors of the Ashmolean and I are grateful to all and confident they will feel their support warranted not only by the spectacular beauty of the exhibition but by the eloquence and originality of the research in this book.

Christopher Brown, Director

# INTRODUCTION

'The colleges of Oxford, for curious workman-ship and private commodities are much more stately, magnificent and commodious than those of Cambridge.'

William Harrison, *Description of England*, 1587

1 (**100**) Decanter, silver, London 1867, mark for George Fox, retailed by R. & S. Garrard. Brasenose.

It is debatable whether the biased opinion of Harrison regarding the relative standing of Oxford and Cambridge is true, but without doubt both possess remarkable holdings of medieval and Tudor silver, and remain treasure houses of eighteenth- and nineteenth-century plate. The silver belonging to the colleges is as rich and rare as that held in any royal palace or cathedral. College silver is rarely seen outside the confines of the institutions to which it was given; it was and still is private, for the use of college members in chapel and at table according to time-honoured traditions. Unlike museum exhibits college silver is still very much in use. The silver is both functional and symbolic, uniting past donors and college members with present day students and Fellows. To dine in Hall and drink from a Founder's cup is to participate in an often centuries-old tradition. These glittering silver and gilt pieces gain meaning and power through use and display, but, scattered throughout the colleges, they are rarely seen together. The exhibition which this book accompanies unites the finest pieces from the Oxford colleges, along with everyday silver, to share a treasured inheritance with the public.

The display is only part of the story of Oxford silver, as it draws only upon the holdings of the colleges, and not the University, which also owns

ceremonial and dining silver. In 1977 there was an exhibition of the Oxford University regalia by the University Marshall, including the three staves all made by the London goldsmith Benjamin Pyne in 1723.[1] We know from the Vice Chancellor's accounts that silver was regularly bought, given and received: Mr Wilkins an Oxford goldsmith was paid for mending the 'Bedell Staves sevrell times' in 1650 and made the 'staffe for the sup[e]r[i]or Bedell in Arts' for £33'. The University gave 'Dr [Christopher] Wren a Present of Plate for his paines about ye modell of the Theater' in 1664, costing £6 17s 6d.[2] Wren had gone up to Wadham in 1650, and three years later became a Fellow of All Souls. The Sheldonian Theatre, commissioned 'for the enactment of University business', which Wren designed, and to which the model relates, was completed by 1669. However the story of the University silver is a separate, if connected, field to that of the Oxford colleges. There is a parallel story to be told of the Cambridge colleges. While there have been exhibitions of their silver, most recently at the Fitzwilliam Museum held in 1975,[3] their documentary history awaits thorough investigation.[4]

It was not until the development of silver scholarship in the mid nineteenth century, that college silver emerged from behind the buttery door and out of the wardens' lodgings to be displayed in public via catalogues and exhibitions.[5] It was in Cambridge rather than Oxford that the first initiatives were taken. In 1845 J.J. Smith published the first substantial work to be devoted to college silver; *Specimens of Cambridge Plate*, an occasional paper written for the Cambridge Antiquarian Society, with 13 engravings. Smith explained that the study of such silver involved 'historical details of customs, manners, wealth and art'. Inspired by the riches that were revealed, Foster and Atkinson published in 1896 a catalogue, *Old Cambridge Plate*, in conjunction with the first exhibition of college silver at the Fitzwilliam Museum.[6] This was the first temporary exhibition in Britain

dedicated purely to silver, and is therefore a landmark in silver studies. Charles Moffatt's *Old Oxford Plate* was not published until 1906, and was the first comprehensive work on the silver belonging to the Oxford colleges. He was a Queen's man, and presented the College with a mounted coconut cup designed by himself in ancient style. Twenty-two years later, in 1928, just over four hundred pieces of college plate were exhibited at the Ashmolean Museum.[7] Some of these exhibits were not on show to the general public again until 1953 when *The Treasures of Oxford*, including silver, were shown at Goldsmiths' Hall in London, part of the celebrations connected with Queen Elizabeth II's Coronation. It was particularly fitting that New College, and others, loaned silver that had been made in the reigns of both Elizabeth I and Elizabeth II.

Thirty-five colleges in Oxford were founded between 1249 (University) and 1977 (Green), as well as five permanent private halls founded between 1896 (Campion) and 1957 (Greyfriars). The silver that survives in these colleges is but a small sample of once greater holdings, the magnificence of which can be glimpsed in records, such as inventories, accounts, benefaction books, and more rarely the original bills. Fortunately for us, many Founders, like William of Wykeham (1324–1404), Bishop of Winchester (from 1367) and Lord Chancellor of England (from 1368), realised the importance of preserving college archives. Wykeham made provision in his foundation statutes for New College of 1379 for a tower, almost a fortress, in which to store the evidence relating to his own extensive endowments, and the silver belonging to the College (Fig.2). It was a pattern that others followed. From these dry rolls, books and scraps of vellum and paper we can reconstitute the contents of butlers' pantries and wardens' strong rooms that have long since been lost, or given up during the Reformation, for the 'superstitious and idolatrous images' these pieces bore, were 'loaned' to King Charles I during the Civil War, were plundered by the Parliamentarians,

2  D. Loggan's bird's- eye view of New College in *Oxonia Illustrata, etc,* 1675.

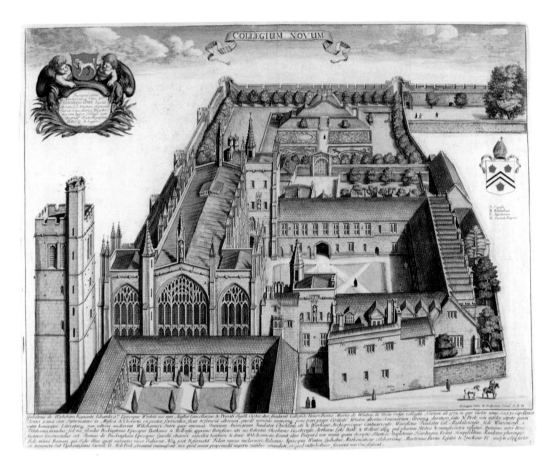

or more often still, were melted down and re-fashioned to recoup the bullion value as part of the usual and regular recycling of silver. These records enable us to track the passage of individual items of silver from creation, through various phases of use and redundancy, and represent a richness for the historian comparable to the wealth of the silver itself. The exhibition with which this book is associated is based on a two year Leverhulme funded research project dedicated to recording all the archives in the Oxford colleges relating to silver, from foundation to the end of the nineteenth century. Information gained from these sources has enabled the 600-year-old social life of Oxford college silver to be recreated. The story continues into the present, with new commissions recently made by New College, Pembroke, St Cross and Wadham offering vital patronage to the goldsmiths' craft, which like the colleges has a history that stretches back into the Middle Ages.

Whilst the silver, silver-gilt, and gold was designed to be displayed, the accounts, bills, inventories and statutes, and other archival documents are more difficult to exhibit; they are simply less glamorous. Yet their contribution to our understanding of the making, purchase and use of silver in the colleges is great. The following section attempts to explain the purpose of the key types of documentation that have been used in this book, and how important they are. It is significant that the colleges kept their silver and the archives together, as they were both deemed integral to college affairs. Land titles and other such documents were of major financial value. The silver and the archives are parallel treasures, kept alongside each other in secure towers in multiple padlocked iron-bound chests. Several of these chests survive, including the University Chest, or the Chest of the Five Keys, with five locks for five different key holders (**142**. frontispiece).

This imposing chest, used since 1668, replaced an earlier one of 1427, and was intended for the University's money and plate. It was in regular use until 1756, when the University opened a bank account.

The arrangements devised by William of Wykeham for New College, because of their early date, scale and detail, served as a blueprint for other colleges. The Tower, completed in 1386, was placed physically and symbolically at the centre of the College. According to the very detailed description of the Tower given by Wykeham in his 50th statute, the rooms were used in ascending order, the ground floor secured by two locks, for the brass, pewter and less valuable silver regularly used in Hall, the second floor with three locks for the chests containing the College's title deed and lease, and the College seal; the third with four locks for the gold and silver used only on feast days in Hall, for the Founder's statutes, and for the College's funds; the highest room with two more locks, for the vestments, relics, ornaments, and plate used in chapel. Elaborate precautions were taken with the keys: for example no less than six people were needed to take the great seal out of custody, three bursars to open the door to the room, and Warden, Sub-warden and Dean to open the three locks of the chest in which it was kept. This type of security system, though effective, could sometimes be a nuisance: as the Butler Griffin Owen at Christ Church noted in 1582, 'xi pieces of plate lefte in the utmoste house because had not the 2 keis of the inner doore'.[8] According to the engraver George Vertue, who visited Oxford in 1737, he was unable to see the Founder's pastoral staff at New College, 'by reason of its being under 9 locks, and Fellows not all in College'.[9] Perhaps the College gave this reason to get rid of an importunate visitor? As a report in the local newspaper *Jackson's Oxford Journal* of 1761 reveals, the system was not infallible. When £600 was stolen from the Corpus Chest, which 'is always secured... under as many Locks, of different Constructions, as there are Bursars,

and the different keys severally kept by each', an inside job was suspected.

The administration of the Tower and its contents was the responsibility of the Bursar, whose office immediately adjoined it on the ground floor.[10] At All Souls the original treasury was the tower over the gateway in which 'plate and other goodes' and 'old writeings' were kept in 'twoe chests plated with iron... wth Lock and Key'.[11] At Jesus College the silver was 'all layd up in a chest that is in the Study over the gate'[12] and at St John's a note was made in 1586 that the ewer and basin 'was brought up into the Tower, & laid in the chest there bound wth iron'.[13]

Important assets needed to be carefully monitored, and all the medieval Founders stipulated that regular inventories should be kept of college goods. A statute of 1292 at University College (founded 1249) declared that 'all the goods of the College, movable and unmovable, above two sterling in value' should be listed in a register, 'one part of which shall be kept in the Common Chest, and the other by the Bursar, and every year shall be viewed by all the Fellows'. The first inventory of silver at the College to survive is dated 1423 and lists 57 pieces of plate. The Liber Albus or White Book at New College records inventories made between 1396 and 1509. The different headings under which the silver is listed help us recreate the varying environments in which the silver was kept and used. Like the college structure itself, silver was subject to a strict hierarchy. An inventory of silver from St John's College of 1591 is divided between the Tower, the Buttery, and the President's Lodging.[14] The Tower (or Treasury) plate comprised large items such as a ewer and basin, a standing cup and cover, and a salt, to be used at High Table on special occasions. The St John's College Buttery plate was made up of mostly spoons, small pots, and wine bowls, for everyday use. This silver conforms to the type that could be found within the buttery of a noble household. An old dictionary of building terms *The City and Country*

3 Bursar's Long Book,
begins 1655. New College.

4 (**146**) Calculus or
Bursar's Long Book, 1724.
Lincoln.

*Purchaser*, published in 1703, described the buttery: 'In Noblemen's and Gentlemen's Houses, 'tis the Room, belonging to the Butler, in which he disposes all his Utensils, belonging to his Office as… Pots, Glasses, Tankards… Cruets, Salvers, Pepper-Boxes, Sugar-Box, Mustard-pot, Spoons, Knives, Forks'.[15] The President of St John's had largely drinking bowls for his own use. Most was gilt, or double gilt (two layers of gold), and had been given by the Founder, bought by the College, or given by Fellows, students, and servants. These three main locations of silver in St John's are common among all the colleges. Some silver was loaned out to various members of a college, and books survive which record the signing in and out of silver, helping us reconstruct who was allowed to use it, of what type, when and for how long.

Other colleges adopted similar methods of accounting. Two or three Bursars elected from the Fellows were made responsible for receipts and expenditure, and were required to report quarterly. Every last detail is recorded: for example at Balliol in 1622 we know that 1s was paid 'to a ratt catcher for destroying myse in the buttery'. On a specific day each year receipts and invoices for all the year's income and expenditure were drawn together in the form of a single account. The earliest of this type of record to survive are the Subwarden's rolls at Merton, which date from 1277.[16] At Queen's College they are called the Compoti, and date from 1340,[17] at New College the Bursar's Rolls survive from 1390 (**144** & **147** & Fig.3) and at Oriel the Style from 1409, at Lincoln the Compotus from 1456–1600, and the Calculus 1603–1880[18] (Fig.4), and at Magdalen the engrossed accounts from 1481.[19] These early accounts were kept in the form of parchment rolls, which were superseded in the early sixteenth century by vellum and leather bound books. At Corpus Christi College the accounts are called the Big Books, the Libri Magni, which survive from 1521 (Fig.5).[20] Audit or Count Day was a very important date in the college calendar, and was frequently accompanied by a review of the silver. The information from which these final accounts were drawn up include tradesmen's bills (Fig.7), variously called bills or vouchers, some of which survive in colleges like Brasenose from 1614, Corpus from 1625, New from 1649 (Fig.6 & Fig.7), Wadham from 1660 and Worcester from the nineteenth century, and notes taken by the

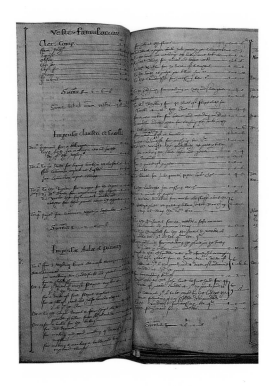

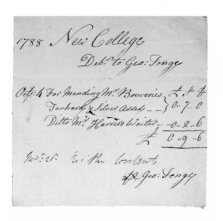

5 (**145**) Liber Magnus or Bursar's Long Book, 1622. Corpus Christi.

6 (**152** & **159**) Receipt and bill for silver supplied to New College in 1788 & 1712 by Oxford goldsmiths George Tonge and John Wilkins.

7 (facing page) Goldsmiths' Bills 18th and 19th centuries to New College and Corpus Christi.

bursars in the form of day books. Some bills, like one for a decanter, supplied to Brasenose by the London goldsmiths R. & S. Garrard in 1868, can be connected with surviving silver (Fig.1).

All the accounts commence with a summary of the receipts from the estates for the preceding year. Income includes rent from college estates and livings, payment for admissions, room rents, benefactions, money obtained from students for the purchase of silver, and fines. Expenditure included the salaries of the Head of House and Fellows, servants' wages, poor relief, and fuel. Daily maintenance is recorded under separate headings for the garden, the kitchen, the hall, the bursary, and library and chapel. The first surviving accounts at Lincoln College from the mid 1400s show a modest income of £71 0s 7d, and expenditure of £67 9s 2d. The Rector was paid 40s, the Bursar and Cook 13s 4d each. The buying and acquiring of silver can thus be considered in the context of the relative costs of the time. Through these accounts we can see how a college built up its store of silver, maintained and disposed of it.

For example at Exeter College we can see the purchase of a case for spoons in 1360 for 12d, then a tankard, then 18 spoons the following year for 7s 6d. These accounts also reveal how this silver underwent hard use, and was often recycled. At All Souls in 1605 'twoo bages of broken plate… were sold to pay the Lord Cromwell the Money given him by Composition in the end of the Whadborough Suite'. At Christ Church in 1750 the Chapter ordered that '£500 be raised out of the Old Plate for the Hall to be repaired and beautified', and in 1778, £100 of plate was sold to meet the cost of a new grate and stoves for the kitchen, altering the chimney and putting up a smoke jack. At Magdalen in 1711 a different type of recycling happened, select pieces of silver, the Duke of Norfolk's flagon, Mr Annesely's basin and ewer, and Sir Thomas Wenman's bowl were 'putt in the Lottery to the value of £100'.[21] Wrought silver was not only important as a means of indicating status, but was also part of the everyday running of a college, following the same pathway as silver belonging to any royal or noble household.

**Bot of HUNT & ROSKE[LL]**

**LATE STORR & MORTIMER,**

JEWELLERS, GOLDSMITHS & SILVERSMITHS,

**TO THE QUEEN.**

TERMS.
7½ Per Cent Discount for Immediate Payment.
5 Per Cent Within 3 Months.
2½ Ditto Ditto 6 Months.

Spoons Forks & Second Hand excepted from Discount
Five Per Cent Charged on accounts
Exceeding Twelve Months

156, NEW BOND STREET, LONDON.

MANUFACTORY, 26, HARRISON ST, GR[AY'S]

1854

Mar 16

The Rev.d The Warden & Fellows of New College

**Bought of Lock & Son,**

**Goldsmiths Jewellers &c. Oxford.**

Repairing
A Cheese Toaster
A Tankard
Half Pint
Another Ditto
Garnish of Cruett

Sugar Castor
Sauce Boats
Desert Knife
Decanter Cork
Fish Knife
cut glass Pepper Castor
large strong cut glass Cruets
a Sugar Castor
glass Soy Cruets

**Oxford**

**Bot of J. Fisher**

SILVERSMITH & JEWELLER,

Corn Market

**GREEN & WARD,**

GOLDSMITHS & JEWELLERS,

20, Cockspur Street.

# *1*

# DONORS & GIFTS
## IDENTITY & MEMORY

8 (**10**) Crozier, silver-gilt, late 15th or early 16th century. Corpus Christi.

The majority of silver belonging to Oxford and Cambridge colleges was acquired via gift, from Founders, their friends, Fellows, students, servants and visitors. 'A noat of all the plate' at St John's of 1591 reveals that 'a lydd of the gylte wyne boale' was of the Founder's gift. Sir Thomas White, the son of a Reading clothier, who became a Merchant Taylor, founded St John's (named after the patron saint of tailors) in 1555. The note continues with 'one silver bason & ewer pcell gylt of the gyfte of Or Founders sister'.[22] A 'standing Cuppe wth a Cover double gylte' and a 'tankerd wth a Cover double gylt' were the gift of two commoners. Only six 'silver spoones wth Apostles' were 'bought by the Collidge' at their own expense. At New College the Bursar Henry Nobes in 1664 divided the silver in his keeping between 'gift plate' and 'colledge plate', the latter bought by the College.[23] Most college silver is therefore an accumulation of individual gifts. Whether given voluntarily, or by compulsion, these objects are remembered not primarily for their form, function or design, but by the name of the donor engraved upon them. It is the names that stand out. A late eighteenth-century bill 'for Beating out', or mending a sauce tureen at Brasenose, does not therefore refer to the object by the date of its making, or its arrival in College, or even by the supplier's name, in this case Paul de Lamerie, but by the name of the Fellow who gave money for its purchase, who was named Bennett.[24] While college plate usually bears the armorials of the college, that given as a gift also bears the donor's arms, as a perpetual reminder of the individual's generosity.

## FOUNDERS' GIFTS

'to remayne… in the said college for ever as a Remembrance of me their Foundress', Extract from Dorothy Wadham's will 1617, referring to her gifts of plate, Wadham College.

The oldest silver within the colleges usually relates to gifts from their Founders. As Marian Campbell has stated, the 'Prime aims of all colleges were to combine the advancement of learning with the furtherance of religious worship. But in a sense, all medieval foundations were also commemorations of their Founders'.[25] Although many Founders left silver to their colleges as part of the essential equipment for running, not all of them possess any of it today. It is only via inventories and bills that we can reconstruct the past splendour of such bequests. We know from surviving bills from the royal goldsmith Robert Amadas that Cardinal Wolsey commissioned many luxurious and expensive items of plate for his new college, now Christ Church, which he founded in 1525. One bill lists £5,002 worth of silver, including a 'payre of goodly altar candilsticks of silver and gilte, a payre of gilte pottys chas'd wth portencullyses and margaret fflowers' and a 'flower of golde wth a great table dyamonde and iii perles'. When Cavendish, Wolsey's biographer, described his personal chapel, when he was Chancellor, it is clear that Wolsey was used to being surrounded by lavish plate, and that the orders for Cardinal College were by no means unusual: 'But to speak of the furniture [furnishings] of his chapel passeth my capacity to declare the number of the costly ornaments and rich jewels that were occupied [in use] in the same continually' which included 'sumptuous crosses, candlesticks and other necessary ornaments'.[26] Yet none of the treasures that Amadas supplied survives at Christ Church today. They were sequestered by Henry VIII in 1529 at the time of Wolsey's downfall, and recycled for his own use.[27]

Yet there are colleges, notably New College and Corpus Christi, which still own impressive amounts of Founder's plate, saved from the Reformation and the Civil War by the cunning and audacity of their Fellows. Richard Fox (c.1448–1528), who founded Corpus in 1517, left to his college his crozier, the symbol of pastoral power of Bishops and

Abbots (Fig.8). Fox's crozier is one of only three in silver to survive from the English late Middle Ages. Although it bears no hallmarks or inscriptions, the cast figure of St Peter in the crook suggests that it was made for Fox when he was either Bishop of Exeter (1487–1491) or Bishop of Winchester (after 1501), as both sees are dedicated to this saint. The staff, which is engraved with a floral diaper pattern, includes a portrait, which just might be that of the engraver (Fig.9) Fox also gave a standing salt and cover (1494–1501), six spoons (1506), two ablution basins (1493–4, and a copy of 1513–14), a chalice and paten of gold (1507–8) and a covered cup (1515–16) supposedly given by Katherine of Aragon to Fox as a gesture of thanks for his involvement in her marriage to Henry VIII (Fig.10). The evidence for this provenance lies entirely with the engraved pomegranates on the lid, Katherine's personal emblem, inherited from

9  Detail from the staff of Fox's Crozier.

10 (**22**) The Founder's Cup, silver-gilt, London 1515–16. Corpus Christi.

her parents, Ferdinand and Isabella, who adopted it to celebrate the reconquest of Granada.[28]

It is the deep desire to be remembered that lies behind these gifts. The personalities behind the plate are reinforced via engraved armorials, enamel bosses, and cast elements that remind the users of the donors. For example, much of Fox's silver incorporates his personal emblem, the pelican vulning (pecking at her breast to draw blood to feed her young), a powerful symbol of Christian self-sacrifice. His pastoral staff incorporates a cast pelican beneath the crook, and in the panelling above it are pelicans set in niello, shining gold against the black. The handsome hexagonal cast salt incorporates plaques once set off against brightly coloured enamel bearing the pelican, with another pelican cast on top of the lid, with pearls hanging from her beak.[29]

11 Portrait of Robert de Eglesfield, Founder of Queen's, from R. Ackermann, *History of the University of Oxford*, 1814.

12 (1) Drinking Horn with silver-gilt mounts, c.1340. Queen's.

At Queen's College, founded by Robert de Eglesfield (d.1349) in 1341, an inventory of 1416 refers to 'aquilae crateris fundatoris'. The eagles allude punningly to the Founder's name: he had been chaplain to Queen Philippa, patroness of the College, and Lord of the Manor of Eaglesfield, a Cumberland village (Fig.11). It is not possible to make a definite link between the large mounted horn described by Provost Henry Airay (Provost 1599–1616), 'Rob. Eglesfield O[u]r worthy foundr is thought to have left the great horn w[i]th covr and garnishing thereof to this Coll', and the surviving example in College, although the cast eagle on the cover is certainly a reference to Robert de Eglesfield's name (Fig.12). The word 'Wacceyle', from the Anglo-Saxon good health, engraved around the silver-gilt brim, reminds us that this horn was for drinking, passed round as a loving cup at the great college feasts. It was this cup that Baron Waldstein was taken to see in 1601 when he visited Oxford. After viewing the manuscripts at the Bodleian he went 'to the Queen's College which has a cup made from a horn and decorated with silver-gilt rings'. It was already a tourist attraction.

Some colleges, like Oriel, acquired their 'Founder's' plate retrospectively. In 1324 Adam de Brome obtained a licence from King Edward II to found a 'certain college of scholars studying various disciplines in honour of the Virgin'. Two years later he had revised and extended his plans, with Edward himself as the Founder, but Oriel remained a small institution with an income of about £60 a year by 1350, and £180 a century later. Yet the cup referred to in the earliest surviving inventory of 1596 as the 'Founder's cupp double guilded with a chain of SS & E & six crownes on the outside of the upper cage & E & a chain of SS in the bottom', was recorded in the Treasurer's Accounts as bought by the College in London in 1493 for £4 18s 1d. This is an unusual example of the acquisition of 'Founder's silver' by purchase rather than by gift. The handsome lobed cup with a cover bears the mark of a Parisian

goldsmith of c.1350, and was thus probably bought second hand, as a suitably impressive cup to honour the Founder's memory (Fig.13). Four years after its acquisition it was 'laid up in the treasury chest' at Michaelmas 1497.[30]

All Souls did not acquire its splendid silver and gilt salt, which had belonged to Archbishop Chichele (c.1362–1443), who founded the college in 1438 (original buildings completed in 1443), until 1799, when it was bequeathed to the College by Mrs Catherine Griffith, widow of Christopher Griffith, whose first wife Anne was a collateral descendant of the Founder. This salt is one of the most important survivals of medieval plate in England and is of unique design (Fig.14). The salt may have been a diplomatic gift to Chichele, who was Archbishop of Canterbury from 1414, and between 1406 and 1420 led a number of diplomatic missions to Rome in connection with the war with France, but it may equally

13 (2) Cup and Cover, silver-gilt, Paris c.1350. Oriel.

14 (5) Standing Salt, silver parcel-gilt and painted, crystal lid, c.1400–50. All Souls.

15 (35) Cup and Cover, silver-gilt, London 1601–2. Magdalen.

have been made in London by a continental goldsmith.[31] Chichele's college had cost him some £9,500, over £5,000 of which went to endow it with estates.

It was not necessarily enough to be associated with a Founder to guarantee survival as a complete object. At Magdalen there is a standing cup and cover, called the Founder's Cup, surmounted by a small cast finial representing Mary Magdalen, hallmarked London 1601–2 (Fig.15). However as William of Waynflete (who had become Bishop of Winchester in 1447) founded the college in 1458 and died in 1486, it is clear that the 1601–2 cup presents a problem if it is to be considered as connected with the Founder. The silver historian John Hayward came up with a plausible theory. He noted that an early inventory of 1580–1 included 'one pece wth a cover gilt haveing the Image of Marie Magdalen called Magdalen boxe', and he surmised that in 1601 the finial was removed from the box and transferred to the 1601–2 cup. It was this cup that the President of the College redeemed from the Oxford Mint in 1643; a receipt survives 'for a gilt bole weighing 42 ounces, and having Mary Magdalen on the top of the Cover the full summe of £11 11s 6d', its melt value. The cup

appears to have been in hard use, the finial is much worn, and extensive mending work is evident, datable to the 1680s, involving the addition of cut card work to support the base of the bowl. Some Founder's gifts simply did not survive the passing of time or regular use. At Corpus in 1736 'broken parts' of Bishop Fox's mitre, which would have been jewelled, were found to be 'so much decayed… that it could not be mended', and along with 'some batter'd plate' were melted down and the proceeds put towards rebuilding projects.[32]

It was Dorothy, the forceful widow of Nicholas Wadham, who saw the completion of her husband's project in 1612, the foundation of a college, its building completed only three years later, at a cost of some £12,000. In her will drawn up in 1617, the year before her death, she bequeathed £100 to the College, plus silver, 'to remayne… in the said college for ever as a Remembrance of me their Foundress'. It is clear that Dorothy had no intention of letting her memory fade. The College has honoured her wishes, and the pair of flagons (1598–9) (Fig.16), and her communion cup and paten (1612–13) (Fig.41) remain in the College to this day.

## THE CUSTOM OF GIFT GIVING

The presentation of gifts can be seen as the oil that lubricated the works, courting favours, sealing friendships, acknowledging assistance and furthering relations. It was part and parcel of a culture of diplomacy. For example the President of Magdalen Richard Mayhew, whom Henry VII made royal almoner and had chosen for his embassy to Spain to arrange the marriage of Prince Arthur to Katherine of Aragon, was given Flemish tapestries made to commemorate the betrothal, which are still in the President's Lodgings today. The key roles that the Founders and heads of colleges played in national and international politics meant that the importance and symbolism of the silver gift went beyond the confines of

Oxford, and connected the colleges with the monarchy and other European courts.

The so-called 'Founder's Jewel' at New College was a gift from a citizen of Winchester, Peter Hylle, recorded in the New College Liber Albus of 1455 as a 'costly and sumptuous jewel'.[33] The gold brooch, formed as a crowned Lombardic letter M with the figures of the Virgin and the Archangel Gabriel framed in the double arch of the letter, is particularly appropriate for a college associated with Wykeham (d.1404), who had dedicated himself to the Virgin's service (Fig.17). His two colleges in Oxford and Winchester were founded in her name, New College is titled St Mary's College of Winchester in Oxford, commonly called New College, and over all the principal gates Wykeham is represented as her votary.[34] The sophistication of design and making of the jewel suggests that it is French work, c.1350, like other items of jewellery connected with the Founder, including a girdle made of linked enamel plaques with emeralds and pearls.

16 (**33**) Pair of Flagons, silver-gilt, London 1598–9. Wadham.

William Warham (d.1532), who was a Fellow of New College 1473–88, and later Warden, Archbishop of Canterbury and Lord Chancellor of England, gave four gifts of plate, including an exotic silver-gilt mounted bowl, which appears in a list of jewels and goods given by him in 1516 (Fig.18). The mount is scratched 'W Warh Cantua' in an early seventeenth-century hand. The bowl is made of a particularly treasured type of green glazed porcelain, the earliest piece of Celadon known to have arrived in England. Porcelain at this time was very precious, 'partly because it was made of an unknown material impossible to imitate in the West and partly because it was widely believed that it was incorruptible by poison; in other words if poison was placed in the bowl, the bowl would break'.[35] As Marian Campbell has remarked, 'The bowl is unique in an English context, the only complete piece and earliest surviving medieval example of porcelain brought to England soon after it was made. It is one of only two or three extant pieces in Europe'.[36]

17 (**3**) Founder's Jewel, gold with rubies, emeralds, pearls and enamel. Possibly French *c.*1350. New College.

18 (**20**) Chinese celadon porcelain bowl *c.*1400–50 with English mounts *c.*1500–30. New College.

19 (**39**) Steeple cup, silver-gilt, London 1610–11. Brasenose.

A primary source of college gifts came from those who were appointed their heads. For example a 1596 inventory from Oriel reveals 'a mazer having a bottom with a rose enameled & an edge double guilded weighing by estimation of a goldsmith six ounces have written about Vir racione bibas non quod petit atra voluptas sic caro casta datur lis lingue suppeditatur', which refers to the surviving mazer. It is said to have been given to the College by John Carpenter, who was appointed Provost of the College in 1430. At Brasenose, the Principal Samuel Radcliffe bequeathed to the College in his will of 1648 'all my plate' including a steeple cup of 1610, 'to be used at our accounts in the College'; this is now referred to as the Radcliffe Cup, and is still used at the college audit on St Thomas's Day (Fig.19). It was in regular use, as there are many accounts for its mending, including one in 1773 by the local goldsmith Edward Lock, who was paid 3s 6d.

Gifts were also exchanged when foreign dignitaries visited. The Dean of Christ Church bought 'a payre of gloves to give to the Ambassador of Spayne lying in Christ Church when the Queen came to Woodstock' in 1602.[37] Over sixty years later when another Spanish ambassador, Count Molina, fled with Charles II to Oxford in September 1665, 'to avoid the sicknesse raging in London'[38] he acknowledged New College's hospitality in accommodating him in the Warden's Lodgings for four months with the gift of a handsome gilt cup and cover. This was stolen in 1675, when thieves broke into the Buttery removing near £200 worth of plate. Molina's successor Don Pedro Ronquillo, replaced the cup in gratitude for his entertainment at the College at the time of the Oxford Parliament in 1681 (Fig.20).

As past students advanced in their careers they did not forget the foundation their colleges had given them. George Hall, who had matriculated from Exeter College in 1628, went on to become Bishop of Chester, and chaplain to Charles II in 1662. He gave a splendid gold cup to his college in 1669 on

the death of his wife, and his own estate of Trentham St Germans. This elaborate pot (Fig.21) is one of only two pre-eighteenth-century pieces of gold in Oxford (the other being the chalice and paten of 1506–7 at Corpus).

John Kyrle (1637–1724), later known as the Man of Ross, because of his generosity to that Herefordshire town, gave to his college of Balliol a handsome silver tankard on his matriculation in 1657 (Fig.22). At its presentation Kyrle issued a challenge, that if anyone could better his gift, he promised to match it. As the present tankard is hallmarked for 1669–70, and weighs a substantial 61oz it seems that he honoured his promise. 60 oz of silver would have made two sets of Apostle spoons or 3 pint mugs; four sauceboats or two large standing salts. The College must have been grateful for the gift as they gave 10s

20 (**61**) Cup and cover, silver-gilt, with engraved arms of Spain, London 1680–81, Jacob Bodendeich. New College.

21 (**51**) Cup and cover, 22ct gold, London 1661–2, Richard Blackwell II. Exeter.

22 (**56**) Tankard, silver, London 1669–70, mark TI. Balliol.

23 Detail of the cast hedgehog thumb-piece.

to the 'messenger who had brought Master Kyrle's Cup'. Today the tankard is simply known as 'The Man of Ross'. The thumb-piece is cast in the form of a hedgehog, the family crest (Fig.23). The lid is of a later date, as the original was probably removed for its bullion value, and replaced fifty years later for the College, by the London goldsmith Gabriel Sleath. This was a quick and common form of realising one's assets, while preserving the gift, and the memory of the donor.

One of the most generous benefactors to an Oxford college was Sir Joseph Williamson (1633–1701), an influential statesman (he was Secretary of State 1674–9), diplomatist, and editor of the first newspaper to be printed in England, the *Oxford Gazette*, which first appeared in 1665; Samuel Pepys, his friend, described it as 'very pretty, full of news and no folly in it' (Fig.24). He marked his career successes with ever more beneficent gifts of plate to Queen's College. His first gift was a silver trumpet in 1666, used every day to announce dinner in hall (Fig.25). He must have had in mind the custom mentioned in the Founder's statutes, and still observed, of calling the members to dinner by the sound of a clarion, as was the custom at court. Three years later this was followed by a rose-water basin and ewer, and two years later a shallow two-handled cup and cover with a coiled serpent handle. These were not his only gifts to his College: Williamson provided £1,700 for new residential buildings and in his will he left the College a further £6,000.

The engraving of the donor's name upon the silver given was deemed an important aspect of the gift, and followed a time-honoured formula. An unusually frank and lengthly letter of 1681 survives from Dr Hall (1664–1709), Master of Pembroke College, in relation to Lord Pagett's gift of a silver tankard.[39] Although it was melted down and re-formed into two sauce boats with spoons in 1771, the sauce boats carry the original inscription, transferred from the tankard: 'Coll. Pemb. Oxon DD GUL PAGETT Hon. Dom. Gul. Pagett Baronis de

24  Portrait of Sir Joseph Williamson in R. Ackermann, *History of the University of Oxford*, 1814.

BEAU DESERT IN COM: STAFFORD FIL. NAT. MAX. et hujus Coll. Sup. Ord. Com', which translates as 'William Lord Pagett, eldest son of the Right Honourable William Lord Pagett, Baron of Beau Desert in the County of Staffordshire and Gentleman Commoner of this College gave as a gift'. Hall's letter to Pagett tells us much about the custom of presenting and engraving plate, beyond the evidence of the inscription itself:

> We have your Lordships most nobl[e] Plate at the College but the Inscription is not yet ingraved, because I would first submit it to your Lordships correction. I find upon enquiry that the inscription of those Plates, which are given by the Nobility to other Coleges are very plain mentioning only the Donor & his Relation. As is that upon your Lordships Plate should be thus Dono dedit D. Gulielmus Pagett, Honoratissimi Domini Dni Gulielmus Pagett Baronis de Beau-desert in Comitatu Staffordia filius natu maximus, & huius Collegiii Superioris ordinis Comensalis.'

Hall was right, there was a standardized university-wide etiquette of acknowledging a

25 (**53**) Trumpet, silver, given in 1666 to Queen's.

26 (**71**) Oval filigree box, silver, 17th century, given in 1686 to Christ Church.

donor, recognising their lineage and place of birth, and position held within the college; so that all who used it would know the standing of the man who gave it. Hall added that the cost of the plate and its engraving would come to less than the sum Pagett had given 'But there is a way to expend it, if your Lordship approv[e] of it ffor Plates are usualy presentd to the Society in the College-Hall with a bottl of wine'.[40] This form of celebration was common among the colleges. At Jesus College for example the arrival of 'Mr James Phillips Plate' was accompanied by 'Wine w[he]n his Plates were received' in 1737, and 1s 6d was spent on 'a Botle of wine on receiving Mr Williams Case of knives and forks' in the same year. The letter written in 1681 is not so different to one written just over 260 years later, from the Rector of Lincoln to an 'old boy'; who had given some silver spoons to the college in 1948, 'The College proposes the enclosed inscription, they are anxious that your name should be associated with the gift, and hope you will agree, I enclose the College coat of arms, the scrol[sic] can of course be omitted or varied as you like'.[41]

An unusual gift was bequeathed to the Library at Christ Church by John Fell (1625–1686), the Vice Chancellor (from 1666). It appears in a register of donors' gifts, as 'Two mandrakes in a silver box'.[42] The mandrake is poisonous, having emetic and narcotic properties, and was thought to have magical properties. Such a curious gift was

appropriately presented in a curious silver box (Fig.26). Filigree work was much admired, and associated with exotic craftsmanship. By 1600 filigree work was associated with Paris, and much of the display plate ordered by James I in 1607–8 was Paris work.[43] So Fell's gift to the College was doubly exotic. Fell is buried in Christ Church Cathedral, where there is a memorial to him with a long inscription recording the events of his life.

Another great benefactor was Sir Watkin Williams Wynn (d.1749) who matriculated from Jesus College in 1710. He gave several gifts of silver to his old college including an enormous silver-gilt punch bowl of 1726–7, weighing just over 2780oz, engraved with his name and date of his gift: 'D.D. Watkin Williams Wynn de Wynstay in Com. Denbigh. L.L.D: olim hujus Collegii Socio Commensalis 1732' (Fig.27).[44] The Bursar recorded 9s 9d for wine in 1733 upon receiving Wynn's fine bowl, and presumably drunk from it. It is so large (it holds ten gallons) that baptisms for the new born of College members are sometimes performed in it. By tradition, although there is no proof, Williams Wynn is supposed to have promised to provide an even larger bowl if anyone could claim to have filled it with punch and drunk it in one go, the current bowl being the prize. It appears that, as yet, no-one has been able to meet the challenge. It was this punch bowl that was probably used at a dinner in the Radcliffe Camera in June 1814 on the visit of the Prince Regent, the Emperor of Russia and the King of Prussia to Oxford. Hakewill, a guest at the event, noted that 'There had been a large gold bowl from – College, which holds – gallons, set before Blucher, filled with punch' from which 'we all took a glass and drank to his health and the sovereigns'.[45]

In 1778 the 5th Earl of Chesterfield gave Queen's College a handsome argyle, a new addition to the noble table and a device for keeping gravy warm, supplied by the London goldsmiths John Wakelin and William Tayler. It takes the form of an elegant vase, the spouts hidden at either side, by hinged flaps over the handles (Fig.28). The Benefactors' Book includes a drawing of it, and the description of this new object as an 'Amplum Vas Argenteum (vulgo dict: an Argyle)'. It is engraved 'D: D: Philippus Comes de Chesterfield A.D. 1778'. The donor's arms are matched by those of the College on the other side, and the words 'Coll: Reg: Oxon'.

In 1960 Father E.B. Louis of Ampleforth, who had been at Balliol from 1919–21, gave to his College a handsome vase on a stand (**93**). It is one of 73 vases of similar, but not identical design called '*Lloyd's Patriotic Fund Vases*' paid for from a fund solicited by Lloyd's underwriters 'for the encouragement and relief of those who may be engaged in the defence of the country, and who may suffer in the common cause; and those who may signalize themselves during the present most important contest'.[46] The original design is based on the fifteen vases designed by John Flaxman awarded to commemorate officers who had served with valour in Nelson's naval victory at Trafalgar on 21 October 1805. It is unclear exactly what relationship Father Louis had with Thomas Louis, Admiral of the White, one of the victors over the French off San Domingo in 1806, to whom this vase was awarded. He is mentioned simply as an 'ancestor'. The Admiral was voted the £300 vase in 1806, although it was not delivered until 1809.

27 (**79**) Punch bowl and ladle, silver-gilt, London 1726–7, John White. Jesus.

28 (**89**) Argyle, silver, London 1777–8, Wakelin & Tayler. Queen's.

On one side of the vase is the seated figure of Britannia, holding in her right hand the figure of Victory bearing a crown of laurel, and in her left hand a palm branch and a shield charged with a British Lion. On the other side is the figure of Hercules fighting a three-headed serpent.

At Magdalen the President, Dr Martin Joseph Routh (1755–1854), received a massive side-board dish, presented to him by Emperor Alexander I of Russia, which he in turn left to the College. By the time of its presentation in 1820–1, Routh had already been in office thirty years, and was to serve another thirty-four (Fig.29). The large circular dish bears six oval panels with symbols of the Arts and Sciences, and at the centre is a large Russian Imperial Eagle. It is engraved with the inscription 'UT IMPERATORIO DONO SIT SEMPER HONOS COMMIS-SUM FIDEI EST MAGDALENSIUM SALVUM CONSERVANDUM A RAPA-CIBUS ET FURIBUS TUTUM' (To preserve forever the memory of this Imperial Gift, it is entrusted to the safe-keeping of Magdalen College, to be kept safe from robbers and thieves). Routh was a scholar in field of patristic Theology, who kept his head amid the frenzies of the Oxford Movement. His dress remained that of the eighteenth century, as did his view of the purposes of the College.

Some college silver came via gifts from students to particular members of a college. John Keble (1792–1866) received a splendid candelabrum from his pupils at Oriel in 1823, which was given by Keble to the college set up with money raised by public subscription in his memory (**96**). John Keble, a shy, retiring and unpretentious man, became one of the acknowledged leaders of the Oxford Movement. After gaining a first from Corpus Christi in 1811 he was elected a Fellow at Oriel, where he was an inspirational tutor.

Gifts of silver connected colleges with all sorts of people and places. An Indian silver tea and coffee service, known as the Armenian Set, was given to St Hilda's College

29 (**95**) Sideboard dish, silver-gilt, London 1820–21. Phillip Rundell. Magdalen.

by Mrs A.G. Francis in 1935 (**98**). The set had been given to her by her grandfather. The tea pot was made in Calcutta, by Hamilton, in 1837, and the other elements were made to match bearing London assay marks for a year later, and engraved with the inscription 'Presented by the Armenian inhabitants of Calcutta to Alexander Russell Jackson MD November 1837. A wise Physician skilled our wounds to heal, is more than Armies to the Public Weal', a quotation from Pope's *Iliad*.

Not all gifts came from Fellows, their relatives, and students, there are numerous references to silver given by college servants. William Drese, 'brother to the Butler' at St

John's, gave 'i dozen spones' according to an inventory of 1591. At Brasenose Robert Danner 'sometimes servant to Doctor Humfrey' gave 'a great standing bowle' in 1611.[47] Balliol seems to have inspired its servants with generosity as well as loyalty as several items of silver are gifts to the College from them. 'Mag' Price, a college bedmaker, gave a two-eared cup worth £5 in about 1640. The Steward's gift of 1713, has since been turned into a water jug (1797), and Jane Wyatt, the daughter of the under Butler, left a piece of silver in 1739 on her death.

Individuals donated silver for many and complex reasons. In an early nineteenth-century note addressed to the Principal and Fellows of Hertford College, the author explains that he is giving 'a large silver three-handle loving cup studied [sic] with coins… to be inscribed as having been presented by me to the said College in memory of my said Uncle as a recompense for the destruction of certain of the plate belonging to Magdalen Hall aforesaid which appears to have occurred through the fault of my said uncle'.[48] On the re-foundation of Hertford in 1874 the medieval Magdalen Hall came to an end as a separate institution. Gifts did not have to be great. In a letter to the Principal of St Mary Hall (a fourteenth-century academic hall associated with Oriel, and dissolved in 1902), a former member outlined the reasons for his gift 'from feelings of respect towards yourself, and of gratitude for your kindness to me during my residence at your Hall, and also from my fondness of old associations I have purchased and engraved a dinner fork, which I hope you will do me the favour to accept, and allow it to be used for the present and future members of the Hall'.[49] A letter to the Warden of Exeter College written in 1959, explains how a past student wanted to give 'some object or other in sterling silver, not, you understand to immortalize myself or anything like that; but simply for the sake of gratifying myself in providing a Thing that would endure. When I say object, I think foremost of a beer mug, because of my own undergraduate bias, but I am not specifying anything'.[50]

## MANDATORY GIFTS AND THE GENTLEMAN COMMONER

Not all gifts were voluntary acts of generosity. The intrinsic value of silver meant that the 'gift' of wrought plate was often made a requirement for entrance to a college, either as a Fellow or as an undergraduate. It was customary for Fellows to present a piece of silver when awarded a Fellowship. The Statute Book at Oriel includes a note of May

1587–8 to the effect that each Fellow had to give a piece of plate for the use of the College 'unum vas argenteum in usum collegii', to be at least the value of £2 10s. In that year Richard Harris and Richard Parkinson were admitted Fellows, and a 1596 inventory at Oriel includes 'a colledge pott with two eares, engraven on the outside with the Coledge armes & the words Coll: Oriel with the name Richard Harris/Parkinson Socii given by them at their admission as Fellows'. From the Restoration Fellows also gave plate on vacating their Fellowships at Merton, usually engraved 'in usum sociorum'. Those proceeding to take up their Master's degree also presented plate. At the back of the Long Book for 1697 at New College is a note of 'The Money arising by the Graduates Donations for Plate', which came to £10. Those who 'proceeded M[aste]rs of Arts There' gave spoons, and by 1641 the College had 59 of them.[51]

In the early seventeenth century in an effort to increase its revenues the colleges created a new category of undergraduate recruited from the noble and well-to-do, the Gentleman Commoner. On the payment of increased fees they were allowed at High Table. As Statute 12 of Pembroke College stated, 'in as much as in a well-ordered house, guests and outsiders should be entertained politely and kindly, it is our decision that commoners living in College at their own expense [that is Gentlemen Commoners] shall enjoy the public amenities of the College, with benefit of the hall, library, chapel, buttery, the common service of staff, and the honour, respect and privilege appropriate to their rank'.[52] At St John's there is a reference in 1606 to a Richard Bellingham, who 'in consideration that he was admitted to sitt at the Masters table' was required to give 'to the Colledge for a gratuitye a white silver pott wth two eares'.[53] At Balliol from 1609 a 'toll' of £5, soon increased to £10 for the purchase of books or plate, was levied on each Gentleman Commoner. At Magdalen a similar fee was required. When Sir William Roberts' son went up to Magdalen in 1655 he noted the expenses incurred: £10 to the bursar, £10 to his tutor, and furnishings for his room including chairs, curtains, a candlestick, a chamberpot, a table and a lock and key, and a gown. He also had to provide a 'College pott', which cost him £10 2s 9d, quite a substantial part of the total £56 expenses.[54] At Brasenose from 1651 'none shall be admitted Fellow comoner except they first deposite in the principals or bursars handes the sum of five pounds or a plate of that valew at least'. At Lincoln it was to be at least £4 'and as much more as they liked'; at Merton £8, and at Corpus Christi £10. At St John's the

30 (**59**, **91**, **81**) Three ox-eyes from Queen's, 1677–8, 1792–3 and 1735–6.

custom was to give spoons. In 1623 the Butler listed 'The name of the Commoners wch have given spoones since 1608 are entred into ye Colledge Bookes are 171 wch being added to the 48 formerly given make upp in the whole 219. So the Colledge now having but 150 there are wanting 69 wch are thus to be accounted for'.[55] These were for the exclusive use of the donors during their residence, and at their departure became the property of the College.

'An Account of Plate given to Ball: Coll: since the first admission of Fellow Commoners There circa AD 1609'[56] includes a flagon given by Wilde, Blouynt and Savage, weighing 44oz 15dwt, but the most common form of gift was a double handled pot. These

bulbous bodied pots with distinctive circular handles, that look like two round eyes or ears, are by far the most common type of drinking vessel in the colleges of the seventeenth century and are referred to in various inventories and bills as 'ear'd potts', 'ox-eyes', and 'college cups'. There are early sixteenth-century examples in both pottery and glass but the earliest mention of this type of vessel in silver in Oxford occurs in a New College inventory as a 'great silver pot wth eares' in 1558.[57] At Balliol the 1598 inventory includes '4 cuppes wth eares'.[58] So it appears that the form existed in silver before 1609, but rapidly became the standard form of 'gift' as the weight of these pots could match the 'toll' of silver required. The list of plate that Balliol sent to Charles I in 1643 includes '25 two ear'd pots small and 5 Great two Ear'd pots: called zegadines'.[59] It is unclear where the word zegadine derives from, and they were not, as legend has it, unique to Balliol. A search through the New College long books reveals the presence of zegadines in 1657, 'two zagadines from Mr Steephens'.[60] The name seems to have fallen into disuse by 1662, as the zegadines are referred to as large 'two eared plates' from that date.

Most Oxford colleges possess cups of this type. Although they had gone out of general fashion by the early eighteenth century they continued to be made throughout the nineteenth century and into the next, as archetypal college vessels that were seen by ex-students as perfect gifts to their colleges. At Queen's College forty-four examples survive dating from between 1677 and 1950 (Fig.30).

By the mid eighteenth century Commoners were giving tankards or mugs, which by then were a much more fashionable item of drinking ware. At Brasenose in 1731 Commoners gave pint mugs of 19–20 oz, Scholars half pint mugs 10–11oz and Battlers quarter pint mugs of 6 oz in weight.[61] In 1738 the London goldsmith Richard Green responded to Mr Howard's request to send a tankard of 'eight or nine pounds value' to Brasenose to fulfill his entry

31  A Gentleman
Commoner illustrated in
R. Ackermann, *History of
the University of Oxford*,
1814.

of student as the result of 'the irresistible influx of commercial wealth... In them extraordinary largesses began to purchase immunities; the indolence of the opulent was sure of absolution, and the emulation of literature was gradually superseded by the emulation of a profligate extravagance; till a [new] order of pupils appeared; a pert and pampered race, too froward for controul, too headstrong for persuasion, too independent for chastisement, privileged prodigals. These are the gentlemen commoners of Oxford' (Fig.31).[63]

## BENEFACTION BOOKS

Silver gifts were frequently melted down and re-fashioned, only the donor's name surviving in the form of the engraved inscription. A more permanent way of remembering the original gift was to record it in word and picture. Ten Oxford colleges still possess large, leather-bound, gold-tooled books which celebrated donations with pomp, in the hope one suspects of attracting more.[64] Their introduction coincides with the rise of the Gentleman Commoner. Fulsome praise was accorded each donor, and a description, usually in Latin, of the object was sometimes accompanied by a drawing of the gift. The earliest to survive is from Oriel and dates from 1635; Brasenose followed in 1642 (**148**). It was however in the 1650s, when the colleges were recuperating after the Civil War that they became more popular. The Liber Albus Benefactorum at Trinity College is perhaps the grandest, and begins with Robert Strange's gift of a silver cup in 1650, and ends with Walter Manners and John Hanborough, who gave a pair of candelabra in 1815 (**149**). The accuracy of the drawings can be seen when comparing the watercolour depiction with the surviving gift. In 1750 Frederick North, who matriculated from Trinity in 1721, gave to the College a ewer of 1713–14. This has been matched with the gift of William Legge, who became the 2nd Earl of

requirement. The goldsmith, writing to the Principal, informed him that he had sent one 'this evening to the Coach, the tankard I have sent is of the newest fashion & comes to more than my Orders, please let the Gent[n] see it and if he approves of it I shall take an opportunity to draw on you for the money which is ten pound and ten shillings'.[62]

By the late eighteenth century the Gentleman Commoner was blamed for the decline of academic standards at Oxford and Cambridge. *The Gentleman's Magazine* of 1798 looked upon the expansion of this class

Dartmouth that year and gave a rosewater dish of 1749–50 (**74**). Each gift is engraved with the arms of the College and the donor. In 1737 North had presented to the College a fine set of iron gates on the Broad Street frontage.

In the St Edmund Hall Benefaction Book Edmund Ashton's cup given in 1650 is the first item of silver to appear. The Book was kept up until 1858. At Jesus a fine silver jug, bearing the mark of the London goldsmith Simon Pantin, assayed in 1711, is inscribed with the name of Robert Price, a Fellow Commoner donor whose name appears in the Jesus Benefaction Book in the same year. The weight of what is described as a 'decanter' is inscribed in the book, a handsome 46oz 14dwt. The rate of acquisition of silver can be clearly read from the Book. In 1711 five silver spoons weighing 8 oz 10dwt, as well as Price's decanter, were given. Nothing was given the following year, but in 1713 a 'tankard of the value of £10'

was presented. 1714 was a bumper year, with the acquisition of a very large tankard weighing 62oz from Charles Harris, the Steward, and a salver of 44oz 16dwt and a two-handled cup and cover, no weight recorded, by two Fellow Commoners. It was not until 1737 that knives and forks appear, when Edward Wilkins, another Fellow commoner, presented 'a neat Case of silver-hafted knives and forks containing two Dozen each for the use of the Common Room'. Gifts of course were not always of silver. Francis Payne gave a marble chimney piece and two marble slabs for the Bursary in 1732, to complement the large marble table given the previous year.

In 1676 Lincoln College acquired its first Benefaction Book, bought for £2 4s, plus an extra £2 for the drawing of an elaborate frontispiece.[65] At Pembroke Mr Clerk was paid £1 5s 'for Writing 10 names in the Book of Benefactions', a high price due not

32 (**150**) Album Benefactorum, 1694–1807, Thornton's gift bottom right. Pembroke.

only to the intricate workmanship, but also to the liberal use of gold leaf, and lapis lazuli blue to embellish them. Silver at this time was cheap in comparison, at 5s a troy ounce. At Exeter College in 1703–4 several accounts appear connected with the Benefaction Book, including £5 'For 24 Skins of velum for a Register of Benefactors', £2 5s 'For ruling and binding the Benefaction book', £10 'To Dudley for a case of Does skin to the said Book' and £1 1s 6d 'To Mr Sury for the frontisp. to the Book of Benefactors'.[66] William Sury was responsible for most of the illustrations in Oxford benefaction books at this time, although they were mostly pen and wash, which cost 2s a piece. Several pieces of silver survive that appear in the Pembroke Benefaction Book. Thomas Thornton gave in 1727 'duo pocula argentea' which survive in College. They are handsome silver tankards that bear his arms, supplied by the local Oxford goldsmith Timothy Dubber, and bought in from the London Goldsmith John Sanders in 1720–21 (Fig.33). With the introduction of new and more elaborate dining equipment in the eighteenth century the description of given objects became ever more complicated. 'Tria vascula argentea cum coperculis perforatis' was a round-about way of describing three condiment casters, introduced to the dining table in the late seventeenth century. 'Duas argenteas cymbulas condimenta capienda' refer to a pair of sauce boats, another novelty for the refined table.[67]

Benefaction books did not die out in the eighteenth century. A new book was begun at Trinity in 1887. It is large, bound in red leather, has metal clasps and is illuminated, and as grand as any earlier example. Recorded gifts include a silver tea and coffee service given in 1920 by Mrs May Cannan in memory of her husband, who had been a Fellow, Dean, Tutor and Junior Bursar of the College. The service had been a wedding present from the undergraduates in 1891.

## SILVER FOR PRIVATE USE

While Fellows and certain categories of student had access to college silver, we also know that many brought their own silver to college, as befitted their rank and status. In the last thirty years of the sixteenth century more and more sons of the nobility and gentry came to Oxford to finish their education, bringing with them appropriate personal silver. It is possible to gain a glimpse of such private, as opposed to corporate, silver via the inventories the University took of members who died intestate. The University undertook the task of inventorying an individual's possessions. Inventories were lodged in the Vice-Chancellor's office and many hundreds survive between 1556 and 1734. Dipping into these inventories at different times we can see the changing fashions in dining and drinking wares, as standing cups were replaced by tankards, and by the late seventeenth and early eighteenth centuries the arrival of wares for drinking tea, coffee and

33 (**75**) One of a pair of tankards, silver, London 1720–21, John Sanders. Pembroke.

chocolate. At Queen's College for example, plate was changed in 1717 to buy 'a Large chocolate pot wth College crest' and a tea pot.[68] At Brasenose a pair of oval tea caddies in a 'neat inlaid chest' were bought in 1777, and are still in use in the College today.

We can also see in these inventories the relative value of goods. Silver outranked even textiles in these inventories. The inventory of Robert Dowe, Bachelor of Civil Law and late Fellow of All Souls, who died in 1588, comprised four pages of books, and four items of silver which suggest a man of wealth: a 'standinge gilte cup wth a cover' weighing an immense 170 oz, 'an old salt p[ar]cell guilt, 3 spoons, a mazer bound wth silver'.[69] The worldly goods of George Ryves, Warden of New College from 1599 to his death in 1613, when the inventory was taken, came to £279, £100 of which was allocated to his silver, kept in a chest in the study next to the parlour in the Lodgings. His 23 shelves of books were valued at £82, his 34 'picketures' were valued at shillings each, and his 'scarlet gowne and hood' at £6 13s 4d. His gift of a pair of silver-gilt flagons to his College in 1602, engraved with his name, and still in the Treasury today, were a handsome personal gift. Edmund Astley, the Butler at All Souls, owned far more and elaborate silver than some of the academic staff and it is possible that he was operating as a pawnbroker to supplement his college wages. His inventory of 1636 lists 'six gilt bowles with covers, a gilt tankard and a double salt gilded, six pieces of ungilt plate and twelve spoons'.[70] Thomas Hare, a Bachelor of Physic at Brasenose possessed on his death in 1650 £50 worth of silver, comprising 'a gilt tankard, a parcell gilt tankard, 2 gilt salts, 2 gilt bowls, with covers, 2 gilt wine cups, 2 white bowls, 12 silver spoons, a mazer garnished with silver and gilt'.[71] Rev Charlett, Master of Arts at University College, left behind him in 1722 'a plate, a lesser plate, a pair of salvers, 2 casters and mustard pot, a tea canister, a candlestick, 2 tumblers, a tea pot, a tankard, 5 flat handle spoons, 5 gilded tea spoons and strainer and

tongs, 1 porringer, a soup spoon'. Some 177oz, just over the weight of Dowe's single standing cup,[72] and reflective of the new equipment for dining and drinking introduced in the late seventeenth century.

This personal silver could be put to financial use. Students and academics have always been short of money, but with the introduction of 'university chests' in the early fourteenth century they were able borrow cash on the security of plate, books and other property; no interest was charged.[73] One of the earliest recorded was founded in 1316 by Ralph Germyn. In 1562 Sir Thomas Bengen pawned 'a standing lvyery potte prcell gilt, a cuppe for bear, bowle wth cover gilt, magdeleine cuppe gilt and a standing cup'.[74] The following year William Chamberlain pawned 'a nest of gobletts, parcell gyllt, a goblet gylt, a cuppe and a salte with a cover gylt'.[75] The same objects appear to go in and out of the chest on a regular basis, providing a very useful source of money for the hard-pressed student or Fellow.

The tradition of using private silver in one's rooms continued into the nineteenth century. In Cuthbert Bede's *Adventures of Mr Verdant Green,* published between 1853 and 1857, he describes the preparations for sending the hero up to Oxford 'His mother was laying in for him a new stock of linen, sufficient in quantity to provide him for years of emigration; while his father was busying himself about the plate that it was requisite to take, buying it brand-new, and of the most solid silver, and having it splendidly engraved with the family crest, and the motto 'Semper virens'.[76] As late as 1927 the *Manual for Prospective Rhodes Scholars* explained 'Your Scout hurries back and forth in and out of your study. White linen and silver toastracks begin to appear from his closet and yours... Breakfast begins... Fish with strangely coloured sauce, sausage rolls, or breaded lamb chops, coffee in tall silver pots, tea for those who wish it'.[77] Standards of etiquette, extending to the use of personal silver, had to be maintained.

# 2

# CHAPEL SILVER
## REFORMATION & REVIVAL

### BEFORE THE REFORMATION

All colleges were primarily religious, epitomized by the fourteenth century foundation, Queen's College, founded 'to the glory of God, the advance of the church, and the salvation of souls'.[78] Daily chapel attendance was required. Founders frequently gave chapel silver and vestments. Although Richard Fleming, Bishop of Lincoln (d.1431), left no money to finance his foundation of 1427, he gave a silver-gilt chalice, a paten, an altar frontal and a silver cup to the College. They were housed in the Chapel on the first floor of the north range of Lincoln College, the floor was trodden earth, an image of St Hugh of Avalon, the patron saint of those who came from Lincoln, stood on a pedestal at the foot of the chapel stairs, the walls were limewashed, the windows glazed, and the silver, vestments, and books kept in a locked chest.[79] At St John's in 1566 the Founder granted 'pcells of church plate and ornaments of the church… fyrst a chalice wth a paten gilt waying xxoz iii quarters, Itm one other chalice wth paten pcell gilt xiiioz do Itm a pax garnyshed wth sylver and gylt set wth some stones'. Chapel silver always formed a distinct category of silver, and was inventoried separately. In many colleges the earliest piece of silver still in their possession is the communion cup. At Christ Church, for example, an Elizabethan silver paten of 1566–7 is the oldest piece of silver owned by the College.

The story of English church plate depends as much on theology and sacramental devotion for its forms as on artistic taste, so the type of chapel silver in the colleges changes quite distinctly over time. The possession, and more importantly use, of older forms of vessels indicate a college's devotion to earlier forms of worship; while the adoption of new methods, or revival of old types of worship are represented by the arrival of different items of plate. A pre-Reformation college chapel would have been equipped with a large number of silver and gilt objects essential for ministering to the spiritual welfare of its members. Many of these are included in

34 (12) Pair of chalices and patens, silver-gilt, London 1498–9. Brasenose.

the gifts of John Knyght to the Warden of New College in 1403, comprising a silver-gilt thurible (or censer), a missal with silver clasps, a silver-gilt chalice, a paxbred silver-gilt enamelled with images of Jesus crucified, Mary and John, two basins with enamels of St Martin in the bottom, a silver-gilt vessel to hold holy water with a silver sprinkler, and a silver-gilt monstrance to contain the consecrated body of Christ, scattered with triangular enamels.[80] Knyght also gave 'three cloths of Ragona with a red field and three cloths one red, one blue and one green to make chasubles for the chapel'. The antiquarian John Gutch in his *Collectanea Curiosa or Miscellaneous Tracts relating to the History and Antiquities of England and Ireland* usefully describes these 'Church Utensils' in 1781 for his post-Reformation reader. The fact that Gutch needed to explain the use of these once common items indicates how far the instruments of Catholic worship had passed from use in England. They included:

a pyx, or box for wafers; a paten or silver plate gilt, on which the wafer was placed after it was taken out of the box; a corporas, or cover for the wafer, which had a case; a chalice or cup for the wine, which was in silver or gold, or at least to be gilt inside; cruets for water or wine to mix; a little bell to be rung before the Host or wafer, when it is carried to any sick persons and at the elevation at the time of the mass; a wax taper to be lighted at the elevation of the Host, and a candlestick for it; a little bason and Towel on a side board for the priest to wash his hands; a chrismatory to put the chrism or holy ointment in; a vessel for the holy water, a censer to burn incense in with a spoon; two candlesticks with lighted candles at each end of the alter; and a monstrance of silver, by its name it should be for show.

Early inventories of chapel plate in Oxford reveal that in the fifteenth century a college

chapel was furnished with at the least a chalice and paten. All elements of the chalice were prescribed by the Church. By the fourteenth century it was considered important to have chalices of precious metal, as befits the container for the blood of Christ. The order that the chalice should be laid on its side on the paten to drain, meant that the circular foot was replaced by a lobed one to ensure stability. In medieval symbolism the chalice was frequently said to represent the tomb in which the body of Our Lord was laid, and the paten to represent the stone laid over it. Up to modern times it was designed to fit on the top of the chalice, and was regarded as a part of it. The knop was for the priest to grasp when he lifted the chalice high to consecrate the wine. As it was the priest rather than the congregation who drank the wine, only a small bowl was necessary. College accounts are full of references to the mending, maintenance and exchange of chalices, which were clearly in

regular use. At Oriel the Treasurer's Accounts refer in 1469–70 to 8s paid for the repair of a chalice, in 1478–9 for 'making 6 knoppes to a chalice' costing 1s 4d; and in 1525 'for the exchange of 9 chalices with covers'.

Yet there are only five pre-Reformation chalices left today in the possession of Oxford colleges. The pair with their matching patens at Brasenose are the earliest, bearing London hallmarks for 1498–9, and are rare survivals, with a characteristic sixfoil foot and knop with quatrefoils (Fig.34). The chalice and paten of 1507–8, part of Bishop Fox's chapel plate at Corpus, are exceptional because they are made of gold, and are the earliest known examples of hallmarked English gold work (Fig.35). Magdalen College has a chalice of the same date, with a paten of 1527–8, although this was presented to the College much later by the great silver collector Sir J.H.B. Noble, and said to have come from a church in Hampshire (Fig.36). Chapel plate was essential for a Bishop, and gold chalices are mentioned

35 (**21**) Chalice and paten, gold, London 1507–8. Corpus Christi.

36 (**24**) Chalice and paten, silver-gilt, London 1527–8. Magdalen.

37 (**9**) One of a pair of Ablution basins, silver-gilt & enamel boss, London 1514–15. Corpus Christi.

38 Detail of spout on reverse.

frequently in the wills of medieval bishops. It has been suggested by Marian Campbell that Fox was either given the Corpus chalice, or bought it 'ready-made', as it bears none of the emblems connected with Fox which would suggest a special commission.[81] The red enamelling of the pierced Gothic knop adds an exotic touch of colour.

A pair of circular ablution basins from Corpus are also likely to have been used in the chapel (Figs 37 & 38). They each bear a circular enamel boss with the arms of Richard Fox as Bishop of Winchester; one is hallmarked London 1493–4, and the other evidently a later copy of 1514–15. Pairs of ablution basins were an important item of pre-Reformation church plate and were used for the ritual cleansing of the priest's hands before the consecration during mass. The most distinctive feature seen on the 1514–15 basin is the small spout under the rim of one of the dishes, through which water was poured from one basin into the other. This was one of the many aspects of Roman Catholic worship excised from the mid-sixteenth century Protestant liturgy, when most were melted down. As Timothy Schroder has noted, the 'Fox basins… have no religious decoration and were not necessarily made for church use'.[82] They could have originally been used for 'the ceremonial washing of hands before a banquet', a ritual that was observed at royal and noble tables. Many objects like basins and flagons shared similar forms for both secular and chapel use, and sometimes moved between these contexts.

At New College a silver and gilt pax survives which bears the cast figures of the crucified Christ, the Virgin and St John, and a delicate engraved foliate border (Fig.39). At the back is a simple silver loop that enabled the priest to pick up the pax, to be kissed in turn by the congregation at the Eucharist. This custom was introduced after 1250, and a pax became part of the furnishing of all churches, although only the wealthier would have had one in silver. Only two Pre-Reformation silver paxes survive in England.

An inventory of Chapel silver at Brasenose of 1519–20 gives some impression of the richness of a pre-Reformation college chapel. It includes 'a crosse of silver & gylt, a fote for the same, iii chales [chalices] of silver & gilt with foure pattennes, i censar of silver & gylt, ii cruettes of silver & gilt, ii cruettys of silver, ii candelsticks of silver parvell gylt, a paxe of silver & gylt, a little paxe of silve & gylt, a shippe of silver [vessel for frankincense], a pixe of silver and gilt, a standing cuppe of silver & gylt, an oder cupp with a cover sylver parcell gylt', and 15 corporas cases. The grandeur of Wolsey's chapel can be glimpsed via one of Amadas's bills (the Royal Goldsmith), which includes 'one high cross new made after the fasion of the cross of Cardinal Campegius, silver and parcel gilt £26 10d, oone cross of silver and gilte wth Mary and John with a greate foote of silver, with a flying Angel' and 'making two images of Peta and Pawle'. Elaborate crosses were a common feature of the pre-Reformation chapel. At Magdalen the accounts refer in 1484–5 to 'Grase a goldsmith' who was paid 7s 4d for making a cross weighing 5 oz, and 56s for 'repairing a cross with two images'; in 1504–5 'a silver cross was b[rough]t from London' costing £2 6s 8d, and 8d for the carriage. At the time 32 sheep were valued at £2 8s.

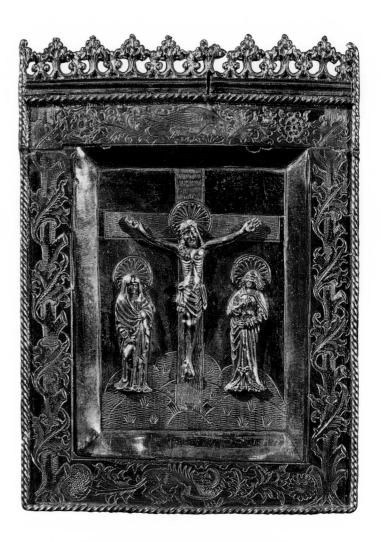

39 (23) Pax, silver and silver-gilt, c.1520. New College.

## REFORMATION AND RESISTANCE

Henry VIII's desire for an heir and divorce from his first wife, Katherine of Aragon, led him to declare his independence from the Pope, and in 1534 the Crown became the supreme head of the Church of England. The changes in the service that followed the introduction of Protestantism were neither simple or swift, and were adopted or resisted according to the religious leanings of each college. Response to the Reformation was therefore complex.

At St John's College, founded in 1555, there survives a note of 'such old superstitious church ornaments as were gyven and delyvred' to the President, Ralph Hucheson. The vestments of black velvet with embroidered borders were converted into cushions for the use of the chapel.[83] Condemned as Popish, the remaining vestments are now treasured. Balliol, like other Oxford colleges, was staunch in its allegiance to Rome and tried to resist Henry VIII's demand for acknowledgement of his supremacy in place of the Pope. Exeter College continued to be strongly Catholic in its sympathies, partly because it drew most of its members from the religiously conservative counties of the south-west and partly because the College's greatest benefactor William Petre's religious sympathies were with Rome. Yet Henry VIII's political and personal desires combined with an already growing movement for the reform of the monasteries resulted in their suppression in 1538. The pillage of the monasteries in 1536 and 1539 brought nine tons of gold and silver to the King's Exchequer. At the time of the Dissolution of the Monasteries Oxford University underwent visitations to tighten the discipline of students in monastic colleges, although the college chapels were left untouched for several years.

Yet, according to the church historian Eamon Duffy, late medieval Catholicism was neither decadent nor decayed, but was a strong and vigorous tradition, and the Reformation represented a violent rupture from a popular and theologically respectable religious system. The 1549 Articles specifically repudiated those sections of the 1547 Injunctions which refer to, or seem to allow, the 'popish mass', chantries, candles on the altar 'or any such things'. There was a determination to stamp out immemorial devotional customs, even at the cost of preventing those who continued to use them from 'taking their rights', by excluding them from Communion.

However, after the arrest of the Lord Protector Somerset in 1549, traditionalists all over England hoped that Roman Catholicism would be restored. The Mass and other Catholic ceremonies were revived in Oxford. Such optimism was misplaced. In the reign of Edward VI (1547–53) colleges where Masses were said for Founders or other benefactors had to submit to visitations from government officials who were authorized to alter statutes, to remove Heads and Fellows, and to do everything necessary to secure obedience to the new Protestant Order. The visitors rooted out those images and symbols of popery which were not successfully concealed. On Christmas Day 1549 bishops were instructed to call in all Catholic service books. In January 1550, the order was enshrined in an Act 'for the defacing of images and the bringing in of books of old Service in the Church'. All Souls chapel lost its altars, its reredos statuary, its organ, and some of its vestments and ornaments.[84] At Magdalen the college resisted some of the changes ordered in 1549, notably the suppression of the choir and the grammar school, but a radical party among the Fellows procured the resignation of the President Owen Oglethorpe in 1552, and proceeded to purge the chapel of its medieval furnishings and vestments.

In 1553 the Privy Council introduced a levy on cathedral and church plate. Although college plate was exempted, they took the secular and chapel plate from Winchester College, the feeder school to New College. When Mary (1553–58) ascended to the throne she attempted to return plate, but it had already been flattened at the collecting centres and so could not be returned to use. During her reign Sir Thomas Pope gave to his foundation of Trinity College three consignments of chapel silver which give no impression of the changes in religious practice. The first grant of 1556 included two gilded chalices with patens, a pax of silver garnished with silver and silver-gilt and set with counterfeit stones, a pyx and a gilt pot.[85] A second batch of chapel plate came the following year and included a carrying bell of silver, and another pax gilt with a crucifixion, which must have resembled the surviving example at New College, a holy water stock and sprinkler of silver parcel gilt, two basins of silver parcel gilt, a cross of silver and gilt 'with Mary and John garnished wth chrystal and stone' and

40 (**41**) Communion cup and paten, silver-gilt, London 1612–13. Wadham.

41 Wadham College altar showing the Foundress's flagons and communion cup (one 1612–13, the other a copy of 1634–35) in front of the new screen of 1832, by Delamotte & Jewitt.

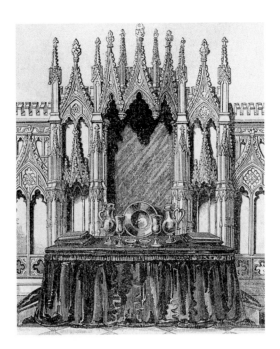

two silver-gilt candlesticks.[86] The third grant added a monstrance of silver-gilt. Such, Gutch explained, 'were the trinkets or implements of Churches in those days of ignorance and superstition, when toys and baubles to please and divert children were admired and valued as if they were the principal part of Religion'.

One of the first acts of Queen Elizabeth was the restoration of the communion cup of the laity in 1559. The plate of college chapels still remained intact, although offensive to the Protestant hierarchy. The Visitation of Oxford carried out soon after her accession, to reform the University, was conducted tactfully. The instructions issued in Mary's reign by Cardinal Reginald Pole, were quietly withdrawn; papist symbols which had reappeared in his time were removed. Since the Crown showed no disposition to get involved, it was left to the Visitors to bring pressure. It was not until 1561 that the bishops began to insist on the change of the 'Massing Chalice into a fair and comely cup', and the colleges like the parish churches were required to give up their chalices. Under Archbishop Matthew Parker's visitation article, 'any prophane cuppes, bowles, dishes, or chalices heretofore used at Masse' where to be replaced with a 'decent Communion

cuppe, provided and kept for that purpose'. There are examples of these new communion cups at All Souls of 1564–5 (**30**), at Wadham of 1612–13 (Fig.40), and at Balliol of 1614–15 (**42**). Parker's successor, Archbishop Grindal, on his translation from York to Canterbury, framed articles of enquiry, one of which expected the use of 'a fair and comely Communion cup of silver, and a cover of silver for the same, which may serve for also for the ministration of the Communion bread'. As a result many of the pre-Reformation chalices were melted down and re-formed into such decent communion cups, in accordance with the changes in the the form of service, which meant that instead of only the priest taking the Sacrament the whole congregation did, requiring larger cups and flagons. As Andrew Gilchrist has noted, 'Of those silver chalices made between 1160 and the Reformation there are only seventy-seven examples left', and, of these, five, as we have seen, are in Oxford.[87]

'The Orders of the Queen's High Commissioners for Defacing the Church Plate in the College' of 23 April 1567 relating to All Souls gives a dramatic impression of the transformation of chapel silver. The 'whole Fellowship' were ordered to gather 'together and upon the Commmon Consent of all or the greater part of the said Fellowship gathered shall cause to be defac'd and broken such church plate as is then in the College or custody apertaining to the use of the Church or Chapel, excepting 6 silver basons with their ewers or cruets, one tabernacle gilt'. Some colleges converted chapel silver to secular use in order to save it. It is likely that at this time the cast figure of the Annunciation on Wykeham's crozier was removed, and placed inside the staff, where it was discovered in the eighteenth century, and returned, rather crudely by means of a copper scroll. The 'Ave Maria' Coconut cup of c.1480, at New College, reputedly survived the Reformation because the wings of the six angels, holding scrolls bearing the engraved words 'cristus', 'ihesus' and 'maria' for Christ, Jesus and Mary, had their wings clipped, transforming them from 'idolatrous' images to secular mortals, and thus escaped the furnace (Figs 42 & 43). The altars in the chapel at New College were removed in 1560, and some of the medieval glass was destroyed in 1564, the niches in the reredos were plastered over in 1566, and the rood screen was dismantled in 1571–2.

Some were astute enough to profit from the Dissolution. When Sir Thomas Pope resolved to found a college in Oxford he decided, like some other benefactors of his period, not to build from the ground but to profit from the upheavals of the Reformation. Accordingly he bought in 1554 the surviving fabric of Durham College, a monastic college begun in 1291, and used it as the basis for building Trinity College.

Despite the Visitations many outspoken adherents of the old religion contrived to remain in office: for example James Brookes, Master of Balliol, was made Bishop of Gloucester by Queen Mary. There was a hard core of resistance in Oxford to the new form of service. Bishop Gardiner, who visited Corpus Christi in 1553, 'found that College was such as if no Reformation at all had been there... Those yesterday that had visibly nothing, the next wanted nothing for the celebration of the Mass, all utensils required for it being ready at hand'.[88] Fox its Founder had been instrumental in Katherine of Aragon's marriage to Henry VIII, so it is not surprising that there were attempts to evade the visitations organized to inspect parish churches and the college chapels. Captain James Wadsworth, giving evidence to the House of Lords, testified that 'there are divers Reliques of Superstition and Popery of a very considerable value in the power and custody of the President and Fellows of Christ Church and Corpus Christi College of Oxford'.[89] At Corpus mutual recriminations followed. In 1588 it was revealed that Hieronymous Reynolds a Fellow, George Atkinson the chaplain and Richard Joyner the clerk of accounts had conspired to conceal chapel plate and vestments when 'the Church Jewells and other ornaments [were taken] oute of the vestrye against all order of Statute'.

42 (**17**) Ave Maria coconut cup with silver-gilt mounts, late 15th century. New College.

43 Detail of the clipped wings of the angels on the Ave Maria coconut cup.

44 (**43**) Recusant chalice and two patens, silver-gilt, London 1641–2. St John's.

Reynolds had 'kept theme... VIII yeres together in his owne privye custodye, part undergrounde, part above grounde, And hathe denied the having of it, being asked by Mr President in the last scrutiny'.[90] Other colleges also showed willingness to observe the older form of service. At Exeter College Mr John Goldon priest and sometime Fellow 'gave to the use of the Master & Fellows that sang mass pretende in divers parcels twenty pound sterling whereof 10lb 2 oz be bestowed upon a chalice of silver to be used at the said pretende mass principally' the other £10 'to be bestowed to prepare a room for an altar in the south side of the chappel for the cotidian mass or pretende'.[91]

William Laud (1573–1645) who became President of St John's in 1611, in the same year that he was appointed royal chaplain, and was from 1633 Archbishop of Canterbury, zealously imposed religious uniformity, and while raising standards in the Anglican ministry, provoked the hostility of the Puritans. The two chalices and patens made in 1641–2 for St John's College are a memory of his Laudian reforms, and rare survivals of silver made at the time of the Civil War (Fig.44). The sexafoil feet, the small decorative knops on the tall stems, and the compact bowls are a return to Pre-Reformation form. They were made just after Laud and King Charles I attempted to impose Anglican practices on the Scots, which caused the Bishops' Wars, and resulted in Laud's

impeachment in 1640 by the Long Parliament. Laud was executed for treason in 1645, and his remains removed to St John's in 1663. When Charles I requested the loan of college silver to support his efforts against Parliament, it is clear that chapel silver was exempted. A note at Brasenose of 17 January 1642 expressly declares that Communion plate was not required. At Wadham there is a memorandum 'That all ye plate of this College shall be Lent unto the King according to His Matie request, expressed in His letters above written reserving only our Communion plate'.

Laudian or pre-Reformation customs took a long time to die. A.C. Benson remembered in 1906 that the chapel service at Brasenose retained 'several peculiar little ceremonies: the candles are lit at celebrations. The Junior Fellows bring in the elements with solemnity from the antechapel. When the procession leaves the altar, the dignitaries who carry the alms and the vessels bow at the lectern to the altar, and to the Principal as they pass his stall. The Vice-Principal bows to the altar on leaving his stall, and the Principal as he passes out. These little observances date from Laudian or even pre-reformation times'. Although none of these observances are still maintained, candles are still lit for celebrations.

By the early seventeenth century there is evidence in the college account books that the colleges were re-assessing their chapel silver, although the word 'chalice' was slow to disappear. Queen's College in 1637 sent their old chapel plate to London to be exchanged for two new 'challices and two pattens guilt' and a 'paire of Potts guilt', all were marked 'Deo et Sacris Regin'. Of the total cost of £58 11s 2d, £38 4s 9d was met by the melting down of the old chapel plate.[92] An inventory of Exeter College chapel silver in 1638 comprized two flagons of silver, two chalices and two plates of silver.[93] By 1659 at Magdalen the altar was now referred to as a communion table, as indicated in a listing of 'a faire large green velvet gold-laced carpet for the Communion table wth gold fringe'.[94]

## RESTORATION

Soon after the Restoration many colleges began to make good their losses. Conspicuous among the replacement of chapel silver was the purchase of a richly embossed service of plate by Dean Fell and the Chapter for Christ Church. The service, all London made and hallmarked between 1660 and 1662 comprises a pair of candlesticks, a large alms dish, two communion cups and patens and a pair of flagons, all richly embossed with floral decoration and silver-gilt (Fig.45). A.C. Pugin's depiction of Christ Church Cathedral Choir for Ackermann's *History of the University of Oxford*, published in 1814, provides the context for the regular use of this rich service (Fig.46).

There is continuous evidence for use of lights on the altar, as upholders of the Anglican tradition point to the injunction of Edward VI in 1547 referring to the retention of 'two lights upon the high altar, before the sacrament, which for the signification of Christ is the very true light of the world, they shall suffer to remain still'. There is also evidence that during the reign of Elizabeth I

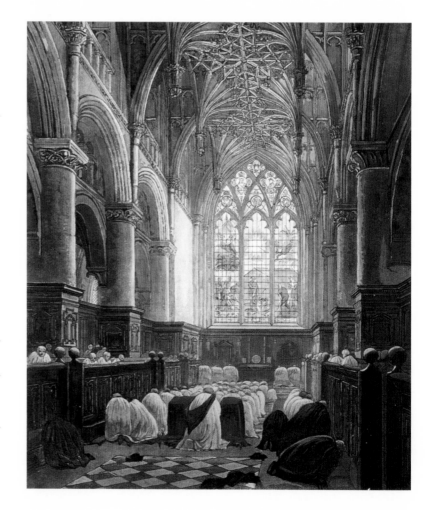

45 (**50**) Chapel set given by Dean Fell to Christ Church, silver-gilt, London 1660–2.

46 Christ Church Cathedral showing the altar with silver, from R. Ackermann, *History of the University of Oxford*, 1814.

not only were candlesticks in use in the Queen's chapel, but 'in many cathedral churches, besides the chapels of divers noblemen' according to Bishop Cosin in his *Notes on the Book of Common Prayer*, *c*.1640.[95] While the candlesticks represented a continuity in chapel plate, the use of larger cups, from which communion wine was drunk not sipped by the whole congregation created the need for large flagons, like those given by Dorothy Wadham to her college (Fig.16), and the fine examples which are part of the Christ Church set.

## THE EIGHTEENTH CENTURY

While the eighteenth century represented a rather low point in the history of the acquisition of chapel silver (as well as in academic prowess) in Oxford and Cambridge there were some notable exceptions. At St John's a 'Gilt Offering Bassin and two large Gilt Candlesticks given by John Taverner of London Gent 1720' were added to the Chapel plate, and were 'kept in the wainscot Box lined with green Bays in the Audit House'.[96] In 1729 William Stratford, Canon of Christ Church and Professor of Theology, bequeathed his 'gilt communion plate to the Dean and Chapter for the use of private communions which may be in that society'. The Stratford Sacramental Service, made between 1699 and 1710 in London by the French Huguenot maker John Chartier, is bold, simple and well made and comprizes a chalice and paten and a plain alms dish.[97] It can be seen in the Cathedral Treasury today. The Benefaction Book at Jesus College records the gift of a pair of altar candlesticks in 1736 from Rt Hon Benjamin Parry, Privy Councillor and Register of Deeds in Ireland. He bequeathed 'the Sum of Forty Pounds to purchase a Piece of Plate for the Altar for kind reception and treatment of his Uncles' who were both afterwards Bishops in Ireland during the troubles. This, together with £18 given by the Principal, went towards the purchase of a large pair of silver candlesticks.

During the eighteenth century much seventeenth-century altar plate was mended and gilded, part of a wider campaign of refurbishment. At New College in 1741, for example, the Oxford goldsmith John Wilkins was paid to mend a pair of flagons and chalices and make two new patens. He then gilded the lot.[98] At St John's in 1759 George Tonge, another Oxford goldsmith, was paid 10s 6d for 'Mending & boiling the silver work and silver added to the Crosier'. Christ Church paid a goldsmith named 'Pearce' in 1764 'for reguilding the Communion plate'. All the colleges record in their bursarial records the termly cleaning of the chapel silver, a task quite distinct from the cleaning of the dining plate. At Lincoln in the 1770s there are payments first to Edward Snelling, and then John Hawkshead for 'cleaning the chapel and plate' which cost 10s a term.

## THE HIGH CHURCH MOVEMENT

The High Church Movement originated in Oxford in 1833, and had as its major objective a return by the Anglican communion to a 'Catholic' church, not Roman Catholic, but faithful in doctrine and ethos to the pure Church of the Early Fathers, disavowing the undue influence of the State in Church affairs. The Movement, whose adherents were often known as Tractarians or Puseyites, was at its height between 1833 and 1845. The most famous of the figures connected with it are John Henry Newman (1801–1890) and John Keble (1792–1866), Richard Hurrell Froude (1803–1836) and Edward Bouverie Pusey (1800–1882).

While Keble's interest in primitive and medieval Christianity was for purely intellectual and theological reasons, that of the Cambridge Camden Society, founded by J.M. Neale in 1839, allied the artistic with the theological and directed the liturgical and ceremonial revival in the Church of England. The High Church, or Oxford Movement revived many pre-Reformation elements of the service, providing goldsmiths with the opportunity to make more elaborate 'chalices', based on medieval examples like those that had survived in Oxford at Corpus (of 1507–8), and Trinity (of 1527–8). The architect William Butterfield voiced the Society's dislike of 'the long deep cups in general use' which were no help in the reverent administration of the sacrament, in preference for the shallow circular bowls and large knops of pre-Reformation chalices. In a letter published in *The Ecclesiologist* in 1842 he wished 'your Society [Camden Society] would engage some goldsmith in the manufacture of chalices of the ancient form… The chalice at Corpus Christi, given by Bishop Fox, the Founder, is exceedingly beautiful, and would be an admirable model; and also that in the possession of Trinity College'.[99]

The 1527–8 chalice at Trinity College became one of the 'icons' of design for the High Church Movement, an example of Oxford drawing upon its reserves of historic plate to inspire design (**25**). The legend engraved around the bowl of the chalice, foot and paten (CALICEM + SALUTARIS + ACIPIAM + ET + NOMINE + DOM[IN]I) (I shall take the cup of salvation in the name of the Lord) proved inspirational to the High Church Movement. Knowledge of the chalice was disseminated via Henry Shaw's *Specimens of Ancient Furniture*, published in 1836, and in an anonymous publication by members of the Oxford Architectural Society and the Cambridge Camden Society *Specimens of Ancient Church Plate* (1843–45). Many reproductions were made, including examples by John Keith, who had been appointed the silversmith of the Ecclesiological Society (formerly the Cambridge Camden Society, founded in 1839) in 1843.[100] Keith made work to the designs of Butterfield, and from 1856 George Edmund Street, who were both busy refurbishing the interiors of churches and chapels. An article on Keith and his firm in the *Art Journal* of 1863 heralds them as 'extensive and meritorious manufacturers of CHURCH

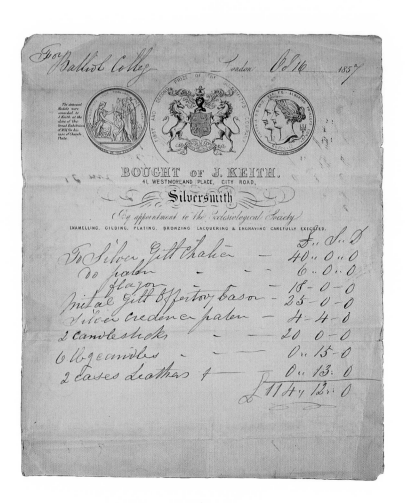

PLATE and other objects in metals. They work from designs supplied by artists who are thoroughly conversant with the style required; and they are especially aided by the Ecclesiological Society.'

Keith supplied Balliol College with a handsome and extensive chapel set, designed by Butterfield, and featured in *The Ecclesiologist* for 1858 (Fig.48). The architect had completed the new chapel in 1857 costing £8,000 and replacing that of 1522–9.[101] Keith's bill for the chapel set remains in the College and lists a 'Silver Gilt chalice' and paten, a 'Metal Gilt Offertory bason', a 'silver credence paten', '2 candlesticks' with 6lb of candles and '2 case Leathers', costing in total £114 12s (Fig.47). The high cost of the chalice reflects its elaborate workmanship. Keith's engraved bill head advertises that he had been awarded medals

47  Bill from John Keith to Balliol for the Chapel set, 1857.

48 (**99**) Chalice, paten
and flagon, silver-gilt,
London 1856–7, designed
by William Butterfield,
made by John Keith.
Balliol.

at the Great Exhibition of 1851 for his case
of Church Plate. Keith also supplied a
parcel- gilt and richly jewelled chalice and
paten of 1874 to Christ Church. His name
and 'pattern No 41', suggesting a standard
design, is stamped on each piece.

At the time that Keith was working, many
of the college chapels were undergoing
redecoration in accordance with High
Church ideals. At Worcester College the
chapel was refurbished by the architect and
decorative art designer William Burges
(1827–1881) in 1863–4, the year he became

Superintendent to the Ecclesiological Society.
The rich and complex decoration of the
chapel is deeply symbolic and remains one of
the most fascinating examples of Burges's
luxuriant medieval-inspired design, incorporating animals and birds at the end of the
pews, elaborate floor mosaics and rich ceiling
patterns. Burges had conducted a protest
campaign of several years' duration about
Keith's standards of metalworking, and at his
suggestion Jes Barkentin (born in Denmark
c.1814) of Regent Street was appointed the
Society's manufacturer in 1867. Burges had

given him and not Keith the Worcester College chapel commission to provide handsome silver bindings to a pair of Old and New Testament bibles, incorporating seventeenth-century Roman plaques, in the year of the completion of the chapel refurbishment.[102] It was the Revd C.H.O. Daniel (1836–1919), a printer and bibliophile, and Fellow of the College and later Provost, who supplied the silver-bound Testaments. Daniel has been described as 'in a quiet and unassuming way a thorough-going high churchman and supporter of ritualism. He worked particularly closely with Burges on the iconographic scheme for the chapel', which is carried through in the design of the covers.[103] The Old Testament binding incorporates at the front a silver panel illustrating the Meeting of Elizer and Rebekah, and the back panel of copper

shows the Adoration of the Magi (Fig.49).[104] The New Testament incorporates two silver panels, at the front the Meeting of Jacob and Rachel and at the back the Baptism of Christ (Fig.50).

Carl Krall (born in Heidelberg, Germany 1844 of Czechoslovakian origin), joined Barkentin's business in 1868, assuming control in 1883 when his partner died. There are several examples of the work his business completed in Oxford, including an altar cross of 1890 for Trinity College chapel,[105] another cross of 1901, converted by Reignbeau of Birmingham into the Oxford Cathedral Church of Christ's processional cross in 2000, and the restoration of William of Wykeham's pastoral staff in 1907.[106] The headed paper on which the report of the restoration was made shows how Krall kept the name of Barkentin and Krall throughout his directorship of the

49 (**101**) Bible cover (Old Testament) by Barkentin & Krall, silver, London 1867–8, incorporating copper plaque. Worcester.

50 (**102**) Bible cover (New Testament) by Barkentin & Krall, silver, London 1867–8, incorporating a 17th century silver Roman plaque. Worcester.

business until he retired. Magdalen has several pieces by Barkentin and Krall, two cruets of 1897–8 given by R.L. Ottley a Fellow (1890–97), a chalice and paten of 1923 given in memory of Thomas Trotter Blockley by his wife in 1923, and a staff of 1935.

Another prominent designer of ecclesiastical plate was Charles Eamer Kempe, although he is better known for his stained glass. For Pembroke Chapel, at his former College, which had been built in 1732, he re-modelled the interior in the neo-Renaissance style in 1884, providing a painted ceiling, and

51 (**105**) Communion cup and paten, silver-gilt, London 1885–6, designed by C.E, Kempe. Pembroke.

designed the Communion cup which is hall-marked for 1885, and inscribed '*Venerabili Corpori Jesu*' and '*Venerabili Sanguini Jesu*' (Fig.51). It replaced the 1696–7 chalice & patens which were 'somewhat clumsy for reverent handling' according to Rev. Douglas Macleane, former Fellow and Chaplain and historian of the College.[107] On the altar are copies in silver of the four bronze candlesticks at the Certosa of Pavia in Lombardy, made in 1580 by Annibale Fontana (*c*.1540–87), and considered to be among the masterpieces of late Renaissance bronze work, and a cross with a rayed centre designed by Kempe to match them (**106**). Ten years later Kempe was busy in Brasenose chapel, adding decorations to the plasterwork fan-tracery of 1659.

By the 1830s the demand for the admission of Dissenters to the University began to grow. This was impossible so long as all matriculands had to subscribe to the Thirty-Nine Articles, instituted in 1581. Attempts to overthrow them were forcibly countered by the High Church Men, who in 1834 protested against 'the notion, that Religion can be taught on the vague and comprehensive principle of admitting persons of every creed'. They felt that 'uniformity of faith upon essential points is absolutely necessary; and that the admission of persons who dissent from the Church of England would lead to disastrous consequences'. It was not until 1854 that religious tests at matriculation were removed, and not until the opening of Mansfield College and Manchester College that there was specific provision for Oxford's Nonconformists. The communion plate at Manchester College was given by 'over eighty old Students of the College', and presented at the opening of the College buildings and dedication of the Chapel in 1893.[108] The engraving on the paten records their 'gratitude' for the College's 'free teaching and reverence for its interpretation of the Christian Life'. At the foundation meeting it was decided that it should be 'open to young men of every religious denomination, from whom no test, or confession of faith, will be required'.[109]

## THE TWENTIETH CENTURY

Chapel silver continues to be an important part of college life. The Founder of St Peter's College, F.J. Chavasse, Bishop of Liverpool (1846–1928), gave his viaticum set of 1837 to the chapel, when it opened as a private hall in 1929 (**97**). St Peter's is the youngest undergraduate college in the University. The Founder's son, C.M. Chavasse (1884–1962), later Bishop of Rochester, was the first Master, holding the position from 1929 to 1939.

While many colleges received old silver from past members, others chose to commission new. At Balliol a silver-gilt altar was made by the London-based art metal-worker W. Bainbridge Reynolds (1855–1935), to the design of Michael Tapper in 1927 as a memorial to those who gave their lives during the Great War.[110] His work was featured in *The Studio*, a progressive Arts and Crafts journal which was published from the late nineteenth century to promote excellence in modern design, as opposed to the endless reproduction of historical decorative art. The Guild of Handicraft's communion cup for St Edmund Hall, made in 1945–6, draws upon the medieval chalices with its sexafoil foot and faceted stem, and shares the aesthetic of Reynolds' altarpiece (Fig.52). Charles Boyton's communion cup for Exeter College, although earlier, dated 1931–2, looks towards more modernist influences (Fig.53). He was clearly influenced by the Danish silversmith Jensen, and had, at the time this cup was made, just changed from dealing in replicas and cheap productions to making contemporary designs of his own.

The twentieth century has seen a great revival in interest in commissioning, and much new silver has been acquired in connection with the college chapels. In the 1950s and early 1960s the Goldsmiths' Company organized several exhibitions to promote contemporary silver, and the opening of cathedral treasuries to the public, aiming to provide a setting for the exhibition

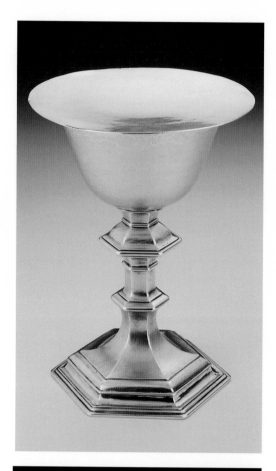

52 (**115**) Communion cup and paten, silver, London 1945–6, Guild of Handicraft. St Edmund Hall.

53 (**110**) Communion cup, silver, London 1931–2, Charles Boyton. Exeter.

54 (**118**) Chapel set,
silver-gilt, London 1953,
designed by Alex Styles for
Garrard. Corpus Christi.

of some of the best pieces of plate owned by churches in a diocese.[111] At the opening of *British Silver Work*, at the Goldsmiths' Company in 1951 G.R. Hughes, an indefatigable supporter of contemporary silver, stated that 'the spirit of patronage on which medieval craftsmen depended is still alive, and… the future of [the Goldsmiths'] craft is, on a long view not unhopeful'. Businesses, corporations and colleges responded by commissioning. To celebrate the Coronation of Queen Elizabeth II, Corpus Christi College went to the Crown jewellers and Royal goldsmiths Garrard for a new silver-gilt chapel set consisting of a wafer box, wine and water cruets, flagon and lavabo (Fig.54). It was designed by Garrard's in-house designer, Alex Styles, who was to become a leader in the field of new commissions in silver. He was honoured with a major retrospective

exhibition at Goldsmiths' Hall in 1974. The design is an inspired combination of tradition and innovation. The smooth matted surfaces, and simple elegant shapes reflect a subdued and elegant conservative modernism. The emblems of pelican, fox and owl connect the commission with the Founder of the College, Richard Fox, whose personal emblem was a Pelican in her Piety. He founded the College in 1517 with the support of his friend and advisor Hugh Oldham, the word 'owl' humorously referring to Oldham ('Owl-dham'). The design was made-up by John Bartholomew, then working for Wakely and Wheeler the well known London goldsmiths. Bartholomew went on to be the influential technician at the Royal College Art, under whom many now famous goldsmiths and silversmiths, like Rod Kelly, have worked.

He currently teaches at Bishopsland, a post-graduate silver and jewellery workshop where young talent is given time to grow. Past Bishopsland students include Peter Musson, who made a finger bowl for New College (2002) (Fig.144), and the Pembroke Double Head of the River Trophy (2004) (**164**).

Altar plate from the Rev. E.S and Mrs Talbot was the first gift of silver to Lady Margaret Hall,[112] founded in 1878 for girls to be prepared for university examinations. The Book of the Benefactors to the Chapel includes in 1955 a silver ciborium designed by the Birmingham designer Eric Clements (b.1925), 'In memory of the parents of the then Principal, Miss L. Sutherland' (Fig.55). It was a statement of faith in the present and the future to buy contemporary, as opposed to antique, plate. Clements also designed and made the communion cup for Nuffield College in 1956, another new foundation with modern ideas about university education. Clements has recently been honoured with a major retrospective exhibition at Birmingham Museum and Art Gallery (2002), and like Alex Styles was one of the great designers of the 1950s–70s. Clements however turned his hand to the wider field of product design, producing tape measures, cutlery, door furniture, and kitchen wares, as well as maces, ceremonial cups, and church plate. Many of the smooth organic lines of Scandinavian modernism found their way into his work as a student at the Royal College of Art, and, as his work

55 (**119**) Ciborium, silver, London 1954–5, designed by Eric Clements. Lady Margaret Hall.

56 (**121**) Communion cup, silver, Birmingham 1966–7, designed by Cyril Shiner. Exeter.

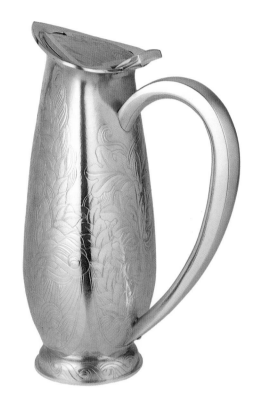

57 (**129**) Lavabo, silver, London 1998–9, Rod Kelly. New College.

58 (**130**) Altar cruet, silver, London 2002–3, Rod Kelly. New College.

reflected the new spirit of the age, many commissions followed.[113] Clements' tutor at Birmingham was Cyril Shiner, who supplied another communion cup for Exeter College in 1967 (Fig.56).

The commissioning of chapel silver continues into the present in the Oxford colleges. The generosity of five different couples who married in the chapel at New College enabled the Dean to commission a new lavabo and one of a pair of altar vessels from the Norfolk-based silversmith Rod Kelly, whose work he saw on display at the Goldsmiths' Company. So far Kelly has completed the lavabo in 1998, and one of the pair of altar vessels. The lavabo is made of silver inlaid with gold, chased with three trouts in water representing the Trinity (Fig.57). The decoration reinforces the function of this piece, as a bowl in which the chaplain washes her hands before preparing the sacrament. One of a pair of altar vessels was completed in 2003, and is chased with a wheatear design and a Green Man adorned with oak leaves (Fig.58). The design on the handle is inspired by one of the misericords in the chapel. Lavabo and altar vessel are united in their triangular form, subtly reinforcing the idea of the Trinity. The vessel for water is not yet finished, and forms the last object in this exhibition of Oxford college silver. Kelly's lavabo and vessels take their place amongst silver of the seventeenth, eighteenth, nineteenth and twentieth centuries on the altar of New College providing four centuries of silver in a chapel that is over six centuries old.

# 3

# SILVER & THE CIVIL WAR
## SACRIFICE & SURVIVAL

'And we doe hereby desire that you will lend
unto Us all such Plate of what kinde soever
wch belongs to your Colledge'.

Extract from Charles I's circular letter to the heads
of Oxford colleges, Oxford, January 1643

### 'LEND UNTO US ALL SUCH PLATE': THE LOAN OF SILVER

59  Charles I,
engraving after
Anthony van Dyck.
Ashmolean Museum
(Hope Collection
inv. 1188).

It is a commonly held belief that 'practically the whole of Oxford's silver was
sacrificed to Charles I'.[114] The evidence for this lies in the relative paucity of
pre-Civil War secular silver in Oxford (there are now under forty pieces) and
the writings of the Oxford antiquarian Anthony Wood (1632–1695), who
wrote in 1674: 'When the Parliamentarians took over the city the colleges
were much out of repair by the negligence of Soldiers, Courtiers and others
that lay in them. Their treasure and plate was all gone'. Samuel Butler in his
poem *Hudibras* conjured up the wholesale destruction of plate when raising
money for the Civil War: 'Did they coin Piss-Pots, Bowls and Flaggons,/Int
offices of horse and dragoons;/And into pikes and musquetteers,/Stamp
beakers, cups and porringers?'.[115]

However, as the silver historian Philippa Glanville has argued, 'the
universally accepted truth that the rarity of early English silver is
'attributable to the Civil War when all old plate was melted down, does not
stand up to close scrutiny'.[116] Although the most important royalist mint was
in Oxford, set up at New Inn Hall (a fourteenth-century academic hall,
re-built in the later fifteenth century) in December 1642, now the site of St
Peter's College (Fig.60), the administrative records that survive in the Oxford

colleges provide plenty of evidence to show not only how much plate escaped both King and Parliament (by being hidden, transformed from secular to chapel use, or from corporate to private property), but also a continuity in the acquisition and use of silver before and after the Civil War. Oxford's melted plate contributed only an insignificant amount to the total coin supplies. As Nicholas Mayhew from the Ashmolean has revealed, £15,000 was struck at the Oxford Mint in 1643, and if we assume that all of it was formerly plate, that compares very modestly with the about £1 million which was struck at the Tower Mint in London during the same period.[117]

After seizing £300,000 worth of silver and gold from the London Mint in 1641, Charles I must have realized the seriousness of the prejudice against him that it caused, and although he settled for £40,000 in precious metal, the damage had been done. It may also explain why Parliament, although desperate for money, waited until June 1642 to issue an order requesting its supporters to contribute horses, cash and plate to finance a fighting force. They offered a generous rate of eight per cent interest, and allowed for the plate 'a consideration' to cover the value of the fashion, of not more than 1s an ounce, a most unusual step. Despite this the Parliamentarians found the Treasury at Christ Church barred against them, but eventually forced an entrance. On searching the place they found nothing but a single groat and halter at the bottom of an iron chest. Enraged they next visited the Deanery, where they found a certain amount, which they locked up in the Dean's chambers. When they returned for their spoils next morning they had vanished. The Deanery plate was later discovered in a trunk in a house in St Ebbe's, and was carried off to Lord Saye's lodgings. More was later found 'hid in walles behinde wainscote & in the sellet'. This was also taken away.[118]

As the winter of 1642 closed in, Charles I retreated to Oxford, himself taking up residence at Christ Church, and proceeded to hold court there. From then, until June

60  New Inn Hall from the Garden, engraving from J. Skelton *Oxonia Antiqua Restaurata* 1818–21, after George Vertue (1750).

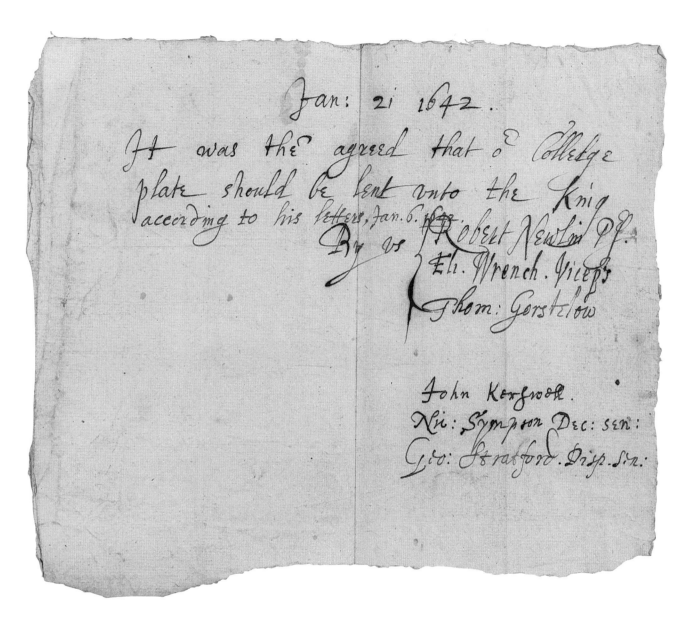

Jan: 21 1642.

It was then agreed that ov Colledge plate should be lent unto the King according to his letters, Jan.6. 1642.

By us    Robert Newlin Pr.
Eli. Wrench. Vicepr
Thom: Gerstelow

John Kerswell.
Nic: Sympson Dec: sen:
Geo: Stratford. Disp. Sen:

61  Note from the President and Fellows of Corpus Christi agreeing to lend Charles I their plate. Old style date Januuary 21 1642, new style 1643. Corpus Christi.

1646, when he surrendered to the Scottish army at Newark, Oxford was his military headquarters. There is plenty of evidence to show that many college butlers removed the plate customarily used at table. Although the colleges entertained royal guests according to their state, it was presumably seen as worth risking offence in order to preserve the plate. At Jesus College the bursar ordered quantities of earthenware for the Hall on the same day that he packed up the dining plate. The Queen lodged at Merton, at Lincoln college rooms were taken as lodgings by cavaliers, the University Parks became the exercise ground for the royalist troops, the Law and Logic Schools were converted into granaries, and New College cloisters and tower were used as powder magazines.

Charles, in response to Parliament's request for plate, issued a circular letter dated 7 July 1642, in which he asked each Oxford and Cambridge college for 'any sums of money that either any of our Colleges, out of their Treasuries, or any person thereof out of their particular fortunes' at the same rate of interest as Parliament had offered. The University came up with a total of £1,360. Parliament on hearing of this 'wicked purpose and intention' demanded that the colleges 'do forthwith put their plate and money into some safe place under good security, that it be not employed against the parliament, certifying us in whose custody it doth remaine'.[119] According to Edward Hyde, Earl of Clarendon (1609–74), who became leading advisor to Charles I during the 1640s, and was author of *The History of the Rebellion*, the King must have had doubts about calling on the colleges a second time, for their property, rather than their cash. Charles is supposed to have received advance information, gleaned from a secret visit to Oxford, that the University, which was very Royalist, would not be too shocked if asked for their plate. This is not surprising as it seems the colleges, like any other institutions and wealthy households, regularly sent their plate to be melted to meet pressing debts, to pay for new building work, the buying of books, or to be re-made. Plate was perceived as a useful reserve, a quickly realisable asset. Oriel College for example regularly sold its silver, in 1544 to buy books, in 1553 to pay a benevolence to the King, and in 1621 to finance building work. What is interesting is that the King, if Clarendon is correct, should have hesitated to ask for the plate, for it implies that he thought that it was valued above and beyond its worth in metal.

According to Anthony Wood's *Annals* for 10 January 1643 'The King's letters [of 6th January] came to all Colleges and Halls for their plate to be brought to the Mint and turned into Money. Many copies of the letter and receipts for the plate given survive in college archives. The letter asked each college to lend to the King, 'all such Plate of what kinde soever wch belongs to your Colledge promising to see the same justly repaydd unto you after the rate of 5s the ounce for white and 5s 6d for guilt Plate Whereupon all sent, except New Inn' where the Mint was set up, under Thomas Bushell. The total

62 (**44**) Oxford Crown, silver, 1644. Ashmolean Museum.

63 (**45**) Triple Unite, gold, 1643. Ashmolean Museum.

64 (**46**) Oxford Crown, silver, mounted, 1644. St Peter's.

amounts of plate surrendered are partly given in Gutch's note of plate loaned to the King by the colleges. Twelve colleges are listed, with a total of 1,610lbs 1 oz 18dwt of plate given. Magdalen gave up the most with 296lbs 1 oz 15dwt, and Balliol the least with 41lbs 4 oz. Exeter, New, Corpus, St John's, Wadham and Pembroke are not mentioned, although we know that many complied with the demand as receipts survive in their archives for plate given. Corpus for example sent in a note of 21 January agreeing to give up their plate (Fig.61). Although the weight might appear to amount to a great deal to modern eyes, it represented only 25% more than the average turnover of exchanged plate per year in the colleges. At Christ Church during the eighteenth century at least 4,280 ozs of plate was traded in for the sterling equivalent, over double the amount sacrificed to Charles I. The regular exchange of plate had cumulatively a far more devasting effect on the survival of silver than the consequences of any national calamity. The eighteenth-century antiquary Joseph Gutch's note is highly misleading, as many colleges submitted plate after the list was drawn up, and others provided the ready money equivalent to the value of their silver. Balliol for example submitted a second load of plate in April and a third in May. It is clear that some believed that the King would honour his agreement and pay the colleges for the silver they had 'loaned'. Sixsmith's bequest in 1651 to Brasenose

directs that the value of his previous gift of a bowl, 'if it can be recovered' is to be added to his legacy of £10 to purchase a new piece of plate. The Mint receipt was always kept in the college chest, and was clearly regarded as a bill upon the Royal Exchequer.[120]

It is clear that many colleges did not trust the Master of the Mint to give an accurate account of the weight of plate given. Jesus College, though loyal to the King, had a goldsmith weigh their loan before it was sent off to New Inn Hall. A note relates that the 'Goldsmiths weights & mynt punctually agree', in fact the Mint calculated 86lbs 10 oz and 15dwt, while the goldsmith returned 86lbs 9 oz 10dwt, a discrepancy to the College's advantage of 3d.[121] As well as a limited amount of gold coinage, a full range of silver denominations, from one pound to one penny was struck at New Inn Hall. Amongst the most famous and attractive of the Mint's products was the Crown struck by Thomas Rawlins in 1644 (Fig.62).[122] It shows a view of the fortified city, with recognisable seventeenth-century houses and medieval spires. The Oxford mint also produced gold and silver coins up to 1646. The gold Triple Unite worth £3 was the largest denomination ever coined in seventeenth-century England (Fig.63). The silver denominations were a pound, half-pound, crown, half-crown, shilling, sixpence, groat, threepence, half-groat and penny (Figs 65 & 66).

65 (**47**) Oxford Penny, silver, 1643. St Peter's.

66 (**48**) Oxford Penny, silver , 1644. St Peter's.

## STRATEGIES OF
## COMPLIANCE AND EVASION

There was no single unified strategy of compliance; each college responded to the call for plate in a different way. The Queen's College was happy to comply with the King's request for help, as early in his reign Charles I had generously given the College six Hampshire livings. However, many colleges sought to evade giving up all their silver. The wording of Charles I's letter sent on 6 January 1643 certainly reveals an awareness of possible areas of dispute. He acknowledged that the founding statutes of many colleges included the protection of college property from appropriation, 'well knowing' the plate 'to be the Goods of your Colledge that you ought not to aline'. Charles argued however that 'no man will doubt but in such a case you may lawfully assist your King in such visible necessity'. The Rector and Fellows of Exeter College decided to exploit this loop-hole, and their response to the King explained that 'This lending of our Plate to be melted downe is against our Statutes, which not only forbid the alienation from it from our College; but also require that the severall peeces thereof bee preserved whole & entire without any change, under the names, & formes in which they were first given'. There is no evidence for such respect and reverence for the College silver in previous years. Inventories in the Rector's accounts between 1566 and 1639 show plenty of plate being melted and exchanged for new. Despite their pleas the Fellows of Exeter were forced to submit to the King, but they clearly decided to try some delaying tactics, asking that 'Some time bee allowed them for takeing out the names and title of the severall donors, together wth weight of the severall pieces, that so their memories, as they well deserved, may bee preserved to Posterity'.[123] Charles grudgingly agreed but urged that they 'will take care [it] may be speedily done, out of the sense of His

pressing occasions'. This excuse is echoed by the House of Lords, who demurred giving up the contents of the Jewel House in 1644 to the Parliamentarians, on the grounds of 'The fastion of it and the badges upon it', which made it, in their eyes, 'more Worth than the Plate itself'.[124] The dons of Exeter also asked that 'reservation bee made of their Communion Plate'. It has been assumed that Charles I automatically exempted chapel plate from the call-up, although no written evidence supports this. Some colleges did give up their communion plate, but most kept it back, and still others turned secular flagons and bowls into liturgical use to protect them. Dorothy Wadham's graceful livery pots (Fig.16) made in 1598, and bequeathed by her to the College in 1617, appear in inventories made before the Civil War with the Treasury plate, and after it in the Chapel audits.

Corpus Christi College seems to have suceeded in giving the monetary equivalent of the weight of plate to the King, rather than the plate itself. There is a record of the College paying £400 to the King in July 1642, which corresponds to the first request for money, and a further payment of £300, which may have been a ransom for the silver. By handing over the money equivalent of the plate the President and Fellows retained a greater degree of control over their property, although they ran the risk of the King demanding the plate at a later date. The College hid a portion of its silver. According to J.G. Milne, who wrote the history of the College in 1946, an old chest had been discovered in the bursary in the early 1940s, which was stuffed with crumpled papers, the latest dating to 1642, which he suggested were used to wrap and hide the College plate. A surviving memorandum dated 21 October 1653 refers to a 'basket wal'd up with cords & stuffed with strawe wherein was two silver flagons, two Cuppes with Covers &... two Common Seales' as well as documents relating to the foundation... brought 'from the wharfe, in

Mr Rowney's [the Steward] Malthouse'.[125] The Rev. H.N. Barton, a Tesdale Scholar at Pembroke (1840–44) and then Fellow (1844–56), questioned the completeness of his college's loan of plate to the King, and wrote that he had 'heard, but heard only, that a quantity of plate, supposedly hidden during the Civil War, was found when the New Buildings were under construction in 1847–8, hidden in an old privy'.[126] Jesus College Cambridge adopted a similar strategy, as the silver was hidden in the Master's orchard.[127]

New College clearly discriminated between plate which was used for exchange, and that which was retained for regular or ceremonial use. The silver held in store in the Bursary was given to the King, but some of that held in the Treasury was kept, hence the survival of the spectacular examples of fourteenth-, fifteenth- and sixteenth-century silver there. However, a later inventory reveals that parts, such as lids of Treasury plate, were given up: a list of silver dated 1664 includes: 'An Indian Nutt garnished with a cover gilt, 21oz and a quarter. The Cover of the Nutt aforesaid may seem to have been given unto King Charles ye first at the siege of Oxon wth the other Coll Plate then given unto him'.[128] St John's made a similar distinction between plate for use at table, and that which could be melted down. A note of 1633 refers to 'Unserviceable plate put into the Chest' and 'Plate to be used uppon extraordinary Occasions' similarly left in the chest.[129]

Another strategy was to divide important college silver and documents between the Fellows. This tactic was adopted by Corpus Christi College Cambridge, and at Magdalen College Oxford. At Corpus it was unanimously agreed 'in consideration of the danger in these times' that the plate should be 'removed out of the treasurie… and every Fellow residing in ye college shall have in his custody two or three pieces of plate for his peculiar use'.[130] This involved absolving individuals of the responsibility for replacing the plate (as directed in the wording of Archbishop Parker's indentures) 'in case any casuall miscarriage of ye said plate should happen', or that it should 'violently be taken', their 'best care and diligence is only requested'. Most of the plate was returned to the College between 1650 and 1670. The untrustworthiness of the Bursar at Magdalen was to be the College's downfall. John Dale, having escaped to London from Oxford, received as planned, a barrel of books from his College, in which was hidden some of the college silver, the College seal and the foundation register.[131] It was not until 1661 that the College discovered that Dale had pawned the college salt, which had been subsequently melted down by a London goldsmith, Leonard Collard. Dale professed in a statement to the courts, where the case was finally referred (and as a result, why legal documents survive to tell us about it) that he 'could not believe a Longe Time that the goldsmith he had pawned it to' would be 'so foolish to melte downe a salt, in which the workmanship was only pretious and remarkable'. Although he asked Collard to 'make another like it', 'haveing no Patterne but what the rude idias remaininge in our memory's would suggest, he could make nothing of it'.[132]

At Jesus College Oxford, the authorities distinguished between that which belonged to the institution, and that which was privately owned. Daniel Evans, the Vice-Principal, had to rescue from the Mint 'a litle peece of plate of another mans wch was in my study, & by mistake taken out wth the Coll: plate & lent to his Matie'.[133] Evans had to pay the £2 for the melt price. Even the expenses incurred in taking the College silver to the Mint is recorded: 'for Coards for the Trunke wherein the College plate was 1d', 'For carriage, weighinge & keepinge of the Coll: plate 3s 6d'. Dr Frewen the President of Magdalen College (1626–1642) retrieved the so-called 'Founder's Cup' from the Oxford Mint for £11 11s 6d.

## VISITATION, IMPOSITION AND RESTORATION

The impact of the Civil War on college silver did not end in 1646 with the King's surrender. The University was subject to a Visitation, which was intended to 'reform and regulate it'. The Vice-Chancellor Samuel Fell, who was also Dean of Christ Church, was dismissed from both his posts, as were several other heads of houses and recalcitrant Fellows, who were replaced by men ordered by the Visitors. In all between 300 to 400 members of the Univeristy were expelled. At New College the drama of the Civil War is vividly recorded in an inventory begun in December 1649. A list of silver was about to be made by the Warden, Dr Pincke; he had entered one line, then another hand appears, explaining: 'Mr Warden began to make an inventory, but being in danger of sequestration all this Time, & at last turned out, He only wrote Emprimis &c and there ended'. It was not until nine years later that the next inventory was made listing the silver 'for Mr Wardens use & in his Lodgeings taken Dec. 17 1658'.[134] In the intervening years George Marshall had been imposed upon New College as their Warden, contrary to their statutes, which laid down that the Warden must be a Fellow or ex-Fellow of the College. It appears that the Fellows had packed up their departing Warden's silver, and made sure the unwanted new arrival remained ignorant of its whereabouts. Pincke himself had claimed his 'true right to that plate during my life, residing in my selfe, and none else'. An inventory of silver made in October 1657 lists all the 'severall peeces of plate belonging to the True and Lawful Warden... for his Use, as they were found in a Truncke wherein they were putt (when they were removed out of New College) at the first opening of that Trunck taken by Henry Stringer, the then true and legall Warden'. A document has just come to light in the Hertfordshire Record Office that reveals that Sir John Halsey, a descendant of

67 (**49**) Cup and cover, silver-gilt, London 1660–1. Magdalen.

William of Wykeham's sister Agnes, from Great Gaddesdon in Hertfordshire, took charge of this plate until it was reclaimed by the College from Halsey.

In the same year that Warden Pincke was expelled from New College, Lincoln invested in a new 'lock and key for the Tresury and for a lock and staple for the great chest'. They must have been substantial as they cost £6 7s 8d, at a time when three dozen pewter spoons, a dozen pewter porringers and a chafing dish only cost £1 5s 11. Lincoln College was clearly making their valuables safe against further appropriation.

Several of the colleges bought handsome loving cups to celebrate the return of their Fellows at the Restoration of Charles II. The example from Magdalen (Fig.67) bears the names of those who were reinstated, their memories forever handed round amongst the Fellowship as a constant reminder of the Civil War and its impact on the College. It is referred to in College as 'The Cup of the Restored Fellows', and is engraved with the inscription 'Pars non minima Eorum / Qui cum per duodecim continuos annos exulassent / Eo quod turbatis rebus Parti Regiae studerunt / Regnante Carolo Primo / In monumentum perenne / Ipsorum Restitutionis postliminio factae / Anno 1660 / Auspiciis Caroli Secundi' (not the least among those who for 12 years continuously had been in exile, because in that turbulent period they supported the party of the King in the reign of Charles I [they presented this cup] as a lasting commemoration of their own reinstatement from exclusion in the year 1660, under the auspices of Charles II). The bowl bears the arms of the College, and on the cover the Royal Arms encircled by a Garter under a crown and 'C.R.'. When the Parliamentary troops had entered Oxford, Magdalen, a college under royal patronage, and whose Warden had been marked out by Charles I as a high churchman, suffered greatly: the chapel was stripped, its ornaments sold off, and the medieval glass destroyed. Most of the Fellows, Demies, clerks and choristers had refused to acknowledge the new regime and were expelled, and replaced with Presbyterians. At Brasenose the College Gaudy, St Chad's day, 2 March, was 'sometime after the Return of Charles the Second wch was in 1660 May 29th, this Gaudy was put off till then to make ye 29th of May ye greater Gaudy'.[135] Today the Magdalen cup is used when the toast 'jus suum cuique' is drunk at the yearly commemoration, on October 25, of another restoration, that of 1688.

Accounts from the colleges from the early 1660s give little hint of a shortage of plate, and many like Magdalen still had much to spare. A note of 1663 notes that 'such plates as are in the President's Lodgings of which there are many of the same sort and not so usefull, and which are decayed and to be mended, be converted into such other plates as may be of more use, ingraving the names and coates of the donors of such plates on the plates into which they shall be converted, and a catalogue of such plates so altered to be written in two copyes'.[136]

# 4

# DRINKING & DINING
## STRUCTURE & COMMUNITY

68 (**27**) Cup and
cover, silver-gilt,
London 1533–4.
Corpus Christi.

Apart from the chapel, the community of a college gathered together as a
whole in the dining hall, which was therefore a central arena for display, and
for the reinforcement of the administrative and social hierarchies within a
college. Junior members of a college had to attend dinner under penalty of
a fine. Vivian Green's vivid reconstruction, from the College accounts, of
dinner at Lincoln College in the second half of the sixteenth century
conjures up what must have been the daily ritual within all the colleges.[137]
As the whole body of the College gathered in the Hall, the Butler rang the
bell, after which a scholar said grace, which was followed by a reading from
a chapter of the Bible. The Rector, or the most senior Fellow, who entered
from the lodgings from a side door, presided at high table garnished with
silver and covered with a linen table cloth. There were two other tables,
ranked according to the grading of their members, Gentlemen Commoners,
M.A.s, B.A.s, scholars, commoners, battelers or servitors. The main dish, a
piece of meat, was brought into the Hall, laid on the service table and carved.
The servitors then took the trenchers to the table for the commons of meat
to be placed on them. At the conclusion of the meal, the 'grace-cup' was sent
up the Fellows' table, and after grace had been said the Fellows filed out of
the hall, each turning to bow to the High Table as he reached the doorway.

It was not so much the things you ate and drank which defined your
position, but as where you sat and with what you consumed them. Individuals
were marked out by the utensils they used, to which they were allowed access.
Not everyone was privileged to drink and eat from silver. It was only the head
of the college, Fellows and their guests who dined off silver and silver-gilt,
others drank from pewter and earthenware pots. There are regular orders in the
accounts of college cooks for the purchase of wooden trenchers, several dozens
at a time, from which the servitors, the lowest order of student, both served and
fed. At Jesus College 130 dozen wooden trenchers were bought for 46s 8d in
Michaelmas 1737. Used for the year, they were then burnt, which was both
hygienic and an economical form of re-use as fuel. These wooden trenchers had

replaced those of stale bread in the sixteenth century.[138] Some Scholars and Commoners ate from pewter. New College still possesses dozens of eighteenth-century pewter plates, and the buttery at Queen's is decked with them today. As late as 1817 John Henry Newman wrote home from Trinity that fine food was 'served up in old pewter plates and misshapen earthenware jugs'. It was not until the second quarter of the nineteenth century that crockery was generally introduced into the college dining halls in place of pewter.[139]

Not everyone found Oxford dining congenial. A visiting German scholar to Oxford in 1710 found dining at Christ Church grim, although he appears to have been determined not to find anything to praise during his stay in England. The hall he described as 'fearfully large and high but otherwise poor and ugly in appearance; it also reeks so strongly of bread and meat that one cannot remain in it, and I should find it impossible to dine and live there. The disgust

was increased (for the table was already set), when we looked at the coarse and dirty and loathsome table cloths, square wooden plates and the wooden bowls into which the bones are thrown; this odious custom obtains in all the colleges'. A Christ Church undergraduate over 140 years later described his dinners there as 'disgraceful', beginning at five, 'men were divided into messes, and a batch of about half a dozen men occupied each table... Though the forks and spoons were of silver (some very old, the gifts of former members of the House, whose names were engraved on them), the plates and dishes were of pewter' (Fig.70).[140]

## THE ACADEMIC AND SOCIAL STRUCTURE OF A COLLEGE

The strict social divisions within a college community were remarked upon by foreign visitors. In 1598 Paul Hentzner commented that at Oxford those that dined in Hall were 'divided into three Tables: the first is called the Fellows' Table, to which are admitted Earls, Barons, Gentlemen, Doctors and Masters of Arts, but very few of the latter; this is more plentifully and expensively served than the others; the second is for Masters of Arts, Bachelors, some Gentlemen, and eminent Citizens; the third is for people of lower condition' (Fig.69).[141] Nicholas Fitzherbert writing in 1602 remarked that to confuse these ranks was regarded 'in the light of a crime'.[142] Different ranks within a college were made physically clear by where you were allowed to sit in hall.

Dining at High Table, literally raised above the rest, was the Head of House, variously called Dean, Master, President, Principal, Provost, Rector, or Warden, and with him the Fellows (some of whom had particular roles, like the Bursar). The country diarist and clergyman Francis Kilvert, who had come up to Wadham in 1859, came back in 1876 and dined at High Table, 'an object of my under-graduate ambition realized at last'. The silver

69  A servitor from R. Ackermann, *History of the Univeristy of Oxford*, 1814.

70 The dining hall of Christ Church, one of the largest medieval halls in Oxford, silver in the foreground, R. Ackermann, *History of the Univeristy of Oxford*, 1814.

was engraved with who was permitted to use it. At Corpus silver for the President was inscribed 'in usum Principalis' At Pembroke the words 'in usum Magistri et sociorum' or 'in usum commensalis superioris' indicated silver designated for the use of the Master, Fellows and later the Gentlemen Commoners. 'Commensalis' roughly translated means a table mate. At Jesus silver for the use of bachelors of arts, is engraved 'in usum Artium Baccalaurorum'. At Exeter silver for the battelers (those of 'lower condition') is engraved 'in usum Battellariorum in aula publica' (for the use of the battelers in the public hall [of the college]).

The use of silver for drinking and dining was an important privilege of rank. The Head of House was allocated plate from the College for his private use, which was separately inventoried. At St John's in 1633, 'Plate delivered to Mr President for use' included 'a standing Cup dubble gilt' and tankards, pots, a trencher salt, a standing salt, three silver goblets a gilt basin and ewer and 18 spoons.[143] According to an inventory listing the President's plate at Corpus of 1640, President Jackson would have had for his own use two silver flagons, two silver cups, two salt cellars, a mazer and eighteen spoons, as well as a quantity of pewter, including '5 dozen trencher plates, 18 dishes greate & small, 2 pie-plates' and four porringers. At New College in 1659 the Warden was allocated one ewer and basin, 2 'great flagons', 'two stoopes or lesser flagons, one flagon of middle size, a sugar boxe with a spoon, a double bell salt, four beer bowls, six other bowles, two wine goblets, 24 slip spoons', and six more 'with gilt heads'; to this was added a smaller quantity of gilt plate, including 'a salt, 3 goblets, and a great bowl'. So the 'minimum kit' in the early seventeenth century comprised at least a large covered cup, a ewer and basin for washing the fingers, a set of spoons, various types of lesser drinking vessels and a standing salt. The Warden at New College kept his silver in 'the Studie by the Dineing Roome' in a 'wooden chest wth a cover, Locke & Key to keep the plate in'. Silver reserved for the head of the college was symbolic of his power and status and was fiercely defended. The importance and impact of the Warden's silver does not seem to have diminished in time, although the types of silver used did. Mrs Campbell remembered dining with Warden Spooner (1844–1930) in his Lodgings at New College in 1905, she recorded in her diary 'Dinner table filled with things. Elaborate flower piece, two enormous silver mugs, tankards, I suppose, little clear glass pitchers of water, old silver, large salt cellars and pepper mills, silver dishes with dessert round the flowers, candles and silver mugs'.[144]

Fellows were permitted to sign out plate for private use in their rooms and rules existed for its allocation and control. At Lincoln College the Butler reminded members 'That the Plate which is borrowed by any Fellow be returned clean by his servant'.[145] At Brasenose it was decreed 'that no Person not Fellow be allowed to keep any plate above 24 hours in his room'.[146] Merton was the first Oxford college to provide its Fellows with a common room in 1661, copying Trinity College Cambridge, which had instigated this new form of social space eleven years earlier. At Merton the room over the kitchen with the 'cockloft' became 'in communem usum sociorum' (for the use of the fellows in common) and a man was hired at a shilling a week to keep it order. Lincoln College followed suite in 1662, and Trinity three years later. The changes in dining arrangements and the acceptance of other forms of social etiquette are reflected in the invention of new rooms, for new and different pursuits using new types of silver.

The introduction of the Common Room created the need for a whole new class of silver, and it is clear from college regulations that it was seen as quite separate from other plate. At Brasenose it was resolved in 1788 that 'the Common Room wine shall not, on any pretence whatever, be allowed to be drunk, nor the Common Room decanters, glasses, knives etc be used out of the Common Room'.[147] At Lincoln 'wine, fruit, beer and punch' was bought for the Common Room costing 14s 9d to celebrate Christmas.[148] In 1780 the Common Room silver at Christ Church was the specific target for a burglary; a report in *Jackson's Oxford Journal* reveals that the booty was 'thought to have been hidden under water' and the two felons were committed to the Castle.[149]

Chocolate, coffee and tea equipages were bought for these new rooms from the mid-eighteenth century. A note at Brasenose College of 1749 explains that 'Green Tea Bohea & Coffee & Chocolate are of late years thought fitt for Philosophers and a glass of white wine may not be amiss'.[150] At Queen's College, for example, plate was sold in 1717 to buy 'a Large chocolate pot wth College crest' and a tea pot.[151] The early arrival of coffee in Oxford is explained by John Evelyn, who went up to Balliol in 1637: he mentions in his journal the arrival of 'Nathaniel Conopius out of Greece… He was the first I ever saw drink Coffe, which custome came not into England til 30 years after'. In fact the first coffee house in England was opened in Oxford fourteen years later, in 1651, by Jacob the Jew at the Angel Inn. By 1740 there were some thirteen coffee houses in Oxford, and by 1800 twenty. The 1740s also brought tea wares to Oxford: at Brasenose in 1741 a pair of oval tea caddies, a 'neat inlaid tea chest', a 'polished engraved and beaded tea pot', a 'pierced sugar basket wth bason', and a pair of tea tongs were purchased. By 1821 the tea chest 'was decayed and valueless' having been put to such regular use.[152] The 1770s brought a later invention, the tea urn, or vase. St John's acquired its tea urn and matching pair of caddies from George

Tonge, made by John Rowe of London (**88**), and Exeter bought a tea urn via a gift from Langley in 1778, retailed by the London goldsmiths Peter and Ann Bateman.

The undergraduate body of a college was divided between Scholars, Commoners, Battelers and Servitors. Each rank of student, bar the lowest, the servitor, was expected to give a different type of gift of silver, or money in lieu. Scholars were of the foundation of a college. At Pembroke College in the 1760s Scholars gave spoons that cost about 15s each.[153] Commoners were not on the foundation of a college, but allowed to take their commons, that is their board and lodging, at their own expense. The influx of undergraduates during the reign of Elizabeth I, especially after the matriculation statutes of 1565 and 1581, transformed some of the colleges from small exclusive bodies into large communities. The newcomers were different from the old type of students. They were less clerical and more numerous. There were four classes 1) The Gentlemen or Fellow Commoners, sons of noblemen, knights or esquires; they were admitted to the Fellows' table, paid higher fees, which were allocated at various times to the purchase of silver, the library and new buildings 2) the Commoners, the sons of ordinary gentry, clergy and trades-men, who formed the bulk 3) Battelers, ranked below Commoners, but above Servitors, and distinguished by different scales of caution money (money deposited on arrival to stand as credit against charges incurred).[154] They were entitled to no commons but purchased their own meat and drink, unless they served a Fellow or Gentleman Commoner, and then they were allowed the dishes that came from their tables. The fourth and lowest category of undergraduate were the Servitors (Fig.69). In return for reduced fees they would perform such menial tasks such as calling Fellows and other undergraduates before morning prayers, waiting at table, and lighting fires.

An inventory of silver at Magdalen College made in 1623 gives a clear indication of these distinct categories of college membership. Pots, bowls, salts and elaborate knopped spoons were reserved for the Fellows' table. The Sojourners' (the College's specific name for Gentlemen Commoners) plate comprised mostly silver drinking pots, while the Battelers' silver was confined to beakers.[155] An inventory of silver at Christ Church of 1679 similarly makes the different divisions clear: the Dean and Canons were not only given tankards, but also candlesticks, chafing dishes (for keeping food warm), salts, and spoons. A less diverse range of silver was allocated 'for The Use of the Nob: & Gent Comners in the Hall', including tankards and spoons.[156]

If silver was used as a means of classifying the college body, it was also used to unite it, a means to remember the Founder, Fellows and friends, to link the present community with that of the past. The dining hall was also an opportunity to assert unity, and the corporate identity of the college. The latter was made possible through the proliferation of the college arms engraved on nearly every piece of college silver, as well as on the wooden panelling, the stone carving, and on occasionally on the picture frames. The circulation of grace cups like the one at New College c.1480 (Fig.82) was a physical underlining of the shared experience of the members of a college. It is still customary on Gaudies (after the Latin *Gaude*, Rejoice) to hand round a grace cup; the term Gaudy by the seventeenth century referred to a commemorative feast, providing an oppor-tunity for former members to return to their college. The drinking from a communal cup was a very direct way of emphasizing the unity of the college and its members. Richard Cook in his *Oxford Night Caps* (1871) explains that 'before the removal of the cloth... the cup is handed round the table, no one presuming to apply his lips to it until two persons have risen from their seats... the persons standing being the sureties that the one holding the cup should come to no harm whilst taking it!' The frequent refurbishment of these cups is proof of their regular use. George Tonge the Oxford goldsmith was paid by St John's to gild their grace cup, and provided 'a new Lather Case to ye Same' in 1784.

## THE MEDIEVAL AND TUDOR TABLE

Early English silver is very rare; fewer than 300 pieces made before the 1520s survive, and many of those 300 pieces come from Oxford and Cambridge colleges.[157] We can reconstruct what furnished the medieval college dining table from inventories, and draw upon paintings and engravings of royal and noble tables, which the colleges emulated. The number of individuals catered for in some of the colleges is equivalent to that of a moderately-sized noble household. For example Exeter College, founded in 1314 by Walter de Stapledon, Bishop of Exeter, was a relatively small college and comprised at the time of its foundation thirteen Fellows, including a Rector and chaplain. Magdalen, founded in 1458, by contrast, was larger, the foundation consisting of a President, forty Fellows, thirty Scholars called Demies, eight Clerks, and sixteen Choristers. The space in which they dined usually survives, although altered over time according to circumstance, fashion and wealth. At Magdalen the hall or 'Magna Aula' was built in 1470, where Fellows and scholars ate together. Straw and rushes were scattered on the floor, which was renewed at feast days. A great table, and table cloths are also mentioned.[158] Lincoln College, founded in 1427, retains its fifteenth-century hall, and although restored in 1891, it is substantially the building of 1437, with noble beams and a fine smoke louvre.

Hugh Rhodes's *The Book of Nurture* (1577) provides us with an early description of a complete table setting for a lord, which would have been appropriate for the head of a college and his Fellows and guests. On spreading the table cloth a salt cellar was placed to the right hand of the lord, to the left one or two trenchers (first made of bread, then wood or pewter) then a knife, then white rolls, then a spoon resting on a folded napkin. The most important pieces of silver at the medieval table were the salt, a covered cup, a set of spoons and a ewer and basin for washing one's fingers. Until the mid-seventeenth century, the standing salt,

71 (**11**) Standing salt and cover, silver-gilt and red glass, *c.*1475–94. New College.

72 (**13**)  Hexagonal standing salt and cover, silver-gilt with crystal, pearls and enamel, c.1494–1501. Corpus Christi.

an essential centrepiece of the dining table, was a symbol of luxury and status. The extraordinary value set on salt appears to have been peculiar to England, and perhaps related less to its cost and more to its ritualistic purifying qualities, which were religious in origin.[159] Of the many salts that appear in household and college inventories, only 'a handful of important late medieval salts survive, notably in Oxford colleges'.[160] They were display items par excellence, and often incorporated armorials, and rare and exotic materials, like crystal and jewels. In Hunt's *Exemplars of Tudor Architecture*, published in 1830, the author notes that 'salt-cellars were also pieces on which taste and fancy of goldsmiths were severely exercised, these artists it may be observed, were, at the period of which we treat, held in high estimation, and ranked with architects, sculptors and other professors of the fine arts'.[161] A small group of salts from the late fifteenth and sixteenth centuries survive at New College, All Souls, Corpus Christi, and Trinity.

Walter Hill, who was Warden of New College 1475–1494, gave a lobed salt to the College. His name appears in a version of the Vulgate Psalm 104, verse 6 and engraved round the base 'Super WA montes TER stabunt HIL aque M' (Fig.71). Of a similar date is a hexagonal salt from Corpus Christi College (Fig.72). It bears the Founder's symbol of the Pelican Vulning, or plucking at her breast, in the cast plaques, which were originally mounted over red and green enamel. An inventory of 1640 of the President's plate includes two salts, one described as a 'silver salt seller with a round peece of christall in the middle with a cover', the other 'guilt with a cover': either could be the 'pelican' salt. The list of Buttery plate reminds us that the plates were of pewter and wood, even at High Table. There is very little mention of silver dishes or plates; the precious material was mostly reserved for the serving of food, or for drinking within a college.

An inventory of 'iocalia et certa bona' given to New College by Archbishop Warham in 1516 includes 'unum salinum deauratum sumptuose factum cum una simia quais sedente super pulvinate cum coopertorio ponderis li unc', that is 'a gilt salt, sumptuously made, with a monkey seated on a cushion with a cover, weight 51 ounces' (Fig.73). It sits on three feet in the form of wild men, or woodwoses. The word 'sumptuous', like the word 'curious' which appears in inventories, implies elaborate and detailed workmanship. William Warham had been a Fellow of New College before becoming a diplomat and Archbishop of Canterbury (1504–32). His salt was used at table during the seventeenth century, as there are records for its mending. For example in 1619 Walter Wilkins was paid 6s for 'mending the ape salt'.[162] The cover was lost at an early date, as it is not recognisable in the later sixteenth-century inventories, nor is it mentioned amongst the plate lost or saved at the time of the Civil War. The monkey salt, referred to as 'the Ape salt' in College inventories, was put away and rediscovered during the eighteenth century, when the guilloche band was added.

Another distinctive and later form of standing salt, of 1549–50, survives at Trinity College (Fig.74). Three caryatid brackets support a rock crystal tube through which can be seen a cast female figure, repeated as the finial.[163] There are only a few examples of these 'architectural salts', like the 1577–8 example in the Museum of Fine Arts in Boston.[164] As Hugh Tait has observed, the large number of objects incorporating rock crystal in Renaissance goldsmiths' work suggests that this rare material was salvaged from monstrances and other medieval ecclesiastical objects that had been seized from churches and monasteries. In the 1640s John Dale the Bursar of Magdalen pawned a college salt whose 'workmanship was… pretious and remarkable', and remembered that when he was a boy in the College 'it was reckon'd a Thing of greate value'; it was

probably a fine example of one of these elaborate standing salts.[165] In the mid-sixteenth century the standing salt was losing its status at table, as salt became cheaper and it became smaller, a good example being the drum salt of 1554–5 at Corpus (Fig.75). Although no other medieval and Tudor salts survive in the colleges, we know that once they were common to all the high tables in Oxford. At St John's College in 1591 'a Salt wth a Cover double gylt O[u]r Founders gift', is listed. This salt like most of the other surviving salts of this period is gilt, that is covered with one, two, or even three layers of gold. At Exeter College in 1592 'one little salt with a cover duble gilt, a greater salt parcil gilt [part gilded] wthout a cover' are listed, and at Balliol in 1608 there was 'a greate white Salte wthout a cover', that is silver, ungilded.

73 (**18**) Standing salt, silver-gilt with garnets and bowl of crystal, known as the 'Ape Salt', early 16th century. New College.

74 (**29**) Standing salt and cover, silver-gilt and crystal, London 1549–50. Trinity.

75 (**28**) Drum salt and cover, silver-gilt, London 1554–5, mark TL. Corpus Christi.

Towards the middle of the sixteenth century the more imposing pedestal salts went out of fashion and a simpler style, known as the bell salt, was introduced. Often in two or three tiers, on less formal occasions the two lower parts served as individual salt holders, and the top as a pepper caster, and when needed all three parts fitted together to serve as a ceremonial salt. 'A duble bell salt silver' was bought by Magdalen College in 1589.[166] An inventory of 1596 from Oriel records a 'Double bell salt with a cover the bottom standing on three balls'; it was double gilt and weighed 22oz.[167] None survive in the colleges. Alongside these grander salts there were smaller uncovered ones for everyday use, or for the less important guests at table.

During the sixteenth century knives and forks were used at table for serving food rather than for eating. At Lincoln College we know there was a pewter sink in the Hall, with running water where diners could wash their hands, an essential when hands were used, rather than forks.[168] It was the spoon which predominated for personal use, and there was an etiquette for use. Rhodes in 1577 prescribed that the spoon should never be filled full when being lifted from the porringer to mouth, and never left in the bowl or leant against its side. When finished with, it was to be licked clean.[169] From the mid-fifteenth century English inventories regularly list spoons, generally silver, some pewter.[170] Although yeomen, parsons and tradesmen owned spoons, it was in merchant and noble households that the most elaborate are listed, and the colleges were certainly on a par with them. Only rare examples such as those at Corpus Christi, given by the Founder's friend Hugh Oldham, bearing cast owl knops, survive in colleges. In the college accounts however we get a much fuller picture of the importance and prevalence of the spoon. In 1556 Thomas Pope left Trinity 'thyrtene spoones whereof xii pcell gilt and one complete gilte'. These are undoubtedly apostle spoons, the 'master' bearing an image of Jesus, and the others the twelve apostles. St John's College bought 'halfe a dozen of Apostle Spoones' in 1587.[171] They would have looked like the 1595–6 examples given to Pembroke in the nineteenth century (Fig.129). Oriel owned a 'dozen spoones one whole guilded the rest guilded on the endes have the pictures of the twelve apostles' in 1596, while Dr Samuel Radcliffe the Principal of Brasenose rescued 'six apostle spoones' from the Mint in 1642. Other sorts of spoon are recorded. St John's owned 'one dozen spones with maydens heds' and a further 'one dozen spoones wth the holy lamb' bought by the College c.1590. They were carefully monitored. Magdalen possessed a total of five dozen and nine spoons in 1598, which were variously marked,

76 (6) Mazer, maple wood with silver-gilt mounts, before 1437. All Souls, on loan to the Ashmolean Museum.

nine with 'MC pricketh on the knob' and '20 wthout marks on the bowl but marked with MC in the outsie of the bole'.[172] By 1623 St John's College listed 63 spoons in the Bursary, 17 in the Lodgings, 58 in the Buttery and 102 in the Tower, while 'two... have beene antiently lost'. Griffin Owen the Butler at Christ Church was preparing the silver 'wont to be used on festival days' in 1582, and listed '2 dussen of silver spoones, one with long knoppes the other with slippes wth round knopps'.[173] Slip spoons were declining in popularity during the Stuart period, so the Christ Church examples were old-fashioned at the time of the inventory. Christ Church won a further three gilt spoons with virgins' heads in 1615, having put £10 into the Virginia Lottery. It was not until the early eighteenth century that forks, although introduced in the 1630s, came into regular use, displacing the importance of the spoon. They do not appear in college inventories in any quantity until the 1720s.

There were many types of drinking vessel on the medieval and Tudor table. One of the earliest forms was the mazer, a turned maple

77 (**26**) Standing mazer, maple wood with silver-gilt mounts, London 1529–30. All Souls, on loan to the Ashmolean Museum.

78 (**16**) Coconut cup with silver-gilt mounts, late 15th century, known as the 'Palisade Cup'. New College.

wood bowl, usually with a cover, mounted in silver-gilt, and often bearing the arms of the owner as an enamelled boss in the base of the bowl.[174] It is clear why so few survive: in an inventory of Magdalen College silver of 1662 it was noted that 'an old mazor wth sylver brims & ye wood rotten' was changed 'for some other plate usefull for the Lodging'.[175] Examples survive from All Souls and Oriel, although from inventories we know that in the fifteenth century many more survived, both in these colleges and others. A mazer is mentioned in an inventory at All Souls of 1437, given by Thomas Ballard (d.1465), Sheriff of Kent in 1452.[176] This must be the surviving mazer which bears an enamel roundel with his arms (Fig.76). Three other fifteenth-century mazers survive in the College, one with a cover mounted with gold leaves, an uncut ruby and pearls, and inside the bowl a setting for a stone; and two others without lids. The College also possesses a large mounted mazer on a standing foot, the silver-gilt mount hallmarked London 1529–30 (Fig.77). Scratched inside the foot is 'R. Hovenden Custos 1571' which was the year

Hovenden was elected Warden of All Souls. Moffatt mentions that the silver historian Cripps believed the signature to be that of Hovenden himself, as it corresponds to his hand, as seen on an inventory of 1583. A list of plate in the President's Lodgings at Corpus of *c.*1640 includes 'a broade wooden dish or Mazir with silver brims', which has long since left the College. Mazers fell out of fashion in the sixteenth century, and John Evelyn refers to them as curiosities in his diaries by the 1660s.

Coconuts, imported from the Middle East as exotic rarities and known as 'Indian Nutts', were often turned into drinking cups with silver-gilt mounts and stems. Rowland Byres, Provost of Queen's College in 1427, 'gave a gilded nut', mentioned in a list of plate made in 1650–60. The 'Palisade' cup at New College, *c.*1480, is an unusual surviving example described in 1664 as 'An Indian Nutt garnished, and gilt impalled', referring to the silver-gilt fence around the base, from which the coconut is supported via what look like hawthorn branches (Fig.78). It is one of four coconut cups to survive in the

College. Another cup from Oriel is of a similar date, and is by tradition said to have been presented by the second Founder Bishop Carpenter (**14**). Exeter College also possesses a coconut cup, dating from the early sixteenth century (Fig.79) as well as an ostrich egg cup, whose silver-gilt mounts are engraved '1610' (Fig.80). The egg shell is supported by three ostrich legs, and the cover has as its finial a cast ostrich standing on three plumes, which Pevsner was to describe as a 'uniquely witty and elegant vessel'.[177] The 'rich Aggatt Cupp' given to Jesus College by Lady Bramley and listed in 1629, could well have been a much older piece, part of some wealthy cabinet.[178]

Although only the lid survives, the All Souls nautilus cup must have been as grand as any within a noble collection. Silver, gilt and richly enamelled with five panels of heraldic diaper pattern, it is of French work, dating to *c.*1300.[179] The lid from All Souls is not the only example of early

79 (**15**) (far left) Coconut cup and cover, silver-gilt mounts, early 16th century. Exeter.

80 (**40**) Ostrich egg cup and cover, silver gilt mounts, engraved '1610'. Exeter.

81 (**4**) (above) Pair of pilgrim flasks, silver-gilt, Paris c.1400–40. All Souls.

continental silver in Oxford, although the college holdings are predominantly London made. A pair of wine bottle or flagons, c.1400–40 of Parisian workmanship, from All Souls are the 'sole survivors from medieval Europe of a type of plate well known from inventory description and illuminated illustrations' (Fig.81).[180] The swan heads that form the stops for the chains refer to the supporters of Archbishop Chichele's coat of arms. The flasks, used for serving wine from the sideboard, may have been either acquired in Paris, where Chichele frequently went on diplomatic missions, or given to him as a gift. There are occasional references to French silver in inventories, such as the four 'french boules' and a 'french gilt boule' that appear in a listing of plate at Oriel, dated 1600. Rarer still is German silver, referred to as 'almain' work in the

inventories.There is an unusual piece of South German silver c.1690 at Corpus, studded with coins from Aleppo, the gift of John Halifax (**68**).[181] Coconuts, ostrich eggs, shells and silver from abroad would have added glamour and curiosity and a touch of the foreign to the robust Oxford college table loaded with silver-gilt and gold.

Most of the colleges would have had pottery jugs and drinking vessels, although because of their fragility few survive from before the early eighteenth century.[182] A few examples still exist at New College, mostly Rhenish salt-glazed stoneware flagons, which have lost their metal mounts, and excavated in the twentieth century. References to these salt-glazed jugs are numerous in sixteenth century wills and inventories, 'one stone jugge double gilted' was valued at 30s in 1588.[183]

There were many other types of silver drinking vessels described in inventories, and in some cases we cannot match surviving objects to them. For example we do not know what the 'hye standing cupp called a monsieurs bowl given by Mr Perpoint' looked like, although we know that it had 'his name engraven underneath the bottom and his armes on the side given his admission to the commensalis cum soci 1596, double guilded 18oz'. At Oriel there were several monsieur bowls, as well as french 'bowles' all double gilt, beakers, tuns and goblets.

There were many forms of drinking cup, but it was accepted that those of silver were not only appropriate for those of rank, but that they were more hygienic. 'The cups wherof you drinke' advised Dr Vaughan in his *Fifteen Directions for Health* (1602) 'should be of silver, or silver and gilt'.[184] Perhaps the most important cup was the Grace Cup. The handing round of a grace cup was integral to college dining. A tall, gilded covered cup at New College, which is called the Warden's Grace Cup, has scratched underneath, 'Ric' de Mayhew', who was a Fellow 1457–71 and Bishop of Hereford 1504–16 (Fig.82). It is described in a 1508 inventory of secular plate as a 'gilt standing pece with a cover gilt and partly enamelled on the knop the gift of the Bishop of Hereford'. Although a rare survival, the inventories of various colleges reveal that the large standing cup was a prestigious vessel common amongst the colleges. A list of silver dated 1525 at University College includes 'a great standinge Cuppe wth a Covr syvler gilt iii woodwoses beringe up ye Cupp wthyn ye Cupp ye Xii Apostles graven round about ye Cupp ye cordynge of ye cuppes having a knopp wth our Saviour standing in his sepulchre having his crosse in his hand', another almost double the weight of the former at 25oz, had 'six pillors about the knoppe of ye cover and the knoppe gravyn and enamelde wth grene blew and purple'.[185] Brasenose possessed a 'gilt standing cup with a cover having in the bottom a scutcheon

82 (7) Cup and cover, silver-gilt *c.*1480. New College.

83 (**19**) Flagon or pot, silver-gilt, English early 16th century. Magdalen.

84 (**37**) Rosewater basin, silver-gilt, London 1605–6, mark WI. Merton.

with three black boars heads and a rose' handed in to the Mint in 1642. Drinking vessels came in diverse shapes. The stout two-handled covered 'pot' at Corpus of 1533–4 is elaborately chased with fashionable arabesques (Fig.68). Ralph Kettle's cup of 1603–4 shares related decoration, but is of a totally different form (**36**).

The earliest English silver 'pot' for serving water or wine is at Magdalen College (Fig.83). It is pear-shaped with a narrow neck, and by comparing its scale-chased decoration with that on hallmarked cups, John Hayward dated it to the early sixteenth century.[186] Previously dismissed as a German import of unknown provenance Hayward convincingly suggests that, far from being a rare form in England, it is an unusual and precious survivor in silver of the common English medieval 'potte', of which examples still survive in pewter.

After grace the diners washed their hands in warm sweet-scented water, in a noble household the lord first, and in a college the most senior member present. This required a ewer and basin, and at least one set is listed in most college inventories. As Philippa Glanville has noted, because of their size, their acquisition in terms of silver alone represented a considerable outlay, and this is partly why so few survive today: as fashions changed, the large amount of silver was re-deployed. Many, however, appear in sixteenth- and seventeenth-century college inventories. The sister of the Founder of St John's, Mary Matthews, gave the college 'one silver bason & ewer pcell gylt' listed in an inventory of 1591. A 1596 inventory at Oriel records 'a bason parcel guilded with a rose enameled in the bottom 52oz, and an ewer with a cover in fashion like a tankard 24oz parcell guilded'. An inventory at St John's of 1633 even refers to a special case for their 'Gilt Bason & Eure'.[187] It is now rare for both ewer and basin to survive. Merton possesses a fine gilt basin that is embossed and chased with strapwork and scrolling of 1605–6, although the ewer has long since disappeared (Fig.84).

While college dining of the fifteenth and sixteenth centuries followed courtly fashion, albeit rather conservatively, there are elements of the noble table that simply do not seem to appear in Oxford college silver inventories, most notably dishes, platters, saucers and chargers, that for example appear in Sir John Fastolf's inventory of 1459, or the inventories of other corporate institutions like the livery companies. This may be explained by their presence as part of the 'garnish', the display of plate upon the sideboard, known as the buffet, which the colleges do not appear to have had. The spice plates of the noble Tudor table are also absent. So while the college table followed many common patterns, it also had a distinct identity of its own.

## THE STUART TABLE

The dining hall at University College gives us a good impression of a seventeenth-century hall (Fig.85). A truss next to the central roof-lantern bears the date 1656, and although it was extended westward by two bays in 1904, much of the furnishing, the oak tables and benches, but not the panelling, are original. Elizabethan and Jacobean portraits including those of Bishop Bancroft and Archbishop Abbott (a former Fellow of Balliol, a senior Tesdale trustee for Pembroke, and Archbishop of Canterbury) hang on the walls and the College loving cup dates from 1666–7. College inventories that list furniture and hangings supplement our knowledge. For example, at Jesus College in 1648 the contents of the Hall are listed: 6 tables, 4 moveable forms, an 'olde Arrass Curtaine laying before the Window', and Queen Elizabeth's picture.[188] An inventory of the President's Lodgings at Magdalen includes the contents of the Founder's Dining Room which contained similar goods to those at Jesus: an 'arrace hanging', 'five back stooles and one chaire' 'thirteen stooles without

backes' a great cupboard, two side cupboards and a sideboard table, 'four kidder minster window curtains with rods', and three Turkey carpets, as well as furniture for the fire.[189] The Common Dining Room contained the 'picture of the Founder' and another of Cardinal Wolsey, the Lord Brook's escutcheon, two lists of colleges in Cambridge, a side cupboard, three Turkey work carpets, one Turkey chair, four Turkey stools with backs, and six without, two 'cushions of the same work' 'an old embroidered cushion of the Founders', and four old striped window curtains. The eagerness of the colleges to take stock of their possessions after the Civil War, and the return of Fellows at the Restoration meant there were a host of inventories made, many of which survive; they provide a wealth of evidence to reconstruct what type of silver was refurbished and bought new at mid-century. The type of dining silver and its position in a Stuart college would have corresponded with the 1682 description made by Giles Rose, one-time master cook to Charles II, based on a French advice book

85 Aquatint after A.C. Pugin's drawing of University College's 17th-century hall a few years after it had been re-modelled, from R. Ackermann, *History of the University of Oxford*, 1814.

of 1661.[190] On the table the Butler placed 'first the table cloth, then the salts and the riders for the plates... then the plates with the coat of arms towards the middle of the table... at the right hand of each plate place a knife, with the edge towards the plate, then the spoons, the brim or edge of the spoon downwards, with forks'. What was missing from the college dining hall, but was present in the noble household, is the stately silver wine cistern. As glass from the 1670s often replaced horn, pewter and silver for drinking vessels, the colleges stuck to their more durable plate.

The seventeenth century saw the demise of the standing salt and a preference for smaller salts distributed more liberally around the table, and the continued evolution of the drinking cup. The development of college wine cellars, like that of Lincoln College in 1640, indicates a growing sophistication as wine replaced beer and ale as the normal drink for dinner; there was also a greater variety of beverages which required specific vessels. Lincoln College paid for its new wine cellar by selling some of its plate from the Buttery, including two old tuns, a bowl, an 'eare piece', an old salt and a tankard; this yielded £18, leaving £29 to pay.[191] The colleges owned not only stan-

dardized drinking vessels, like the large bellied and embossed caudle cups, that appear on the tables of the nobility but also specialized forms that are restricted to college use. The two-handled cups and covers from Merton and Jesus are of a common design of the 1660s–1680s. The Merton example is large and plain with a low flat cover, on which there is 'cut-card' ornament in the form of a six pointed star; the three scrolls above form a stand on which the cup can sit (Fig.86). The tumbler cup from Merton is another example of a common form of drinking vessel: hallmarked in 1681–2 and given by John Randolph the following year to St Alban Hall, it is one of the earliest of a sequence of these cups in the College (Fig.87). Pepys refers to them in his diary of 1664 as a novelty, when he went home 'by the way of taking two silver tumblers home, which I have bought'. The form first appears in the mid 1620s, and All Souls College possesses a number of them dating to 1671. One of the earliest examples of this form to survive is dated 1625, the body engraved 'Ye guift of Humphry Whistler gent somtymes Bailiffe of ye Cittie of Oxon to ye Maior of ye same Citte for ye use of ye Master and Wardens of ye Company of Taylers there 1637'.[192]

86 (57) Cup and cover, silver, London 1672–3, mark TK. Merton.

87 (62) Tumbler, silver, London 1681–2, David Willaume. Merton.

Ex dono Eduardi
Capell filij Arthuri Capell Baron[?]
de Hadham in Comitatu Hertfordiensis
A:D: 1669

Fide & Fortitudine

88 (54)  Cup and cover, silver, London 1666–7, mark a hound sejant. Wadham.

89 (58)  Mug with two handles, silver, London 1677–8, mark TC. Exeter.

The 'auricular' cup from Wadham (Fig.88) is a rare and late example of this court style, and the only example of it to survive in Oxford. It was given to the College by Edward Capell in 1669, three years after its making. The auricular style derived from the engravings and silver of the van Vianens, who came from Utrecht. The gristly, cartilaginous style of the embossing transforms the common form of bulbous body with cast handles into something that looks almost liquid. It was a style that had been much favoured by Charles I, and had been promoted by the presence in London between 1636 and 1642 of Christian van Vianen, who had been given a royal pension from the King. The Wadham cup shows how

styles fashionable in London and at Court could take twenty or thirty years to arrive in Oxford. By 1790 it was kept in the Warden's Lodgings along with the Foundress's flagons.[193]

The two-handled beakers from Exeter College diverge from the standard form, showing how the colleges developed their own special shapes in silver (Fig.89). The 1677–8 beaker is the earliest to survive of several versions of this type, which is peculiar to Oxford, but not specific to this College. Oriel have several, the earliest of the same date as the Exeter example. While the straight sides re-call the more usual beaker form which had appeared as early as the fourteenth century, the cast handles derive in

miniature from the caudle cup, so it is a hybrid. The engraving is of standard form, and recognizes it to be the gift of William Hooper, who had matriculated to the College in 1660. As an inventory of plate at Oriel College taken in 1623 shows that there were many different types of drinking vessel being used at the same time. The Butler looked after 7 'eare gobletts' (weighing between 17–23oz), 7 tankards (16–20 oz), 5 tunnes (8–10 oz), 15 bowls (13–27oz) and 4 small wine cups (which weighed a total of 20 oz).[194] The 'tuns' are beakers, the 'bowles' were deep with flat bottoms set on a sturdy stem (and none seem to have survived to the present), while the cups had more sharply tapered bowls. Whereas the coming of glass into fashion and its comparatively easier supply, ousted the silver wine cup from the aristocratic table by the second half of the seventeenth century, it remained in the colleges for longer as a more practical material for institutional use. A list of Exeter College plate taken soon after 1640 lists 25 silver wine bowls (12–23oz), 27 'Eard pots' (14–38oz) 40 tankards (17–44oz) and 11 beakers (7–15oz).

The predominant drinking vessel in the colleges from the 1660s was the ox-eye, or

90 (**52**)  Ox-eye cup, silver, London 1661–2. Merton.

91 (**60**)  Tankard, silver, London 1678–9, mark TC. Oriel.

92 (**73**)  Pair of tankards, silver, London 1710–11, David Willaume. Merton.

'eared cup', which had become the mandatory 'gift' of a Gentleman Commoner to his college during the seventeenth century (Fig.90). Both Magdalen and Queen's still possess over forty such cups. The tankard form was known in the sixteenth century, exemplified by Sir Paul Pindar's gift to Trinity (**31**). It was only in the later seventeenth century that tankards came to outnumber the eared pots, many of which were melted down and converted. One only has to look at any list of benefactions to see their popularity. Richard Wenman's tankard given to Oriel in 1679, holds a gallon, and is the largest in Oxford (Fig.91).[195] George Watson unusually gave a pair of tankards to Merton in 1712 (Fig.92).

## THE EIGHTEENTH- AND NINETEENTH-CENTURY TABLE

During the eighteenth century there were great changes to the English dining table as the influence of French foods, dining equipment, and etiquette took hold. The dinner hour at colleges became later and later as the eighteenth century progressed, in accordance with fashion. At Hertford College the dinner hour was 1pm around 1747, and was later moved to 3pm, while supper was at 7pm. At Merton by 1795 and at Oriel in 1809 dinner in hall was 4pm.[196] The interior of many dining halls in Oxford also changed reflecting the adoption of new styles and inventions. At Brasenose for example an eighteenth-century lantern with Doric columns hangs from the roof, and although the panelling was installed in 1684, the plaster ceiling dates from 1754. The floor was paved in 1763, although now it is floor-boarded. Originally a brazier stood in the middle of the hall, its smoke escaping through a louvre, but in 1748 the Gentleman-Commoner Assheton Curzon donated funds for the installation of a marble fireplace.

While the colleges were dominated by tradition in one way, via the cycle of feast days and often a centuries-old tradition of dining, on the other they slowly adopted the soup and sauce tureens, argyles (for serving gravy), forks and other paraphernalia of fashionable dining that first appeared on royal and noble tables sometimes ten, twenty or thirty years previously. For example, the earliest argyle in Oxford seems to have been the gift of the Earl of Chesterfield to Queen's in 1779 (Fig.28); Exeter followed in 1787, and Brasenose in 1806, although they had arrived in noble households in the 1750s.

The college year was marked by feast days, when special food was served and the most important silver used. The Bursar at Lincoln in the late eighteenth century made extensive notes in his day book of all the major college festivals (Whitsunday, All Saints, Christmas, Candlemas, Easter. Chapter, and Count day), and the food presented at each. At Whitsun the Fellows dined on salmon, lobster, lamb, peas, and marrow pudding; at Christmas they feasted on fish and oyster sauce, beef, potatoes, pickles, and mince pies, and on Count Day when all the college accounts were made up, and hopefully balanced, fillet of veal, roots, celery, potatoes, and plum pudding were served.[197] These delicacies were not uncommon. In 1774 Parson Woodforde 'dined and spent the afternoon with the Warden at New College when he 'had a most elegant dinner indeed. The first Course was Cod & Oysters, Ham & Fowls, boiled Beef, Rabbits smothered with Onions, Harrico of Mutton, Pork Griskins, Veal Collops, New Coll; Puddings, Mince Pies Roots &c. The second Course was a very fine roast Turkey, Haunch of Venison, a brace of Woodcock, some Snipes, Veal Olive, Trifle, Jelly, Blomonge, stewed Pippins, Quinces preserved &c Madeira, Old Hocke, and Port Wines to drink &c. A desert of Fruit after Dinner'. At Brasenose in the mid eighteenth century the 'Buttler hath a Wassail night on Shrove Tuesday commonly he provides a great cake and a copy of verses hanged on a stick… with a bush of bay laurel and rosemary… together with a spiced bowl [to

Butler bringing in the laden salver, and the President and Fellows gathered around (Figs 93 & 94). During the eighteenth century the two-handled cup and cover grew in size and reflected by the mid-century the French taste for the rocaille, incorporating elaborate cast elements drawn from nature, rather than the more standard vocabulary of classical ornament. A large silver cup of 1763–4 given by John Symmons to Jesus is embossed with suitably Bacchic scenes (Fig.95).

The adoption of new dining equipment is vividly presented in the bursars' books where we can see old plate, damaged and old-fashioned, being traded in for new. At St Mary Hall (closed in 1902, when the silver was transferred to Oriel) in 1726 Mr Davenant's large salt was turned into two pepper boxes and a mustard pot. As mustard pots did not become common until the 1750s, this is an unusual example of a college being in the avant garde of fashion. In 1768 a porringer of 1658 was traded in for a soup ladle. In 1777 another porringer of 1679 was turned into four decanter stands, and in 1782 an argyle was acquired in part exchange for old plate

93 (**104**) Standing cup and cover, silver-gilt, London, 1882–3. Queen's.

94 Detail of 104 showing the Boar's Head Dinner.

95 (**86**) Cup and cover, silver, London 1763–4, John Parker and Edward Wakelin. Jesus.

each table] with apples and good ale', and at Christmas 'carpets must be laid on every table, under the cloth'.[198]

At Queen's College the Boar's Head Dinner celebrates a student of the Queen's College who supposedly fought off a boar at Shotover hill by stuffing a volume of Aristotle down its throat. The story is remembered every year at a feast in mid December. After the trumpet is sounded a boar's head is processed into the hall on a large silver salver. The ceremony dates back to at least 1395–6. A handsome standing cup with cast panels shows the Boar's Head, the

which included a late seventeenth-century tankard.[199] At Pembroke the 1681 tankard given by William Pagett was changed into two sauceboats in 1777 and at the same time two large ox-eyes donated by Lord Ossulton and Reginald Bray in 1659 were exchanged for one large tray. The first decades of the eighteenth century are also marked by regular bills for the supply and maintenance of knives and forks by local Oxford goldsmiths. At St John's Thomas Slaymaker provided 'a dozen and ten silver-hafted knives' £6 1s 10d in 1748, with matching forks in a mahogany case for the use of the President. The cost of these can be compared with the £6 13s 4d which New College paid Thomas Combes as his half year's pay for teaching. Two dozen ivory-hafted knives and a dozen forks followed, purchased from John Best of Lombard Street in London for £3 4s.[200]

Nearly all the college inventories include a silver punch bowl, which, as the early twentieth-century collector W.A Young remarked, should be 'regarded as the sun round which a collection of drinking vessels should be gathered', and several survive to show what splendid pieces these were. While they had appeared in wealthy households from the late seventeenth century, they are not listed in college inventories until the early eighteenth century. Sir John Harpur's gift to Magdalen was painted in the nineteenth century by Holman Hunt, in his depiction of 'May Morning' (Fig.96).[201] Its distinctive often detachable scalloped rim was said by the Oxford antiquary Anthony Wood to derive from 'a fantastical Scot called Monsieure Monteigh who wore the bottom of his cloak so notched'. The elaborate gadrooning was replaced in the 1710s and 1720s with highly polished smooth bowls, like those of 1726–7 at Lincoln and 1730–1 at University College (**80**), that must have sparkled in the candlelight, and reflected the drinkers who were gathered around.

96 (**72**) Monteith, silver-gilt, London 1700–01, mark SM. Magdalen.

By the mid eighteenth century pint beer mugs proliferated. At Wadham, for example fifteen 'eared pots' of the 1650s and 1660s were converted into beer mugs by the London goldsmith John Swift in 1757–8. Whereas the Buttery plate of the seventeenth century is dominated by pewter dishes and plates of many different varieties, that of the eighteenth reveals the introduction of silver tureens for soup and sauces, and provision for an increasing choice of condiments, and desserts. A comparison of Buttery silver at Brasenose in 1749 and 1761 reveals the changes in dining equipment. In 1749 there were 12 individual salts, but by 176 there were only 21. In 1749 there were 4 sauce boats, and twelve years later there were 7, while the number of casters had doubled from 5 to 10 over the same period of twelve years. Brasenose College might appear to have been rather enlightened in their relatively early purchase of a fashionable soup tureen in 1750–1, all the more so as it bears the mark of the leading London goldsmith Paul de

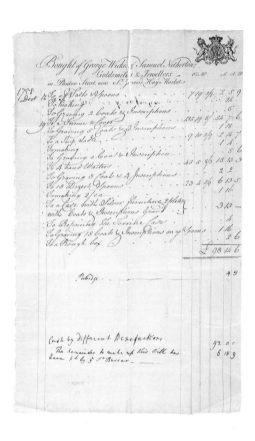

97 (**154**) Bill from Wickes & Netherton for the tureen, 1758. Brasenose.

98 (**83**) Tureen, silver, London 1750–51, Paul de Lamerie. Brasenose.

Lamerie (Fig.98). However on looking through the College bills it is clear that they acquired it second-hand, with a ladle, eight years after its manufacture, from the London goldsmiths George Wickes and Samuel Netherton (Fig.97). It was bought with money donated by three Gentlemen Commoners, William Lloyd, John Sneyd and Richard Gorges, who contributed £20 each. Sir Watkin Williams Wynn's gift to Jesus College was made in the latest neo-classical taste, reflecting his own patronage of the Adam brothers. The handsome tureen and cover of 1806 at Lincoln was made from the silver recycled from gifts given between 1662 and 1720. Some dining wares have names that have simply been lost over time, and we have no idea what they would have looked like. For example an inventory at Corpus of 1720 includes 12 boucher-plates.[202]

The invention of silver items for the serving of special foods and drinks blossomed in the eighteenth and nineteenth centuries. Several of the colleges boast silver toasted cheese dishes, which seem to have been popular among the Fellows. Trinity acquired one in 1806, and Brasenose one in 1815–6, supplied by Paul Storr and retailed by Rundell, Bridge and Rundell (Figs 99 & 100). The small silver trays, standing above hot water in the base, kept the small pieces of toast warm whilst their coverings of cheese are melted and browned by the heat reflected from an open fire by the brightly burnished interior of the lid when held half-open by a handle-attached chain. Toasted cheese was not a novelty in the nineteenth century: it appears as a favourite savoury in *The Closet of Sir Kenelm Digby Knight Opened* (1669) 'you may scorch it at the top with a hot Fire

99 (**94**) Toasted cheese dish (closed) silver, London 1815–16, Paul Storr. Brasenose.

Shovel'. The cook Hannah Glasse recommended in 1760 a pan of tinned iron for browning. At Magdalen there is a silver bottle shade, for protecting bottles or decanters from the heat of an open fireplace, one of several devices in the colleges connected with the service of wine, unusual in that it is made of silver, rather than wood, and hallmarked 1806–7. It takes the form of an half cylinder on a footed stand, and is appropriately decorated with a vine handle.[203]

## DINING IN PRIVATE

Whilst dining in Hall defined the corporate unity of a college there was plenty of opportunity to dine more privately in one's rooms. At New College the Warden lived in

100 (**94**) Toasted cheese dish (open) silver, London 1815–16, Paul Storr. Brasenose.

style and entertained visitors. Accordingly the lodgings contained a spacious hall for meals, a kitchen, bedchambers and a study. Warden Spooner at New College was presented with a large chest of dining silver on his retirement, made up of antique silver, which is still in College in its handsome green baize lined wooden box. Sir William Hayter, a Warden of New College remembered that 'The best provider was Maurice Platnauer at Brasenose (then a Fellow and later Principal [1956–60]). He had those beautiful panelled rooms over the main gate (now part of the Lodgings) and gave very exquisite and lavish dinners, I remember particularly an extra course of marrow bones, accompanied by triple-brewed ale in miniature silver tankards'.[204]

There were also private dining clubs. In 1786 the Phoenix Common Room was founded by Jospeh Alderson, who went up to Brasenose in 1779; it is the oldest surviving dining club in Oxford. Via the gifts of members we can see a steady accumulation of silver; in 1804, 'six silver table spoons' were procured, 'to be paid for by a subscription of the 12 actual members'. The following year 'to defray the expenses of a silver cup' a similar subscription was set up, and 'Messrs Rundell and Bridge… employed for… purpose' of the commission. In 1824 thanks were conveyed to Mainwaring for his very handsome present to the Club of three silver bottle stands; while in 1853 John Gott and George Mallory gave a 'handsome present of a silver punch bowl'. A dozen silver dessert knives, a silver cigar lighter and two pairs of silver nutcrackers were soon added to the Phoenix Club plate.[205] The Junior Common Room wine club at Pembroke was founded in 1794. Election was strictly limited, and its after dinner invitations on Saturday evening a greatly valued privilege.[206] Silver for its use engraved is 'Jun Cam Com', for 'in usum Junioris Camerae Communis' and includes a teapot given by 23 members and in 1824, soup ladles, wine labels for sherry, port and madeira, and a snuff box.

# 5

# THE LOCAL CONNECTION
## KEEPING & CARE OF COLLEGE SILVER

'Have especial care of the Colledge Stocke and Tresure, that you may have herewith to releeve and helpe yourselves uppon all unhappy accidents, or occasions that may befall the Colledge'

Bishop Curle, the Visitor, to Oxford to
Dr Frewen, President of Magdalen College, 1636

101 (**167**) Portrait of
William Palmer,
Butler (1782–1824),
by Stephen Taylor
*c.*1824–5. Oil on
canvas. Oriel.

So far the story of Oxford college silver has consistently focused on the academic community, from the perspective of commissioning, purchasing and using the silver, whether in chapel or at table. There is however a hidden history which connects the silver with those who maintained and cared for it, in the form of local Oxford goldsmiths and college servants. While the material traces are few, the archives enable us to reconstruct their role, bringing these shadowy characters to the fore. Their signatures appear on bills and college inventories, and they were responsible for its everyday use and circulation. The majority of Oxford college silver bears the marks of London goldsmiths, yet if we turn to the bursars' accounts and bills it is the local craftsmen and retailers who dominate, and it is rare until the nineteenth century to see the name of a London goldsmith. How then do we reconcile the apparent contradiction between the object and archival evidence? Local Oxford goldsmiths not only acted as agents between the colleges and the London goldsmiths, but cleaned, mended and engraved it, re-fashioned it, provided cases for it, made inventories of it, and lent money on it.

## THE BUTLER AND THE SILVER AUDIT

It was usual for the Butler to have charge of a college's silver, just as in the aristocratic household, and he in turn was responsible to the Bursar, one of two elected Fellows who had responsibility for receipt and expenditure, who were required to keep detailed accounts, and to write a quarterly view. The old plate book at Brasenose thus has an entry written by the Bursar in 1606 'Edwardes our butler hath in his custodie these severall pcels of plate' which included 'eight standing cups, and six other smaller of the same fashion for wine, eight eared cuppes, five white silver salts & one litle gilt, one salt... A great standinge cupp... and twentie silver spooones', the contents of the Buttery safe.[207] This was for 'daylie use of the colledge & specially for service in the haule at meeles'.[208] After a theft of plate from Christ Church in 1696 the Chapter decreed that the Butler, Thomas Bush, should 'pay ten pounds in consideration for the loss of the aforesaid plates' and allowed him twelve months to pay. However it was his son Edmund who eventually settled the debt, eight years later. The problems caused by this resulted in the creation of a contract. Henry Grant the new Head Butler, as part of the terms of his employment, was required to sign an indenture declaring that he 'has received and may heretofore receive great quantities of silver plate of or belonging to... the Dean and Chapter of all which plate he the said Henry Grant is to take care and preserve the same for the use of the said Dean and Chapter [and] on death give up safe, whole and undefaced or make satisfaction for all such of this silver plate as shall be wanting'.[209] Such was the standing of William Palmer, the Butler at Oriel between 1782 and 1824, that his portrait was painted on his retirement, and he is portrayed by the artist Stephen Taylor, holding the Founder's Cup. At New College there is a portrait of the Butler's son, the college servant William Hodges, c.1768, which hangs in the Warden's Lodgings. The boy holds a large silver tankard, and under

102 (**166**) Portrait of William Hodges, College Servant c.1768. Oil on canvas. New College.

his arm a bundle of clay pipes; he is obviously just on his way to attend to the Fellows. At Brasenose the Butler then delegated responsibility to other staff, recorded by him in 1829, 'the Hall Man, Under Butler, and Common Room Man each respectively be responsible for all the plate under their care, and that the Bedmaker or other servants to whom they deliver each piece of plate be responsible to them for every such piece of plate'.[210] At Pembroke the Bursar acknowledged his appreciation of the servant dedicated to the care of the College silver; he noted 'Since I became Bursar in

103 (**168**) Portrait of Henry Bly, Senior Common Room Butler (1923–46), by R. Schwabe, 1946. Pencil on paper. Hertford.

104 (**169**) Photograph of the Merton Butler, c.1950s. Tollygraphics and Mr J.W. Thomas M.A.A.R.F.S.

Nov. 1894, I have found the College plate excellently attended to by William Gribble', then the Under Butler.[211] Henry Bly would have been there at this time, as he went to Pembroke in 1891 as a scout. Bly left an account of his life as a college servant which helps us to reconstruct what it must have been like to rise from scout to Butler over fifty-three years in service.[212] At Pembroke he received no wage, as he was dependent on the generosity of the 'young gentlemen'. Lamps had to be trimmed daily and water had to be carried up to rooms in buckets, and all meals apart from dinner were eaten in rooms. In 1897 Bly went to work in the Hertford College Buttery, not becoming Senior Common Room Butler until 1923, and retiring in 1946. A photograph of the Butler at Merton taken in the 1960s shows him preparing the silver for dinner, behind him the huge buttery safe, a scene that has changed little over the centuries.

All silver that belonged to a college was required to be audited once a year, and it was the responsibility of the Butler to organize and oversee it. The seventh foundation Statute of University College of 1292 ordered 'that all the goods of the College, moveable and

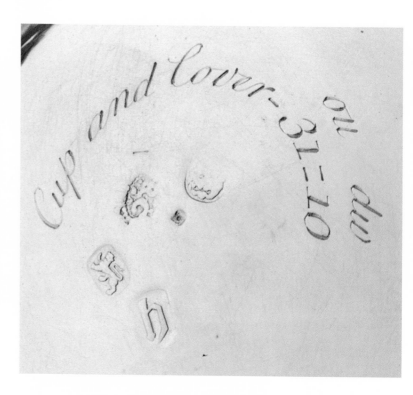

unmoveable, above two sterlings in value' should be listed in 'one indented register… one part of which shall be kept in the Common Chest, and the other by the Bursar, and every year shall be viewed by all the Fellows, before their accounts and every terms all the vessels and instruments and other necessaries shall be viewed by the Bursar'. These annual listings, which survive as separate plate books, like the list of 1631 (Fig.105) and Note of Plate of 1655 (Fig.3) at New College, provide a wonderful glimpse of the ebb and flow of silver, revealing changes in the fashions of drinking vessels, the frequent exchange and loss of silver, and the fortunes of individual items of silver that were lost, found or reported damaged and repaired. In 1678 the new Warden at New College, Richard Traffes, ordered that 'a book bee bought in which a True and perfect Inventory of all ye Goodes belonging to every chamber shalbe registered with their just worth and value'. Silver was listed by the place it was kept, the person who had given it (usually engraved on it), its type and its weight. The silver was inventoried in the buttery, as 'one pair of scales with a nest of weights from lb Troy to 5 penny weight' is mentioned as a part of the auditing equipment there.[213] College silver frequently bears an engraved 'scratch weight' in ounces and pennyweights on the base (Fig.106). At the annual audit the silver was weighed to see if any had been removed; at 5s 6d an ounce it was worth 'clipping' by unscrupulous servants and students.[214] A photograph of the Pembroke College audit in the early 1970s shows what a daunting task locating all the silver, and ticking it off the master list could be (Fig.107).

Plate was listed according to where it was kept in college, and usually divided between white, or plain silver, and gilt plate. Identification was usually via the type of silver, for example drinking bowl, or college pot, but most importantly by name, that is name of the donor. An eighteenth-century note by the Bursar at Trinity makes clear the format of the silver inventory, to be kept in a special book, in which each piece 'is distinguished by its weight and the Years when given, which are entered in columns after those containing the Form of each piece and the Name of its Donor, an intermediate one

105 (**144**) Bursar's Long Book showing an inventory of 1631. New College.

106 Detail of the base of **66** giving troy weight 31oz 10dwt. Magdalen.

107 The Silver Audit at Pembroke 1963. Pembroke.

being left for any future observations'.[215] The extensive 1631 inventory at New College described '3 beare [beer] bowles wth the Colledge Armes in thone side and the Archbishops Warhams Armes on thother side' (Fig.105).[216] Even when re-fashioning occurred several times, as in the case of the Hanbury tankard at Balliol, the donors' names survived, despite the change in form. The surviving tankard was supplied in 1729 by Gabriel Sleath, and was made with silver from a bowl of 1676, which itself replaced two small tankards of 1650 given by the brothers Sir Thomas and John Hanbury. College accounts of 1688 reveal that the bowl, part of 373oz of silver sold, had been exchanged for cash 'for the payment of Colleg debts'.

More rarely the plate was engraved with special marks of ownership. At Queen's the Founder ordered as part of the statutes in 1418–19, that all possessions of the College including animals, should be marked with the sign of a flying eagle. A note in the Brasenose Bursar's accounts reveals that '2 great candlesticks (of the new fashion)' bought in London in 1653 were marked 'BC for Brasenose College'.[217] At Magdalen in 1679, 'all moveables belonging to the College are to be marked MC to distinguish them from other goods that belong to the owners of chambers'. At Trinity some of the silver bears a punch 'CT', for Collegium Trinitatis, indicated in an eighteenth-century inventory as 'PS' for plate that had, as the Bursar explained, 'the Private Stamp of CT on them', PS referring to the Private Stamp.

The conclusion of the audit was always celebrated. One can imagine the relief on finding all in order. At Christ Church in 1650 £1 15s was allowed for the purchase of 'strong beere at the Audit'. At New College £2 was provided for wine at the 1699 audit, and in 1720 'for tobacco at the audit time' 9s.[218] At Lincoln it was called Count Day, for which in 1675 a table cloth was hired for 1s 4d, presumably to show it off. It was one of the regular feast days of the academic year.[219] In 1696 the same college allowed 1s 'for a pot of Coffee at the making up of the accounts'.[220] This tradition of celebrating the conclusion of the silver audit continues to this day. A note of 1947 in the Magdalen archives explains that 'The Vice President may, if he wishes, give a small tea party at the charge of the College in the Senior Common Room to Fellows and their families on this occasion, in order that they may have an opportunity of seeing all the plate brought out for the annual inspection'.[221] At the end of the audit, remarks were usually added to the list; at Jesus the 1626 silver inventory is marked 'All the forementioned Pieces of plate were reviewed and those following were found to be markd and broken and stand in needed of mending'.[222]

Occasionally however the audit did not end happily, at least for the person, usually the Butler, who was held responsible. Any silver that was missing had to be replaced from his wages. At Corpus in 1802, a list of silver 'for which the Butler appears accountable' revealed a 'weight of plate missing 'since his being invested with this charge' and he was required to pay the cash equivalent of its weight by annual instalments, so as to 'compensate the loss in Four years'.[223] Sometimes plate that was registered lost turned up again, as at Exeter, when it was noted that '1 spoone lost by Dr: Prideaux found agayne 1630 under the Binne'.[224]

To avoid such mishaps it is evident that different butlers instigated various rules to minimize the risk of loss. The Butler at Balliol, who maintained overall control and responsibility of the plate, devised a system of regular checking. In his 'Orders for the Kitchen' recorded in 1632 he wrote that 'The Butler every Saturday after dynner to call the Servants that have charge of the any plate to take a view

of it to see where and what case it is, and to present the faults in writing to the Sub-rector'. At Magdalen in 1679 'the Bursars upon their first entrance into their office shall take an inventory of all the College Plate, Pewter, Linen and all other goods in the Bursary, Kitchen, Buttery &c to be entered in the Register that is kept for that purpose in the Bursary'.

## CLEANING AND CARE

It was not simply enough to keep the silver in its relevant place, it also had to be kept serviceable, clean and polished. The report of the Bishop of Winchester, who inspected Magdalen College in 1507, presents a sad state of affairs. Among the complaints made were that 'Pots and cups are very seldom washed, but are kept in such a dirty state that one sometimes shudders to drink out of them'. Most college accounts include the termly cleaning or 'scouring' of plate.[225] Goldsmiths' bills frequently include materials needed for maintaining the silver, abrasive powders, cloths, skins and flat soft-bristled plate brushes. Crocus was a red or yellow abrasive powder made of calcined metals which could be rubbed onto the silver and brushed off. In a similar way grated hart's horn or antler could be used as a source of ammonia. The London goldsmith George Coyte noted in a surviving day book of c.1760 a recipe for cleaning plate: 'Take burnt Hart horn boyl it in water a Hour and put in a bitt of rag boyl it with it rub your plate well with it; and after clean it with a bitt of clean cloth'. The eighteenth-century Birmingham entrepreneur and silver manufacturer Matthew Boulton advised cleaning silver 'in the common way… take a clean soft white brush and wash… with soap, warm water or spirits of wine, & then wash all clean with warm water only & wipe all clean with dry soft linnen cloths'.[226] Mrs Beeton's advice to the housemaid published over a hundred years later follows exactly the same instructions:

108 (**170**) Portrait of a Scullion, c.1680–9, by John Riley. Christ Church.

Wash the plate well to remove all grease in a strong lather of common yellow soap and boiling water, wipe it quite dry; then mix as much hartshorn powder as will be required into a thick paste, with cold water or spirits of wine; smear this lightly over the plate with a piece of soft rag, and leave it for some time to dry. When perfectly dry, brush it off quite clean with a soft plate brush and polish the plate with a dry leather.[227]

Cleaning silver was hard work, labour-intensive, time-consuming and dirty. At Christ Church a servant named Ellis was paid 5s 7d in 1577 for 'scouring the dishes about the hall' once a term.[228] A portrait of a scullion painted over a hundred years later gives an impression of what this type of servant may have looked like. The large plate under his arm is probably pewter, but it, like the silver, was scoured once a term. At Balliol in 1587 a servant by the name of Stary was paid 18s quarterly for 'scouring the vessels', while at Jesus Goodwife Jones was paid 5s 6d for 'scouring the College plate at severall times'. At Lincoln the Butler cleaned the plate. In 1673 Robert Pinson was paid 2s a term for 'scouring the plates', and received 10s a term for his wages. By 1719 the cost of cleaning had risen to 3s a term. At Brasenose the college brought in the local goldsmith's wife and daughter to clean the silver; they are recorded in a list of 'Extra Assistants employed by the Bursar' in 1829.[229]

Bills that survive at New College record in 1811 the purchase of a plate leather and plate powder from Bridgewater and Sheen for cleaning and polishing the silver.[230] If the silver was beyond the elbow grease of the college servants the local goldsmiths were summoned to 'boyle' the plate in a weak acid solution to remove the tarnish. In August 1666 Alexander Wright billed New College £1 2s 6d for 'making clean' some of their silver, including '3 little boles, 1 coll[ege] salt, 3 flagons, 2 wine cups, 2 great flagons, 28 spounes'.[231] At Brasenose in 1753 they paid 7s 6d for 'Two Days work, done by a man at the College' sent by the goldsmith John Wilkins to clean the plate, at the same time buying 'two skins to clean the plate' for 4s. In 1829 the same college purchased '18 yds Russia for 2 doz of knife cloths' for 13s 6d and '20 and a quarter yards Mock Russia' for 9 Plate Cloths' £1 3s 7d. Russia cloth is a durable leather made of skins impregnated with oil distilled from birch bark, which is also used in bookbinding.

The silver like other goods, such as china, glass, and pewter, was moved about in specially-made baskets. A bill from Sarah Plowman, a 'Furnishing Ironmonger' in the High Street Oxford to the Warden and Fellows of Brasenose in 1819 includes the 'Bottoming & mending of 2 plate baskets, which cost 3s 6d, 'providing two new ones at 11s, and supplying brushes to clean the plate'. Important silver came in its own purpose built boxes like that made for the cup and cover at Oriel, acquired in 1743 with its own case made of wood covered with leather, from Phillip Wenman, (82). The cup bears the scratch weight 94oz 1dwt, and the cover 23oz 11dwt.[232] In 1766 the Oxford goldsmith George Tonge supplied New College with 'A mahogany two Dozen spoon case £2 2s, doing ye old case up cost 4s.[233] These cases often became worn, and, like the plate they housed, needed to be refurbished. Edward Lock, an Oxford goldsmith, charged 12s 6d in 1768 for a 'new inside, new lining, new Lace and mending ye Lock Handle & joints and doing up Mr Egerton's case for knives, forks and spoons', for Brasenose. The ledgers of Payne & Son the goldsmiths now in the High Street record the supply of many such specialist cases. In 1909 they sold Pembroke College Junior Common Room 'an oak plate chest, baize lined, bags for larger pieces, fitted for spoons and forks £6 10s'. The 'Large plate chest, iron bound, 2 locks' supplied to Brasenose in 1904 for £5 sounds, from its description, much like the chests that appear in college inventories from the fourteenth century.

## LOST, STOLEN AND FOUND

Apart from the annual silver audit, the whereabouts of plate was regularly monitored, and the memoranda, notes and lists that resulted are valuable evidence for the recreation of its movement both within and outside a college. The Senior Dean's Book, beginning in 1662 at Merton is ostensibly 'An Inventory of all the Plate, Pewter, &c and Linnen belonging to the Buttery, Kitchen &c & Hall in the Keeping of the Senior Butler, and the Junior Cooke & the Porter'. This is interspersed with intriguing memoranda. The first entry notes 'Mr Simonson, heeretofore Subwarden gave £100 with which were bought 20 plates' in 1650. On page 39, there is a reference to 'plates which were exchanged to a tea pott', which in 1678 was a very early example of such a new invention. It was only by the late 1660s that tea became widely available, and the earliest known silver tea pot to survive to the present is of 1670. In 1693 'Mr Edwards of Cuxham tooke a plate sometime since out of the Treasury, ye name [of the donor] not known wch is confessed lost it is supposed to be worth 4 pounds'. In 1713 an overall calculation of the amount of silver the College owned was made 'the weight of the plate in the Lodging 439oz 16dwt value at 5s per oz = £109 19s. In the Dean's Acct the Plates weigh 271oz 14dwt = £67 18s 6d', 'In the Butler's keeping weight 1962oz 1dwt £490 10s 3d' and 'In the Treasury 1658oz = £410 5s' revealing a clear hierarchy of weight. In 1717 Simonsons' 'plates' 'were sent to London', and clearly exchanged for twenty new pots, a sugar, pepper and mustard caster being made with the silver left over, although the one 'mark'd 19 that was lost being since found'. At Wadham a note of 19 September 1837 reported that one of the Scholars' forks, 'was lost some years since and was at once replaced, it has been this day found in the drain from the kitchen pump'.[234]

College property was always at risk, from accident, misplacement, and theft. In 1775 the accounts at Corpus include 10s 6d paid for the

'Expence of Advertising, Search, &c for Lead stolen from Necessary No.3'. At Brasenose the plate book contains 'A note of those parcels of plate that was stolen [in 1626] by braking up of our Treasure house most of them being part of Mrs Joyce Frankland her legacie', which had been given in 1587.[235] Christ Church paid for 'work done in ye Buttry for ye safety of ye plate and other things' in 1607, while a fire in the College in 1630 destroyed 'Hetons pott' which was 'burned att the fire at Mr Tinleys chamber'.[236] A complaint was made at Magdalen in 1679 that 'the College discipline hath not of late yeares been so strictly kept up as formerly it used to be'. The reconfirmation of the College rules provides some startling evidence of what had been happening to the silver: 'That no college plate or dishes be carried out of the College into the Town under any pretence whatsoever, nor any Bedmaker, Servitor or any other Person leave College dishes inn the cloysters; upon Hall stairs, or any other open place, where they may be stolen, or convey'd away'.[237] Notes made by the Magdalen Butler in the early eighteenth century suggest things did not radically improve. In 1702 'the Cook paid 1s 3d 'for finding of stragling plates at the rate of a penny a plate',[238] in 1715 fourteen lost plates were 'brought home' at the end of Michaelmas Term, and at the end of the following term another 29 were rounded up.[239] It was not just the students and Fellows at Magdalen who were lax: at Lincoln College the cook was paid 1s in 1644 'for dishes found abroad gathered up'.[240] At New College 9d was paid to the 'Cooks for finding of stragling plates at the rate of a penny a plate'. A memorandum of 1688 from the Manciple of St Edmund Hall declared that 'there were lost in his time 10 spoons belonging to the Hall, which… were valued by the Goldsmiths at four pounds fifteen shilllings which said sum [was] paid by the said widow Cox'. The College spent the money on 'communion rails & wainscott for the chappell'.[241] A more bizarre finding came in 1760 when the Bursar of Exeter gave 1s to 'Richard Symes… day Labourer for bringing a strey silver cup belonging to the Battlears tabel & found amongst the Dung in a field at Marston'. In 1826 11s was given as a reward from Pembroke College 'to a man for finding a lost Mug'.[242] In 1848 an anxious parent of a student 'enclosed a fork… found among some luggage recently taken out of a repository. It must have been carried away by my son… who was at Balliol in 1837, and accordingly return it to you'.[243] At the same College in 1888 one spoon was lost at 'the luncheon entertainent of certain archaeologists in the College Hall'. The missing spoon was replaced by a new one in May, with much doubt was cast on the honesty of the diners, however in June 1912 'the spoon was discovered in the lift', and the Butler noted '& the archaeologists are above suspicion'.[244] Twenty-five years later the Home Bursar returned 'under separate cover' to Alexander and Company, Sheffield silversmiths and platers, 'four coffee Pots which have been melted by undergraduates who have stood them too long and too near Gas Fires. I presume it is possible to repair them'.[245]

The college authorities had to be on the constant watch for light-handedness. There were many different categories of theft, not only of college goods, but also of the private belongings of dons and students, but they were all an offence which carried the most serious of punishments. On 15 March 1541 the Privy Council examined a William Calcuvey, a London goldsmith, about buying plate stolen from New College, and had him committed to the custody of the sheriff of London. The accounts of Exeter College include several references to peculation: in 1673 the College spent £3 10s 'prosecuting a woman at London that stole plate', and in 1679 'costs for prosecuting a thief that stole a dish' amounted to 7s 4d. On 6 November 1675 'at one or two in the morning New Coll lost most of their plate by people who had a ladder and came over the wall into the buttery window, [Henry] Nobes the Butler being dead about 2 days before'.

From 1746 the Oxford newspaper, the *Oxford Flying Weekly Journal and Circenceser*

*Gazette*, and later from 1753 what came to be known as *Jackson's Oxford Journal*, are a fund of information on the theft of silver, including advertising items lost. Samuel Williams the Butler at Trinity, seems to have turned or at least been found crooked in 1761, when the *Journal* revealed that he had been committed to the Castle for 'having been detected in feloniously stealing three Silver Spoons, a Candlestick, and other Goods, the Property of divers Persons in the said College'. The College authorities seem to have been unwisely lenient, as he appears again two months later having stolen spoons and a whip from two other students. Robert White, sometime servitor of Christ Church, son of Almond White, a barber living near the Mitre Inn, was apprehended for stealing a clock from 'a certaine person at Christ Church, and plate from All Souls and books and clothes from Lethbridge' a student at Exeter College. A haul of plate 'supposed stolen' from Worcester College in 1769 included candle-sticks, tankards and mugs (Fig.109). The following month the Butler's daughter was apprehended at a local goldsmith's for attempting to sell a spoon from the stolen cache; she was transported for seven years for the offence (Fig.110). Spoons, because they were small, light and portable, were a common target for theft. In 1768 six were stolen from Merton, and in 1774 Diana Cripps (alias More) stole a spoon from St Mary Hall, while Thomas Broomfield was condemned to death for stealing silver shoe buckles from a Christ Church gentleman. Oxford goldsmiths were often the first port of call for the sale of stolen silver. Mr Slaughter the Oxford goldsmith was paid 1s by Christ Church in 1659 for 'his pains in recovering the stolen plate', while in 1730 Exeter College gave a substantial reward of £4 4s (which would have bought a suit of clothes for a clerk in public office, or a silver hilted sword) to Mr Wentworth, an Oxford silver engraver, 'for his great care and pains in detecting the cookes boy anno 1723 who had melted down some of the college plate'.

## OXFORD GOLDSMITHS
## AND ENGRAVERS

Oxford goldsmiths worked with the butlers and cleaning boys to keep the college silver up to scratch. As the Brasenose statutes make clear, 'all servants are put in by Mr Principal's sole power' and these included the Goldsmith, as well as 'the Plummer, the Iron-monger, the Glazier, the Brazier, the Chandler, the Smith, and the Butcher'. The colleges appear to have been very selective about which local goldsmiths they patronized. We know from the Oxford freemen's books, called Hanasters, that there

109  Detail from *Jackson's Oxford Journal*, March 1769. Centre for Oxfordshire Studies

110  Detail from *Jackson's Oxford Journal*, April 1769. Centre for Oxfordshire Studies

were many other goldsmiths operating in Oxford, but it is the same select names that keep appearing in the college accounts, linked usually by apprenticeship or family ties, in powerful local dynasties that dominate local affairs.

The first identifiable goldsmith to be mentioned with any regularity in the college accounts is William Wright (*c*.1560/1–1635/6) who was supplying 'standing cups' to Christ Church in 1584, and continued on their books until 1616. In 1598 he was paid for a college pot, charged at 5s 6d per oz and 18d for engraving the names of the donors. In 1591 he supplied eight spoons to Magdalen, and did a great deal of mending work for them including changing a secular cup for ecclesiastical use in 1612. He was also working for Oriel, from whom he rented a property in 1678. Wright, like many other goldsmiths who had access to funds, and therefore influence, was deeply involved in local affairs, being elected successively constable, chamberlain, Justice of the Peace, bailiff, alderman, and Mayor of Oxford in 1614. Goldsmiths could be powerful figures within the local community. One of Wright's apprentices Walter Wilkins (*c*.1584–1623) began supplying colleges in the early 1600s. A receipt for payment from Christ Church in 1607 'to Mr Wright the Goldsmith for duble guilding the Constables sticks of St Thomas & setting the Colledge Armes on it' is signed 'by me Walter Wilkins'. This was three years before he had gained his freedom of the City. The Bursar at Corpus Christi paid 'Walter Wilkins for worke and stuffe about the Colege plate', and for scouring, soldering and polishing '8 peeces 2s one boule broke in the podkin'. Like his master Wilkins took a large role in local affairs, although his early death in 1623, under forty, cut short a promising career, and explains why references to him in the college accounts are so few.

During the second half of the seventeenth century goldsmithing flourished in Oxford, as the colleges were busy replenishing their plate after the Civil War. More names appear in the college accounts, and competition must have increased. The three major names to appear are Thomas Berry, Samuel Wilkins and Daniel Porter Senior. One of Walter Wilkins's apprentices Thomas Berry (1594/5–1670) continued serving the colleges after his master's death: he was paid by Exeter College in 1623. Corpus paid 'Berry the Gouldsmith for mending plate since November 'in the same year, and in 1652 he was paid for the engraving of 'Alderman Nixon's name on the douzen of spoones given by Him'. Berry's name also appears in the Jesus Buttery accounts of 1636 for 'exchanging old plate' and at New College in 1649 when he was paid a handsome £29 9s 6d for new silver including a 'great salte weight 26oz & 3qurts 8dwt two trencher salts, a porringer, and a dozen spoons'. The cost included 'the carriage of the salt and tankard to and from London', which suggests that they were made by Berry, and sent to Goldsmiths' Hall to be assayed.

Samuel Wilkins (1619–1689), a nephew of Walter Wilkins the Oxford goldsmith, began working for the colleges from 1649 when his name appears in the Wadham College accounts, where his cousin John Wilkins was Warden. He was paid for mending, engraving and exchanging plate at Lincoln, Balliol and Trinity, and in 1676 he re-gilded the Brasenose Chapel silver. Daniel Porter (1627–1694) seems to have been busy with college work, as his name appears in many of the Bursars' books between 1659 and 1687. In 1687 Anthony Wood, who was a drinking companion of Porter, mentions that the Fellows of Magdalen had pawned most of their college plate to him, for £700, in order to fund their litigation with the Ecclesiastical Commissioners.[246] His son, also named Daniel, worked for the colleges, but seems to have specialized in loans and banking, and the large debts which emerged after his early death at the age of 33 suggest a none too stable career. A bill from him to New College survives from 1689–90 (**157**).

111 a&b  Centre of a basin, silver, London 1685–6, mark IR, engraved by Lemuel King, detail below. St John's.

112  (below) Bookplate engraved by Richard Wentwoth, 1737. Exeter.

113 (**66**)  (right) Cup and cover, silver, London 1685–6, detail of the engraving by Benjamin Rhodes. Magdalen.

One of Porter's apprentices was Lemuel King, one of the few engravers to be identified in Oxford, via his signature on surviving work (Fig.111B), rather than via the bursars' books, where his name does not appear. The high quality of his work can be seen on three pieces of silver at St John's, a magnificent basin of 1685–6, (Figs 111 a & b) a porringer of 1688–9, and a tankard. It suggests that he was probably a specialist sub-contractor on whom the Oxford goldsmiths called. As engravers were not required to mark their work, their existence is difficult to identify. The high quality of King's engraving can be compared with that of the work of an identified London engraver, Benjamin Rhodes. An account book (1694–1698) belonging to Rhodes for engraving executed for the London goldsmith and banker Sir Richard Hoare reveals that the Clarke porringer given to Magdalen College was engraved by him (Fig.113).[247] On the left hand side of his account book he drew a rough sketch of the arms to be engraved, simplified to a code of his own, or took a counter-proof after completions. Rhodes received 13s 6d for engraving the Clarke cup and cover. According to the account book Rhodes was also engraving silver for Trinity College and King's College Cambridge, as well as many of the great families of England.

114 (77) Tankard, silver, London 1723–4, Humphry Payne, engraved by Benjamin Cole, retailed by William Wright. Pembroke.

Another Oxford engraver to emerge is Richard Wentworth. He appears in the Balliol accounts for 1720 for repairing the plate, for which he charged £7 17s, and in 1737 Exeter College paid him £10 10s 6d for 'a Copper Plate of the College Arms for the Books in the Library' (Fig.112). Prints of the bookplate survive as does the original copper plate. Benjamin Cole's name can be connected to engraving copper plates for printing. In 1738 Jesus College called upon Cole to repair an engraved plate by George Vertue 'from Dr Hugh Price's picture', and in 1749 he 'altered the Plate of the College Arms'. Cole also engraved 'Mr Wynne's Arms, Crest and Inscriptions on a crewet stand and crewets' for 14s, gifts from Sir Watkins Williams Wynn. We know that the Oxford goldsmiths Timothy Dubber and William Wright sub-contracted their engraving to Cole. Yet it was the College who paid Cole 10s directly 'for engraving Mr Thornton's plates' [tankards] at Pembroke in 1720 (Fig.33). Thomas Thornton (1700–1783) matriculated from Pembroke in 1715, and the tankards are marked by the London goldsmith John Sanders, from whom Dubber must have bought it. A standard Latin inscription is placed below an elaborate and very large

rococo cartouche containing his family arms. The College Benefaction Book reveals that £20 had been given by the donor two years earlier in 1718 for '2 poculum argenteum' (see p.33). In 1723 William Wright supplied Norcliff's plate for which Cole was paid 5s for 'engraving the Col: Arms on Norcliff's plate'.[249] Thomas Norcliff matriculated in 1714 and became a barrister at Inner Temple in 1727. The tankard was assayed in 1723 and bears the London goldsmith Humphry Payne's mark (Fig.114).

John Wilkins senior (1685–1728) and his nephew, also named John (c.1690–1757), who had been apprenticed to his uncle, dominate the college accounts in the first half of the eighteenth century: they mended old silver, and engraved and supplied new. New College paid John junior 10s 6d in 1740 'for weighing the College Plate & making a List of the Same'. In the same year he refurbished the chapel plate, regilded the existing items and purchased 'two new pattens to two Challices' from Richard Bayley the London goldsmith whose mark they bear. For Brasenose in 1752 he was paid for 'Taking the Lids & Joints from eleven small tankards 6d each'.[250] The appearance of his wife Katherine's signature in receipt of payment on his bills suggests that she assisted him with the business. *Jackson's Oxford Journal* reported his death in December 1757, 'after a lingering illness, Mr John Wilkins, an eminent Goldsmith of this City, who had twice served the Office of Mayor, and was a senior assistant in this Corporation'.

Two of his apprentices, also worked for him as journeymen, George Tonge (1729/30–1802) and Edward Lock (1730–1813) and they took over much of their master's work for the colleges after his death. In June 1759 Tonge set up his own shop near the Bear Inn in the High Street, and his name appears in the accounts of University, Pembroke and Magdalen, but it was St John's for whom he did the most work. Surviving silver at the College, combined with the bills for it, can help us understand exactly how these local

goldsmiths operated. A long bill from Tonge to St John's covering the period 1773 to 1777, includes the provision of a silver 'pollished Chas'd tea Urn', and the making of two accompanying vases which would have held black and green tea (Fig.116). From the bill it looks as if Tonge made these pieces. However, when we look at the silver the mark of the London goldsmith John Rowe is very clear (Fig.115). Tonge was buying in fashionable new silver from London, and selling it on to the colleges. He was not only buying from Rowe but also from other London goldsmiths including John Robins (1777), Robert Makepeace (1778), and Aldridge and Green (1779).

During the second half of the eighteenth century the name that dominates many of the college accounts is, first Edward Lock senior (1730–1787), then his son Edward (1760–1844). His brother, named Joseph, was a banker and goldsmith and appears in the diary of Parson Woodforde, who noted in October 1793 'called on my Friend Locke the Silversmith this morning who behaved very

obligingly and knew me at first sight. I changed a ten pund Note with him, he keeps a Bank, and does great business'.[251] Sir Joseph Lock became Mayor of Oxford in 1813 and in 1829, and had a fine fifteen acre estate and house at Bury Knowle, at Headington (now the Headington branch library). Surviving bills show how diverse demands on the local silversmith's skill could be. A single bill from Edward Lock the younger to New College in October 1800 includes 1s 6d for 'beating out a large decanter very bad', 3s for 'altering & drilling head of mustard vase for pepper', 'repairing the Alter [sic] candlesticks Do the Crozier for 2s 6d'.[252] Edward Lock exchanged eight old tankards belonging to Corpus Christi in 1808, amounting to some 353oz 5dwt of silver (£93 3s 11d), and purchased with it for the College a pair of sauce tureens and ladels, six cut glass cruets with lables, four silver soy [sauce] lables, a gilt kyan spoon and twenty-five dessert spoons. The sauce tureens were not made by Lock, but bought from Peter and William Bateman, whose mark they bear. Lock seems to have used the Batemans quite frequently to fulfil his college orders. For Brasenose he bought a rich 'Chas'd Tea Urn'. The signature of Edward's wife Ann in receipt of payment from colleges also suggests that, as in many family businesses, the wife managed the accounts.

115 (**88**)  Tea urn & two vases, silver, London 1776–7, John Rowe. St. John's.

116 (**156**)  Detail of a bill from George Tonge to St John's College showing the 'pollish'd Chas'd Tea Urn' and two 'Chas'd Tea Vazes'. 1773–1777. St John's.

117 (**151**) Account book
for colleges, 1885–1916.
Payne & Son, Oxford.

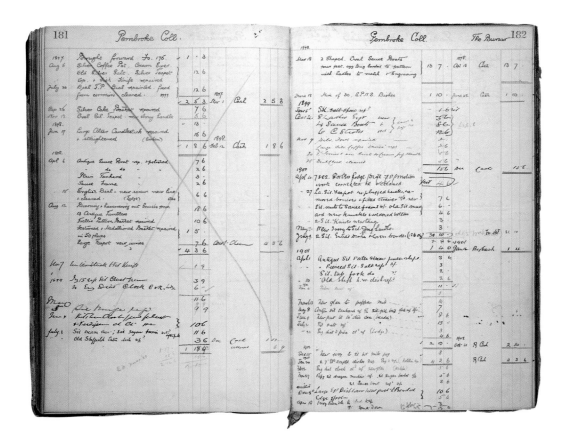

During the nineteenth century Edward Hickman was the Oxford goldsmith responsible for much of the college business. He has been apprenticed to George Tonge in 1766, and by the early nineteenth century advertized himself as a 'Goldsmith, Jeweller, Watchmaker, Engraver and Optician' from his premises in the High Street near St Mary's. As can be seen from one of his bills to New College, much of his work involved repair work. Only one other goldsmith's name appears in the College accounts between 1812 and 1848, that of John Fiske. Rowell & Son Ltd, established in 1797, were watch and clockmakers in Broad Street, not moving to the High Street until 1885, and to Turl Street in 1986. Rowells were used by many of the colleges to maintain their clocks. Payne & Son continue the tradition of the crucial importance of local goldsmiths in the story of Oxford college silver. This family firm dates its association with silversmithing and jewellery to 1790 and had branches in Wallingford, Abingdon, Banbury and Tunbridge Wells before setting up in Oxford in 1888. Geoffrey Payne's employment by Ramsden and Carr in Fulham explains why the business was so open to Arts and Crafts designs, supplying many of the colleges, students and Fellows with 'modern' silver. In 1903 Payne & Son, Oxford, were appointed Ramsden and Carr's sole agents. Paynes' surviving account books from the 1880s reveal the range of work they supplied to the colleges (Fig.117). For Pembroke College in 1898 they supplied sauce boats, 'to pattern' to match. They also cleaned and mended college silver, re-plugging handles, removing bruises and repolishing. They supplied antique, as well as commissioning contemporary silver. Paynes are frequently behind some of the most important modern commissions in Oxford.

# 6

# REVIVAL & REPRODUCTION
## ATTITUDES TO THE ANTIQUE

'a very curious and tasteful collection of those reliques yet remaining of the piety and munificence which distinguished the Founders of several colleges'

Samuel Rush Meyrick, *Ancient Plate and Furniture from the Colleges of Oxford and the Ashmolean Museum*, 1837

118 (**84**) Flagon, silver-gilt, London 1752–3, John Swift. Wadham.

During the eighteenth century there was a growing interest in the shape and form of medieval and Tudor silver, quite separate from its bullion value. The engraver George Vertue had attempted to view the crozier and treasures at New College on his visit to Oxford in 1737. He wrote in his diary 'There is preserved also at New College a Pastoral Staff &c: but this we could not see, by reason of its being under 9 locks, and the Fellows not all in College'. Vertue, who had suceeded in seeing the 'fine Antient Silver pastoral Staff', 'left by the Founder Bp Fox' to Corpus, and the Founder's staff and richly embroidered copes at St John's, was an early representative of antiquarian interest in silver. According to his notebooks, whenever he was working on a job, he inspected the features of local historic interest at the same time. He was probably in Oxford in 1737 preparing portrait drawings of Dr Hugh Price, who founded Jesus College in 1571, which the College received the following year.[253] In 1752 Wadham College commissioned a cup to replace the original Foundress's flagon which had been given up during the Civil War. Interestingly the London goldsmith John Swift, whose erstwhile apprentice John de Gruchy had set up shop in Oxford, supplied them with what he must have thought was an Elizabethan form, rather than one in any currently fashionable style.

From the 1760s the pages of *The Gentleman's Magazine* reveal a growing number of reports of 'old silver', indicative of a new interest in the historical form of silver, above its intrinsic value.[254] In 1768 one contributor commented that 'I have seen in my time, two or three sets [of Apostle spoons], but at present they are scarce, being generally exchanged for spoons of a more modern form, and consequently melted down'. In 1785 a spoon with the date 1654 engraved upon it was reproduced, in 1790 a set of Apostle spoons was reported, and in 1797 a mazer was discussed.

By the early nineteenth century the fashion for making reproductions of old silver became popular as the interest in old plate spread beyond the specifically antiquarian market. Old silver was also 'improved' with the addition of later embossing and chasing. By the 1840s and 1850s interest had spread to seventeenth- and eighteenth-century silver, and scholarly work was undertaken on hallmarks. In 1845 the first catalogue of College plate was published by the Cambridge Antiquarian Society. Admiration for old silver coincided with growing criticism of modern silver design, aired for example in the pages of the *Illustrated London News*, and later the *Art Journal*. Exemplars of silver from the past, housed in the collections of noble families, London livery companies, city corporations, and Oxford and Cambridge colleges became a source of design inspiration for the artist craftsman. As a result Warden Hill's salt and other New College silver was exhibited at the *Manchester Art Treasures* exhibition of 1857, and by the end of the nineteenth century electrotype copies had been made of key examples of medieval, Tudor, and Stuart silver which were circulated amongst British galleries and museums, in an attempt to improve design.

## ANTIQUARIANS AND THE PUBLICATION OF PLATE

One of the earliest illustrations of Oxford college silver to be published appeared in John Carter's (1748–1817) two volume *Specimens of Ancient Sculpture and Painting* (1780–94). Included amongst the carved figurative stonework, were two examples of the goldsmith's craft, the richly enamelled Lynn Cup, said by tradition to have been given to the Corporation of King's Lynn in Norfolk by King John, and William of Wykeham's crozier at New College. Carter's aim was to refute the 'contempt in which the genius of our ancestors has been held' in comparison to continental workmanship, by publishing examples of native English work 'now remaining in this Kingdom from the earliest period to the reign of Henry VIII'. Carter had trained as an architect, but built little and made his career as a polemical journalist and scholar. He was one of the most celebrated antiquaries of his day, and 'his knowledge of medieval art and architecture probably exceeded that of all his contemporaries'.[255] Through his own publishing ventures (*Specimens of Ancient Sculpture and Painting*, 2 vols (1780–94), *Views of Ancient Buildings of England*, 6 vols (1786–93) and *The Ancient Architecture of England*, 2 vols (1795–1814)) and a journalistic campaign conducted in the pages of the *Gentleman's Magazine* he developed a passionate defence of Gothic architecture. He was the most vocal and dogmatic exponent of the view that the Gothic style was indigenous to England and owed nothing to foreign influence. He extolled the mystery and sublimity of Gothic buildings over and above the classical style. Wykeham's crozier was held up by him as 'a singularly sumptuous example of medieval sculpture' reproducing a life-size engraving of

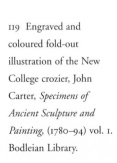

119 Engraved and coloured fold-out illustration of the New College crozier, John Carter, *Specimens of Ancient Sculpture and Painting*, (1780–94) vol. 1. Bodleian Library.

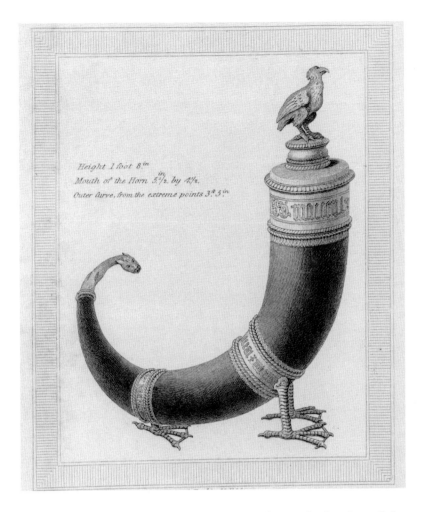

*Height 1 foot 8 in*
*Mouth of the Horn 5½ by 4½.*
*Outer curve, from the extreme points 3ft 5 in*

120 Engraving of the
Drinking Horn from
Queen's, J. & H. Storer
*The University and City of
Oxford*, 1822.

the upper part, with a scale drawing of the whole staff (Fig.119).[256] Drawing on Horace Walpole as his authority, Carter quoted from the great antiquarian's *Anecdotes of Painting* 'Bishop Wickham's crozier at Oxford is an instance of how well the pomp of prelacy was served with ingenious work',[257] proving for Carter that 'ancient sculpture and painting of this Kingdom [were] in their height in the time of Edward III'. *Specimens of Ancient Sculpture* was appropriately dedicated to Walpole, who included old silver in his own collection of antiquities and curiosities at Strawberry Hill. Five years after the publication of Carter's *Specimens*, the crozier was taken down from the tower at New College and put on permanent display in a niche in the chapel, part of Wyatt's restoration begun in 1789, where it can be seen today. Carter's exposure of the New College crozier resulted

in its ultimate elevation to 'the most beautiful example of the period in existence'.[258]

From the date of Carter's publication there was a growing interest in Oxford college silver beyond the world of the colleges and the University. The medieval and Tudor silver began to be valued amongst antiquarians, collectors, and for the first time tourists. J. and H. Storer's *The University and City of Oxford*, published in 1822, was 'in conformity to the reigning taste… enriched with graphic representations', seventy-two views in total, including the Horn at Queen's (Fig.120), the New College crozier and and the All Souls salt. The book, in an attempt to reach a wide audience, is organized in the form of a conversation between various visitors to Oxford and their guides. When Lady Gertrude is taken to Oriel by Falkland the latter comments 'The cup of the Founder is far from inelegant in its shape, the bruises it has met with scarcely apparent. It is silver-gilt, and was found after Cromwell's time behind some wainscotting, where it had been hid for safe custody and forgotten'. In an attempt to laud the representation over the real object, he comments further 'These things never look so well in the originals as in the engraving – And that arises from the pleasure afforded of one art in another'.

The following year Joseph Skelton's two volume *Oxonia Antiqua Restaurata* (1823) was published, accompanied by engravings of select examples of 'the Ancient' plate of the colleges. They were seen to be an integral part of a college's history, intimately connected with individual Founders, and therefore richly evocative of those ancient times with which both specialists, and increasingly the knowledgeable public, were fascinated. Skelton chose to illustrate key pieces of silver to accompany the description of some of the colleges, most notably the Queen's College drinking horn, reproduced in volume 1, and in the second volume the Corpus Christi College salt of *c*.1480 (Fig.121), the Founder's Cup and the mazer and coconut given by John Carpenter to Oriel, and the Trinity College

chalice of 1527, set above an engraving of the Founder's tomb. A bout of interest in college archives also seems to have begun at the same time. At Jesus College the Register of Acts (1752–1824) for December 4 1824 records that 'At a meeting held this day it was unanimously resolved that the contents of the archives… be investigated in order to form a catalogue of the writings & documents'. The following year at Exeter College a Mr Madden was paid £5 'for decyphering old records',[259] and in 1826–7 3s 6d was paid 'for a fragment of old Colege plate'.[260]

Samuel Rush Meyrick (1783–1848), a serious collector, expert on arms and armour and friend of Sir Walter Scott, was an influential antiquarian, whose own collection at Goodrich Castle was held up as an inspiration for 'the intelligent artizans of our manufacturing districts'.[261] Meyrick was a Queen's man, one of a distinguished line of antiquarians from the College including

Thomas Tanner and Thomas Pennant. Meyrick had published 'Remarks on the ancient mode of putting on armour' in 1828, and in 1837 extracted all the references to plate from Henry Shaw's *Specimens of Ancient Furniture*, to which he had contributed the descriptions of the illustrations to publish a separate volume, *Ancient Plate and Furniture from the Colleges of Oxford and the Ashmolean Museum*, arguing that 'Those subjects copied from examples at Oxford, might in a detached form, be highly interesting to the members of the various establishments in which they are preserved, and form appropriate illustrations to many works already devoted to the History and Antiquities of the University'. They 'presented a very curious and tasteful collection of those reliques yet remaining of the piety and munificence which distinguished the Founders of several colleges'. Meyrick's short descriptions of the silver were accompanied by seven sumptuous chromolithographs of Oxford

121  Engraving of the Standing salt of *c*.1480 at Corpus Christi College (**13**), reproduced in J. Skelton, *Oxonia Antiqua Restaurata*, 1823.

122  Chromolithograph of Warden Hill's Salt from New College (**11**) in Henry Shaw, *Ancient Plate and Furniture from the Colleges at Oxford*, 1837.

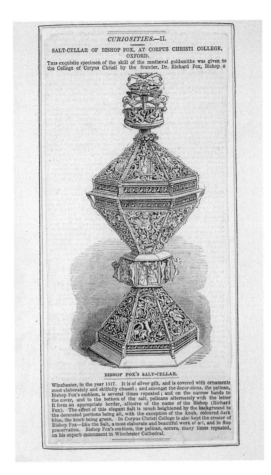

123 Extra illustration featuring the Corpus Salt of *c.*1480 (**13**) pasted into a volume of James Ingram's *Memorials of Oxford* (1832–7).

college plate drawn by Henry Shaw of Chichele's salt from All Souls, Warden Hill's salt from New College (Fig.122), Fox's salt from Corpus Christi, the 'Founder's Cup' from Oriel, Eglesfield's drinking horn from Queen's, the coconut cup and mazer associated with Bishop Carpenter from Oriel, the chalices from Corpus and Trinity, and Fox's crozier. Meyrick's comments convey his opinion on their design, and their date. On Fox's salt he remarked 'the chasing is exquisite, though there be nothing tasteful in the contour'. The Oriel Cup provided an opportunity for debate, 'it had always been my opinion that the ornaments of this cup were not earlier than the middle of the fifteenth century and I am happy to find this conjecture corroborated by the critical acument of the deeply versed architectural antiquary, my friend William Twopenny Esq.' Meyrick refuted the idea that the interlinked letter Es engraved on the body of the cup referred to Edward II (as the collar

of SS also engraved on the cup was unknown before the the time of Henry IV) and suggested that the more likely candidate was Prince Edward, son of Henry VI. Meyrick had begun a debate about the original owner and date of the cup that lasts until this day.[262]

A review of *Ancient Plate* in the *London Literary Gazette* of 1838 reveals the importance of the illustrations in disseminating design information, not only amongst the select world of the antiquarian, but also among a much wider public. 'Mr Shaw continues to gratify the artist, the antiquary and the man of general taste by the publication of his admirable specimens gratifying at once to the antiquary who regards them from their associations, to the virtuoso who furnishes his mansion *a la mode antique*, and to the historical painter, who aims at accuracy of scenery', 'elaborately carved and richly ornamented articles so finely represented compare with the bald and meagre productions of a similar kind in the present day one cannot but become aware of one of the causes of the want of occupation of which the working classes so generally, and we fear, so justly complain'.

In 1832 the first of three volumes of James Ingram's *Memorials of Oxford* appeared. An extra-illustrated version includes not only Ingram's descriptions of some of the silver, but also various engravings and newscuttings, that reveal how widely information about Oxford college silver was spreading (Fig.123). By the mid nineteenth century the taste for the 'old' was even evident among the undergraduate body. Cuthbert Bede's fictional hero Verdant Green (1854) is impressed by a fellow student's rooms at St John's, where, he explained 'there were couches of velvet, and lounging chairs of every variety and shape... There were round tables and square tables, and writing tables; and there were side tables with statuettes, and Swiss carvings, and old china, and gold apostle-spoons... a very gorgeous instance of a Collegian's apartment'.[263]

## THE MANCHESTER ART TREASURES EXHIBITION 1857

In response to the widespread criticism of the design of contemporary decorative arts, including silver, influential figures in the emerging art and design world recommended that manufacturers and artists take their inspiration from examples of the past. Many pieces of old silver were featured in the *Illustrated London Journal* as exemplars of good design. The runaway success of the Great Exhibition in London of 1851 encouraged the growth of further shows, in an attempt to improve manufactures, and educate the public. Although no college silver went to the 1851 show, the Founder's Cup from Oriel and Pembroke Cambridge graced the Society of Arts exhibition in 1850, and were illustrated in the *Gentleman's Magazine* that year. The 1857 Manchester Art Treasures Exhibition was a landmark for Oxford college silver. Examples were borrowed from the colleges to be exhibited publicly outside the University. The aim of the Exhibition was to show 'some of the choicest works of the old masters, specimens of the schools of modern painters, articles of costume, armoury, jewels, household decorations, and other articles which would serve to illustrate the customs and habits of our ancestors'. The site was 'of about twenty-seven acres at Old Trafford, lying about two miles west of Manchester, and completely out of the influence of that smoke-cloud which hovers darkly over the vast Cottonopolis'. The Gallery of Modern Painters commenced with paintings by Hogarth and Reynolds. The Soulages Collection of maiolica, antique metalwork and furniture had a separate space. There were selections from Marlborough House, the British Museum, and gold plate from the Royal Collections. New College lent Wykeham's crozier and Warden's Hill's Salt, receiving in acknowledgement of their 'liberality in contributing... works of art' a handsome colour certificate from the

Executive Committee. The decorative roundels bear images of art workmen, potters, glassmakers, weavers, sculptors and architects, with renaissance names, Michelangelo, Palissy, Cellini paired with later artists, like Stothard, Turner and Vechte. The sumptuous *Art Treasures of the United Kingdom*, published the following year, includes fine chromolithographic illustrations by F. Bedford of Warden Hill's Salt, which stands by a reliquary which in fact was a recent compilation of parts, the base from a sixteenth-century Continental chalice, and the upper architectural section a construction made for Magniac the great antiquarian collector. Other colleges lent their silver too. At Oriel College the three College treasures, the Founder's Cup, the mazer bowl and the coconut cup are still stored together in a single purpose-built box made for their transport to Manchester, the original label being stuck on the side.

124 (**160**)
Chromolithograph showing Warden Hill's Salt, in *Art Treasures of the United Kingdom*, 1858. Private Collection.

125 (**138,139,140**)
Electrotypes of the
Standing Salt *c.*1400–50.
All Souls, the Founder's
Cup 1515–16, Corpus, and
Warden Hill's Salt *c.*1480,
New College. Late 19th
century. Museum of
Oxford.

## ELECTROTYPING AND THE REPRODUCTION OF OXFORD COLLEGE SILVER

At the Committee of the Council for Education the supply of exemplars from the past to improve design was taken literally, in the decision to commission from Elkington and Company, a leading firm of Birmingham goldsmiths, a series of electrotypes of the highlights of English silver. By the time of the Great Exhibition the process of electroplating was well established. Elkingtons had been working on the electro-deposition of silver and gold and in 1840 a patent had been registered. Electrotyping was a spin-off of this process, whereby metal is electro-deposited into a mould and removed when sufficient thickness has been achieved to produce a solid, free-standing object. Exact replicas reproducing intricate detail could therefore be made from originals, and cheaply.

Many examples of historic silver were drawn from Oxford and Cambridge colleges to be electrotyped. Five Oxford colleges gave permission for items of their plate to be reproduced: Exeter (Ostrich egg cup, 1610, George Hall's gold cup, 1661), Queen's (Drinking Horn *c.*1340), New (Portion of Founder's Mitre, *c.*1400, Hour Glass Salt and Standing Cup, *c.*1480, Coconut Cup, 1584–5), Trinity (Chalice 1527), All Souls (Standing Salt *c.*1400–50 and Standing Mazer of 1529–30), and Corpus Christi (gold Chalice and Paten of 1507, and Fox's Ring).

The letters requesting permission to copy and the college replies are still in the Registry records at the Victoria and Albert Museum. All the colleges agreed although, like the Warden of All Souls, they were concerned that the copies be used for educational purposes only. A handbook was published in conjunction with their manufacture. In the words of the author, Wilfred Joseph Cripps, who wrote the *Handbook to the Reproductions of Silver Plate*, published in 1881, the copies were made in order to offer 'the student the opportunity of following at one time and place the whole history of English silver-working, from the earliest times to the present day'. The electrotypes were displayed in the South Kensington Museum, what is now the Victoria and Albert Museum. The Committee for the Council of Education also intended that the electrotypes should be seen by as many people as possible. In order to achieve this reproductions could be bought from the Council. Thus electrotypes were circulated to museums in Accrington, Hanley, Newcastle, Plymouth, Preston, Salford, Stockport and Newcastle, as well as further afield to Sydney Australia and the Metropolitan Museum of Art in New York, who ordered in 1910 copies of two mazers and a cup from All Souls, Warden Hill's salt, a cup and Wykeham's mitre band from New College and George Hall's cup from Exeter College.

The popularity and demand for these electrotype copies must have inspired Elkingtons to sell them commercially. In 1876 they registered a trade mark differing only slightly from that of the Science and Art Department which was stamped on all the reproductions. Surprisingly their request was accepted. In 1906 they seem to have supplied the Laing Art Gallery with a copy of Hall's cup from Exeter College without asking permission. A letter from a Mr Martin to W.W. Watts commented that 'I rather fancy this is one which Elkington's have no right to mould or make a copy of, without special permission', as the College had only given consent for copies to be made for 'the museums at Sheffield, Bradford and Birmingham.[264] The result was that all the type-patterns were called in, and Elkington's had to write to the Department of Science and Art with proof of the original owners' permission to reproduce, before copies could be made.

The combined impact of the circulation of published engravings, the series of art exhibitions staged from the mid-nineteenth century and the distribution of electrotypes resulted in a wave of late nineteenth- and early twentieth-century silver that is clearly inspired by these historic examples.

It was not only exact replica electrotypes that became popular. There are many examples of copies being made of key pieces of Oxford college silver by London and local goldsmiths to satisfy the demand for historic silver, for those who could not afford the price of real 'antiques'. In 1910–11 H.D. Wadham, a distant relation to the foundress, had a third size copy made of one of Dorothy Wadham's flagons (1598) made for his wife. In 1953 it was presented to Wadham by 'their sons and grandsons'. Renaissance shape and

126 Copy of one of the Foundress's flagons of 1598–9, silver-gilt, London 1910. Wadham.

decoration has been copied, but it is embossed not chased (Fig.126).

The pages of Paynes' ledgers reveal many orders for replicas, or rather versions, of college silver including the coconut cups at New College, and the popular 'ox-eyes', like their version of the New College 'Palisade' Cup made in 1903 (Fig.127). In 1933 a Mr Beak, who had been a commoner at Queen's between 1892–5, died and left the College a bequest of £50 to be expended on a single item of silver. In 1937 the College asked Tessiers to mount a wild ox horn, to the design of Mr A.T.C. Carter.[265] It emulates the fourteenth-century founder's horn but in place of his eagle, a consort's crown forms the finial – a reference to Queen Philippa, wife of Edward II, to whom Eglesfield had been chaplain. It is inscribed 'George Bailey Beak, Commoner 1892–5'. Others gave silver that consciously reproduced earlier forms that derived from sources outside Oxford. A letter from the Goldsmiths and Silversmiths Company to the Bursar of Trinity in 1903 reveals the source of the design of a claret jug presented to the College by the Bishop of Madras. It was 'a copy of a chased copper jug which had been washed ashore on one of the islands of Hebrides about the time of the wrecking of the Armada, and is supposed to have belonged to one of the ships of the Armada'.

127 (**107**) Reproduction of the 15th-century 'Palisade' coconut cup from New College, 1903. Payne & Son.

128 (**108**) Drinking horn, with silver-gilt mounts, London 1937–8, Tessier. Queen's.

## EARLY COLLECTORS AND CONNOISSEURS

Many of the early students of silver were educated at Oxford, and maintained links with their colleges, providing some of the earliest examples of scholarship in the field. Wilfred Joseph Cripps, a Wadham man, had published in 1878 *Old English Plate*, 'the first narrative history of the subject, which received universally good reviews'.[266] On visits to Oxford he provided notes on the college silver.[267] He was able to provide some of the first accurate dates for their early silver, 1598 for the communion plate, and could offer comparisons with other examples he had seen, in the case of the communion silver, with that at St George's Windsor, St Margaret's Westminster and at Cirencester. Harold Charles Moffatt, who published the first catalogue of *Old Oxford Plate* in 1906, had been inspired by Foster and Atkinson's *Old Cambridge Plate,* which appeared in 1896. He presented his old college of Trinity with a copy of the publication, as well as with some choice examples from his collection of silver. A.T.C. Carter not only designed new silver that made reference to historic examples, but also gave old silver to Queen's, including an ostrich egg cup, with mounts of 1577–8 which had been exhibited at the South Kensington Museum in 1862.[268] His other gifts included the Winchester porringer of 1675–6 bought with £40 by the Dowager Duchess of Pembroke and Montgomery for her godson the third Earl of Cumberland, and ten seventeenth-century casters. He also left silver to the Ashmolean.

Prompted by Moffatt's catalogue of 1906, which included a photograph of Wykeham's crozier, in a rather bad state of repair, W.H. St John Hope found it 'full of dust and dirt' and 'rickety' and sent for Carl Krall of London, the celebrated ecclesiastical goldsmith. A report on the repairs, the first of its type, survives at New College revealing how its conservation offered the opportunity for investigating the origin of its manufacture. Krall states in the report that 'the construction and its solid hard soldering the delicately worked portions… distinctly proves it as English work in contrast with the French work which in most cases is found to be put together with screws and rivets'.[269] John Carter, the eighteenth-century antiquary who had been the first to publish the crozier, would have surely been delighted. For the first time an item of college silver was not restored via gilding and replacement of parts, Krall carried out 'only such repairs as were absolutely necessary'. While the crozier was in Krall's workshop in London St John Hope used the opportunity to take it to a meeting of the Society of Antiquaries where it was inspected by members, and an article was published by him in 1907.[270] St John Hope had asked the President and Fellows of Corpus if he could borrow Wykeham's crozier at the same time 'but they were not willing to allow their Founder's staff to come up to London'.

Paynes the local Oxford goldsmiths were also asked to attend to the historic plate at New College in 1907, presumably as a result of its exposure via Moffatt's 1906 publication. Paynes did much work to the 'Cocoa nut cup (Palisade) lead removed thoroughly repaired part new wires to base 7 chased leaves and 4 new palings supplied majority of palings rivetted, holes in base patched (6 patches) 6 new pieces to base regilt and restored as originally'. Warden Hill's salt, described as 'twist stem' had 'all the lead removed from salt (not cover), 7 new drop parts supplied by galleries, 1 leaf of centre band repaired, missing part of pierced work and chased band supplied and chased ball, 4 new trefoils ad 5 new balls suplied to loose rim of cover… 2 new coloured and gilt glass sections supplied to cover new tinsel fitted to backs of all the glasses'.

H. Clifford Smith, who had been a Keeper of Woodwork at the Victoria and Albert Museum, returned to University College in 1943 to make an 'Inventory of Works of Art',

129 (32) Four Apostle spoons, silver and silver-gilt finials, London 1595–6. Pembroke.

two 'unicorn's' horns owned by the College. He was art master at Winchester and became Slade Professor of Fine Art at Oxford.[273]

Many more colleges benefited from the interest old members began to take in the antique, as some generously presented their old colleges with parts of their collections. Some gifts were long-standing family plate, like the eighteenth-century silver given by Robert Finch to Balliol on his death in 1830, while others gave silver that had been carefully collected. The late nineteenth and early twentieth century was 'the period of the antique. Prices were continually rising… and bargains could be picked up in the sale rooms… The Hallmark was becoming known as a selling point'.[274] Trinity College for example received a large bequest in 1957 from Charles Cumberbatch (matriculated 1904), an old member who gave silver, furniture and also four fine leaden urns which now decorate the garden quadrangle. Pembroke College greatly gained from the generosity of several of its past students, who were interested in antiques, like James Shepherd Crompton;[275] Crompton was born in 1865, the only son of a Rochdale surgeon and chemist. He was educated at Repton and went up to Pembroke in 1883 to read Theology, but was not ordained. He lived in poor health at home with his father, two servants and his unmarried sister. An assiduous collector of silver, he also bought French paintings, including works by Corot and the Barbizon School, some of which he left to Rochdale Museum and Art Gallery. He began giving silver to his old college in 1907, and by his death in 1925 he had left a large quantity of antique silver. His handsome gifts included four Apostle spoons (1595–1605) (Fig.129), a seal top spoon (1636), a bleeding bowl (1692), and 3 trifid ended spoons (1696), as well as some sugar castors, including one by Paul Crespin, a distinguished Huguenot goldmith, who had only been free of the London Goldsmiths' Company four years when Crompton's caster was made (Fig.130). Crespin is known to have

compiling a special catalogue of the silver.[271] He brought Messrs Crichton Brothers and E. Alfred Jones to help identify the marks, and provided contextual comments on the silver himself: the 'College Loving Cup of c.1670' he notes was 'described in an inventory of Buttery plate as the Charity Cup', and was 'one of the oldest pieces of plate in the possession of the college and was used at High Table daily for two hundred years'. It was at about this time that New College decided to display some of its silver to the public, opening up the ground floor of the Tower. The young silversmith R.M.Y. Gleadowe (1884–1944) designed the interior,[272] and provided a silver mounting for one of the worked in association with Paul de Lamerie, perhaps the best-known Huguenot gold-smith in London in the first half of the eighteenth century, whose reputation soared after the publication of P.A.S Phillips's biography of him in 1935. All the larger pieces Crompton gave have the College shield, his name and an inscription in Latin, and almost all the small pieces carry his initials. Crompton's purchases mark him out as an early and discerning connoisseur of silver. Thomas Barton, who was awarded a Fellowship at Pembroke in 1865, when he became Senior Tutor and Vice-Gerent gave his College a wide range of gifts, from Samuel Johnson's Worcester porcelain tea pot and mug, to a stoneware flagon, mounted in Norwich with mounts engraved 1590 (Fig.131). It was Barton too who gave the sil-ver candlesticks to the college in 1885, copied from the Certosa in Pavia, to embellish the newly refurbished chapel. He also donated much eighteenthcentury silver, including a marrow scoop, five salvers, several pairs of candlesticks, four sauceboats, two salt cellars, four entrée dishes and serving spoons, the total amounting to 675oz 13dwt. He noted 'Of the candlesticks here enumerated I wish to have the use of the two smaller pairs in my rooms, though they will be the property of the College. The fifth pair I have given to the Master'.[276]

Oxford college silver is predominantly of London make, and the few examples of Continental silver that entered the colleges largely came via the gifts of discerning collectors. For example the seventeenth-century Dutch and mid-eighteenth century Swedish beakers at Balliol were given by Lady Lingen from the collection of Sir Robert Ralph Wheeler, Lord Lingen, who had been a Fellow 1841–50. The Scandinavian peg tankard at Queen's of 1782 was given by Edward Bond in 1892; he had been made a Fellow in 1869.

The interest in old plate seems to have inspired many colleges with curiosity about their own silver, and during the later

nineteenth century many re-discoveries were made. The old University staves, dating from the later sixteenth century and now on display in the Ashmolean Museum, disappeared at the time of the Civil War and were not discovered again until the 1890s.[277] According to Moffatt, writing in 1906, the handsome 1605–6 rosewater dish at Merton was 'discovered quite black with dirt and age on the top of an old platesafe about twenty years ago by the present Butler and manciple, Mr C Patey'. A letter from Dr Bloxham to his brother of 1890 describes how 'a chest was discovered in Magdalen Coll: Oxford… which evidently had not been opened for more than a century – it contained (with other things) a magnificent Punch Bowl of silver, entirely gilt & weighing more than 128oz [1700–01] – which had been given by Sir John Harpur of Calke Abbey who was matriculated here in 1697… this is to be used in future as the Wassail Bowl on Christmas Eve'.[278] As Bloxham suggests, the occasion was also an opportunity to invent a new tradition.

Despite the burgeoning scholarship regarding the reading of hall and makers' marks on silver from the 1850s, mistakes were still made. Moffatt tells us that the fat-bellied flagon supplied to Wadham in 1752 by the London goldsmith John Swift (which began this chapter), was, despite its full set of hall-marks considered to be the original sixteenth-century cup bequeathed by the Foundress in 1617 (Fig.118).

130 (**78**)  Caster, silver, London 1724–5, Paul Crespin. Pembroke.

131 (**34**)  German (Rhenish) stoneware tankard with silver mounts engraved 1590. Pembroke.

# 7

# CONTEMPORARY COMMISSIONING
## THE STORY TO DATE

'We… believe that a college could be a better place than an art gallery or museum to house a collection of works of art because successive generations of students and Fellows (and their visitors) would be in daily intimate association with them, getting to know them, and influenced by them.'

W.E. van Heyningen, St Cross College, c.1970

### THE 1928 LOAN EXHIBITION OF OXFORD COLLEGE PLATE

The first public exhibition devoted to Oxford college silver was held in 1928, at the Ashmolean Museum. In the preface to the catalogue the chairman of the exhibition committee explained that up until then the 'only source of information on the subject' was Moffatt's 1906 book, and he hoped that the 1928 exhibition would provide 'an opportunity for the study of so varied a series of examples, covering so many periods and styles' and that it 'would be valued by the designer and craftsman, as well as by students and the custodians of public and private collections'. There were 435 exhibits. The most recent piece of secular plate was a hand candlestick from Balliol of 1836, and the most modern sample of ecclesiastical silver a gilt paten by Paul Storr of 1829 from Brasenose, a

132 (**109**) Rose bowl and basin, silver, London 1902–3 and 1905–6, Gilbert Marks. Hertford.

copy of their 1498 paten. It is significant that the only twentieth-century piece of silver exhibited from a college was the Rucker Rose Bowl of 1920 by Omar Ramsden and Alwyn Carr from Brasenose. The 'modern' section of the display was made up of 35 loans mostly from the Goldsmiths' Company. Yet this was not because the colleges did not possess examples of silver that was of recent manufacture, or of modern design. Hertford College had acquired by gift a fine Arts and Crafts rose bowl and basin of 1902-6, by Gilbert Marks (Fig.132). The injection of 'modern work' from the Goldsmiths' Company was intended to show 'the efforts now made for the production of work of really high quality: silversmiths are still to be

found whose work will bear favourable comparison with that of the past. Efforts in the direction of new forms and decoration are naturally experimental; but the results inspire a feeling of hopeful optimism for the future of this great English craft'. Although the commissioning of contemporary silver was slow to start, the last fifty years have shown a remarkable resurgence of interest involving young as well as established silversmiths working for the colleges.

From college inventories it appears that very little 'modern' silver was purchased or commissioned between the 1928 exhibition and the Second World War. There were a few notable exceptions when new foundations sought to equip themselves with the necessary

decencies of college life. St Anne's College traces its ancestry back to the body that initiated higher education for women in Oxford, the Association for the Education of Women in Oxford, founded in 1878. Land given to the Association between Banbury Road and Woodstock Road, and the bequest of a lease on a house in South Parks Road, gave the 'college' a tutorial and social home from 1936 to 1952. To celebrate their 'home' a four piece silver 'Art Deco' tea and coffee service was acquired in 1937 (Fig.133).

During the War it was difficult to keep up standards. A letter to Balliol from Alexander Clark & Co., the College cutlery suppliers, explained that 'The only types of spoons and forks we have been allowed to manufacture since the commencement of hostilities are the Utility Pattern nickel silver, the quality of which is far below your standards'.[279] After the Second World War the silver trade in particular was crippled by the very high rate of purchase tax levied on the maker's cost price to the retailer; at one time it was as high as 133 per cent. The post-war 'Assistance to Craftsmen Scheme' introduced by the Chancellor of the Exchequer, Sir Stafford Cripps, opened up patronage by granting purchase tax exemption to individual commissioned pieces of silver (although up to five repeats were permitted) provided each piece was approved by two panels of expert judges as a fine example of contemporary design and hand craftsmanship. The scheme remained

in place until 1962, when purchase tax was repealed.[280] Just after the war Keble acquired a handsome glass wine ewer with silver mounts by Omar Ramsden (**113**) and Brasenose College a Standing Cup and cover by the Guild of Handicraft, the design of which is still in the workshop at Chipping Camden (**114**).

## TREASURES OF OXFORD, 1953

The Goldsmiths' Company helped to promote the ailing trade by organizing exhibitions. To celebrate Queen Elizabeth II's coronation in 1953, the Goldsmiths' Company with the Oxford Society under the leadership of Lord Kilmaine organized an exhibition entitled *Treasures of Oxford* including books, paintings, drawings, medals, and silver, which formed the most important group of exhibits.[281] In his opening speech at Goldsmiths' Hall, George Ravensworth Hughes, then Clerk to the Goldsmiths' Company, and an energetic and innovative supporter of the craft, acknowledged the gratitude of the Company for the Chancellor's 'measure of relief' referring to the purchase tax exemption, and hoped that 'our gratitude may rightly be also an anticipation of further favours to come'.[282] It is refreshing to see in the catalogue a cluster of new commissions from the 1940s and early 1950s, prompted by the efforts of the Goldsmiths' Company to promote modern silver, the tax advantage offered, and the need to look forward, rather than back after the War. Leslie Durbin's pair of salt cellars and matching pepper pots with mustard pot were commissioned by Corpus in 1946 from money donated by Sir Alan Barlow, a Scholar of the College from 1900 to 1904, and an Honorary Fellow from 1942 (**116**). They incorporate devices symbolic of past College benefactors; they rest on foxes' heads (for Bishop Fox the Founder) with owls (for Bishop Oldham) under the rim, and a pelican, Fox's emblem, as a finial.

133 (**111**) Four piece tea and coffee service, silver, Birmingham 1936–7, W.N. Ltd. St Anne's.

134 (**117**) Eights Week bowl, silver, London 1951–2, designed by Eric Clements, made by Wakeley and Wheeler, sold by Payne & Son. Merton.

Durbin (b.1913) had joined Omar Ramsden in 1929 as an engraver and chaser, leaving in 1938 to set up on his own. He was to become one of the celebrated modern masters of the craft. Durbin's work appears in the collection of other Oxford colleges including New College, for whom he made a rose bowl and a chalice and paten in 1960–1, and an altar cross and small candlesticks the following year.[283] These acquisitions were not the result of a coherent commissioning policy, but a reflection of the taste of the donors, and the high profile of Durbin at the time. It is likely that the first commission for New College was instigated by John Buxton, who with Dr Juel-Jensen commissioned the altar cross. He was a personal friend of Durbin, who had executed commissions for him in 1952. Lincoln College posseses a rose bowl by Durbin, made in 1966 (**120**).

Another exhibit in the 1953 exhibition was the 'Eights Week Bowl' from Merton. Eights Week is the fifth week in the Trinity (summer) term of Oxford University, when

bumping races are held for four days on the River Thames between coxed, eight-oared boats ('VIIIs') of individual Oxford Colleges. The Friends of Merton decided to commemorate the College boat becoming Head of the River in the Eights Week races for the first time in history, by commissioning a trophy from Payne and Son. The design is by Eric Clements (b.1925), realized in silver in the year he graduated from the Royal College of Art (Fig.134). The gilt finial in the form of a mitre refers to the foundation of the College in 1264 by Walter de Merton, Bishop of Rochester, and the stylized boats and cockle shells symbolize the oarsmen in the water. The 'modern' shape is complemented by seventeenth-century style engraved armorials of the College.

The work of another silversmith whose talent was emerging in the 1950s and '60s is represented at Trinity College in the form of three casters made in 1968–9 (**122**). Gerald Benney (b.1930), who with David Mellor and Robert Welch was at the Royal College of Art in the early 1950s; Benney's work helped create the 'New Look' silver, and he worked with industry to promote good design. By the 1960s his work featured in over 32 major exhibitions, not only in England but in Europe, America, Canada, Australia and Hong Kong. It was in the '60s too that he developed his particular texturing of the surface of the silver shown on the Trinity castors, and known in the trade as 'Bennellation'.

## COMMISSIONS FROM THE NEW COLLEGES

Prominent among the new commissions are items made for Nuffield College, which was founded as a graduate college primarily concerned with Social Studies in 1937, although building could not begin until 1949, with £900,000 for the building and its endowment, given by William Morris, Lord Nuffield (d.1963) of Morris Minor fame. Nuffield gave generously to several other colleges, notably St Peter's, Pembroke and Worcester. By the time Lord Nuffield was eighty he had given away £27 million, much of it in medical benefactions and to found chairs at Oxford. In 1952 Lord Cadman and Samuel Courtauld, who were visiting Fellows at the time, presented the College with a coffee pot, designed by J.E. Stapley and made by Nayler Brothers. It is appropriately minimal in form, the plain polished body raised from a single sheet of silver, the only decoration being applied foliate scrolls at the base. This was followed in 1975 by a pair of wine jugs, designed by Alex Styles, who had been with Garrard & Company since 1947 (Fig.135). As a designer Styles was fortunate to be in an influential position during the 1960s and 1970s.[284] It was an exciting and busy period for new silver, particularly modern pieces. He was kept busy designing silver for the new universities such as Brunel (a mace of 1968), and old, like St Catherine's College, Cambridge (a loving cup of 1961), corporate silver for big businesses like Tate and Lyle

135 (**125**)  Pair of wine jugs, silver, London 1974–5, designed by Alex Styles for Garrard. Nuffield.

136 (**123**)  Globe salt, pepper and mustard, Denmark 1965, designed by A. Michelsen. St Catherine's.

137 (**126**)  Silver, London 1975–6, designed and made by Anthony Hawksley. Wolfson.

138  Wolfson College, David Gentleman, *Oxford Almanack* 1975. Sanders of Oxford.

(sugar casters of 1977), and many sporting trophies, such as the Gillette Cup (1974).

St Catherine's College, designed by the Danish architect Arne Jacobsen, was built between 1960 and 1964. Jacobsen was asked to 'undertake as much as possible of the landscape design and the design of the fittings and furniture', and at the same time retain the traditional features of staircases and quadrangles. It is built of exposed concrete beams filled with plate glass and sand-coloured bricks. The hall is the largest in Oxford, providing seating for 365 dining members. The floor is of Westmorland slate and the furniture is made of oak. Pevsner described St Catherine's as 'a perfect piece of architecture' largely because of the 'geometry pervading the whole and the parts'.[285] The parts extend to the furnishings, including the silver. The cutlery used by the Fellows is designed for the Copenhagen firm of A. Michelsen, and is made of silver. The same design was produced in stainless steel for everyday use. Arne Jacobsen presented the College with a magnificent silver globe salt

and pepper from the same firm which had been established in 1841 by Anton Michelsen, executing designs from the architect Thorvald Bindesbøll in the 1900s (Fig.136). The College has fine examples of modern silver including work by Anthony Hawksley, and many pieces were bought or commissioned via Payne and Son. In 1973–4 the College continued its policy of acquiring contemporary silver by commissioning a water jug from Stuart Devlin given by L.D. Hamilton to the College in commemoration of his visiting fellowship 1972–73 (**124**) The hammered surfacing of the body is distinctive of the period, and the applied circlets that decorate the handle, which is gilt, are characteristically rough textured.

To celebrate the opening of the new buildings of Wolfson College, several pieces of silver were given to the College that matched its modern design. Although founded in 1965 as Iffley College, the University allocated a site in Cherwell and the Wolfson Foundation made a building grant of £1,500,000. The foundation stone

139  Late 18th-century engraving of the Radcliffe Observatory. Sanders of Oxford.

140 (**128**) Pepper mill and
salt, silver and blue glass,
London 1979–80, designed
and made by Rod Kelly.
Green College.

was laid in 1968, and the new buildings formally opened by Rt Hon Harold Macmillan, Chancellor of the University, on 12 November 1974. Silver including a matching bowl, candlestick and jug was acquired from the silversmith Anthony Hawksley in 1975. Shepherd Construction, the firm that built the College, presented a salt and pepper mill the following year; this was added to the 'antique' silver given in 1965 by the Haldane family, the previous owners of the site where Wolfson College now stands.

The last two decades of the twentieth century have seen a renaissance in the commissioning of contemporary silver in Oxford. The latest graduate college to be established in the University is Green College. Via the generosity of Dr and Mrs Cecil Green of Dallas, Texas, building work began in 1977, and the college opened in 1979. It centres on the Radcliffe Observatory, completed in 1794 by James Wyatt, and declared by Pevsner to be 'architecturally the finest observatory in Europe' (Fig.139). The

College commissioned the Norfolk-based silversmith Rod Kelly to make salts and pepper mills from 1979, and a large rose bowl in 1993. Kelly has taken the octagonal form of the Observatory, (inspired by the Tower of the Winds in Athens built c.100–50 BC) and the reliefs of the Winds carved upon it, as his inspiration (Fig.140). On the rosebowl Boreas blows a triton's horn to signify power to raise a storm at sea, and a vessel braves the wind and waves. Zephyrus is represented by flowers, and Notus pours rain from an urn. Eurus has fruit held within his robes. On the top panels are sheets of records covering a funnel used for collecting rainfall, the clock represents Time. A sextant, a thermometer, the end of a telescope with the occasional 'X' marking ten years complete the narrative. Kelly's trademark speciality is his flat-chasing, delicately compressing the surface of the silver to create stylized patterns derived from nature. Two of the eight sides of the each of the pepper mills are chased with depictions of Burus and Ephyrus, continuing the theme of the 'winds'.

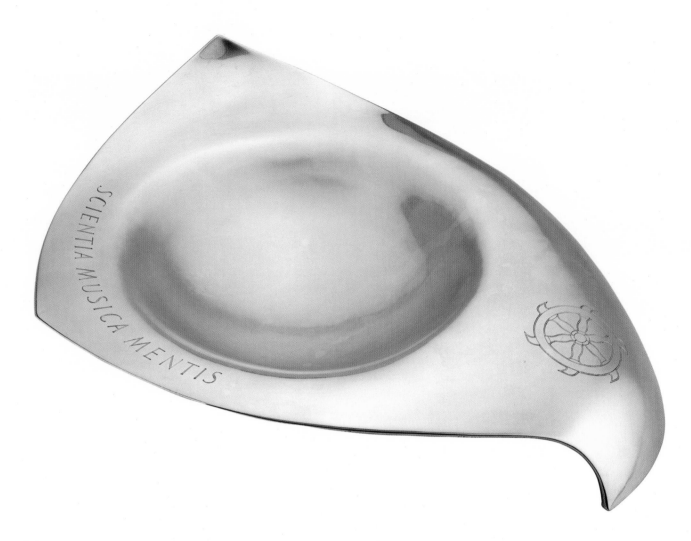

## MILLENNIAL INSPIRATION

St Catherine's has built upon its collection of finely designed contemporary silver by commissioning an elegant and simple yet dramatic bowl for the Millennium, designed and made by the local silversmith Jenny Edge (Fig.141). This is a bold piece that relies on the high sheen that silver takes for its drama. Jenny was approached by Professor M.J.M. Leask, a physicist and Fellow of the College (1965–2000) to make a bowl. She visited the College and decided to make a simple piece that harmonized with the strong clear lines of the architecture. Models in aluminium mesh and pulped paper were made to make sure Professor Leask was happy with the design. The bowl is made from Germanium silver, a new sterling silver alloy which contains 1%

Germanium, an anti-tarnishing agent, invented by Peter Johns from Middlesex University and launched in 2000. The bowl also bears the distinctive millennial hallmark.

Following the theft of College silver in the 1990s St Cross College, founded in 1965 as a graduate college, decided to commission new silver from Rod Kelly and Rebecca de Quin. This enlightened idea is characteristic of a College that had already made a commitment to acquiring first class examples of late Victorian, Edwardian and modern design. The founding Master W.E. van Heyningen had taken the advice of the Handley-Reads, early and knowledgeable collectors in this period of the decorative arts (which in the '60s was only just becoming recognized as an important

141 (**131**) Millennium Bowl, Germanium silver, London 2000, designed and made by Jenny Edge. St Catherine's.

period in design), in acquiring silver, glass and ceramics for the College. Rebecca de Quin, who teaches at the Royal College of Art, specializes in the working of flat sheet silver, and the exploitaiton of the brilliant polish silver can take. The dishes for St Cross are made from the simple cutting, scoring and manipulating of sheet silver (**135**). Her intentions are clearly demonstrated in the silver paper models and designs she made for presentation to the selection committee in 2003 (**164**). The simplicity of form belies great technical difficulty to achieve the fluid form and reflectivity. Rod Kelly's design for a large dish to sit at the centre of a table is in the form of a cross potent, appropriate to the name of the college (Fig.142). In the deep border are chased skipper butterflies, after Dr Skipper, the donor, and mulberry bushes, which were there before the new buildings were erected.

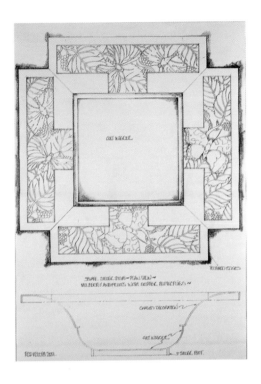

142 (**163**)  Design for St. Cross bowl by Rod Kelly, 2000.

143 (**134**)  Bowl, silver and gilt, London 2004, designed and made by Rod Kelly. St Cross.

The millennium inspired several other colleges to commission new silver including Wadham and Pembroke. Dr Robert Stevens, Master of Pembroke 1993–2001 donated two candlesticks in 2000 from the Guild of Handicraft, bearing the double Millennium hallmark (**132**). Their shape, hand-hammered finish and simple decoration are at once contemporary and redolent of the Arts and Crafts lineage this firm has. To celebrate Pembroke's success of Men's and Women's Eights being Head of the River in 2003, an event unique in Oxford rowing history, the College commissioned a trophy to mark the event (**136**). The project was proposed at a College Gaudy, with money raised from donations from Friends of the Boat Club and College alumni. A design brief was circulated, outlining that the College wanted a trophy of a modern design, of a size and weight to match an earlier trophy of 1872 which commemorated the first time the College became Head of the River, that it should be able to accommodate a shield bearing 20 names with the details of the event ('Head of the River VIIIs Week 2003. Two Heads are better than One), and be robust enough for regular use at College, especially Boat Club functions. Four silversmiths expressed interest and three submitted designs, one of a tall, narrow, oar-shaped ewer, a second of a rather traditional two-handled trophy cup on a wavy base and the third submitted three slightly different designs all comprising a closed silver object mounted on a wooden base. Peter Musson's computer-aided design of the sleek oar-shaped ewer, exploiting the rippling sheen of

144 (**133**) Finger bowl, silver and gilt interior, London 2002–3 designed and made by Peter Musson. New College.

145 (137) Altar cruet, silver, in process of making by Rod Kelly for New College. Photo Toby Hough.

highly polished plain silver won unanimous praise and the trophy was made in time for inclusion in this exhibition (136, 165). The design is based on the shape of oar blades, and the concept of the river. Musson used card and copper models plus digital photographs during making. He is one of the new generation of silversmiths to emerge from the Royal College of Art; he graduated from the College in 2003, and his first work for an Oxford college was a silver and gilt finger-bowl for New College made in 2002 (Fig.144). Back at Pembroke the new commission will share space with nine other Boat Club trophies, largely from the nineteenth century, taking the celebration of sporting success into the twenty-first century.

At New College there is an on-going programme of commissioning that has been influential within the University. Rod Kelly, who designed the New College Millennium Medal, which bears the image of the 'Founder's Jewel', the gold 'M' shaped brooch of c.1350, has made a lavabo and altar cruet for the chapel (see chapter 2) and he is in the process of finishing the second jug to complete the set. It is fitting that this part-finished object, suspended in the last stages of chasing, should be the last item in the exhibition (Fig.145). It does not bring the story of Oxford college silver to an end, as many more new commissions are in process, and it may be hoped that this exhibition will inspire many others.

# CATALOGUE OF ITEMS EXHIBITED

## WEIGHTS OF SILVER

The Troy Pound replaced the Tower Pound in 1527 as the recognized measure of precious metals. The *Troy Pound* was abolished by the Weights and Measures Act of 1878, except for weighing precious metals and stones, and its place was taken by the older *Avoirdupois Pound* for ordinary commercial use.

| TROY WEIGHT | [1 lb Troy] | 12oz Troy | 240dwt Troy |
| --- | --- | --- | --- |
| | | 1 oz Troy | 20dwt Troy |

| | |
| --- | --- |
| Skelton 1823 | Joseph Skelton, *Oxonia Antiqua Restaurata*, 1823 |
| Shaw 1836 | Henry Shaw, *Specimens of the Ancient Furniture*, 1836 |
| Moffatt 1906 | H. Moffatt, *Old Oxford Plate*, 1906 |
| Jones 1938 (Q) | E.A. Jones, *The Silver of the Queen's College*, 1938 |
| Jones 1938 (M) | E.A. Jones, *The Silver of Merton College*, 1938 |
| Jones 1940 | E.A. Jones, *The Plate of Magdalen College*, 1940 |
| Jones 1944 | E.A. Jones, *The Silver of Oriel College*, 1944 |
| Oman 1979 | C. Oman in John Buxton & Penry Williams (eds), *New College Oxford 1379–1979*, 1979 |
| Ellory *et al.* 1999 | C. Ellory, H. Clifford & F. Rogers, *Corpus Silver*, 1999 |
| Marks & Williamson 2003 | R. Marks & P. Williamson, *Gothic. Art for England 1400–1547*, 2003 |

**1** Drinking Horn with silver-gilt mounts, *c.*1340, cover with mark HP in monogram, given by Robert Eglesfield the Founder to Queen's: Moffatt 1906, cat. no. XXIII; Skelton 1823; Shaw 1836. H. 49 cm, L. 46 cm. *Fig.12.*

**2** Cup and Cover, silver-gilt, Paris *c.*1350, referred to as the Founder's Cup, Oriel: Skelton 1823; Shaw 1836, pl. LXIII; Moffatt 1906, cat. no. XVII; Jones 1944, pp. 1 and frontispiece. H. 23.6 cm, Dia. 14.5 cm. *Fig.13.*

**3** 'Founder's Jewel', gold, with rubies, emeralds, pearls and enamel, possibly French *c.*1350, given by Peter Hylle *c.*1455 to New College: Oman 1979, p.295. H. 5.6 cm, W. 4.9 cm. *Fig.17.*

**4** Pair of Pilgrim Flasks, silver-gilt, Paris *c.*1379–1493, each marked three times with a crowned fleur de lys, All Souls: Moffatt 1906, pl. XLIV; Marks & Williamson 2003 cat. no. 101. H. 40.7 cm, Dia (base). 12.7 cm. *Fig.81.*

**5** Standing Salt, silver parcel gilt and painted, crystal lid, *c.*1400–50, All Souls; on loan to the Ashmolean Museum: Shaw 1836; Moffatt 1906, pl. XLIII; Marks & Williamson 2003, cat. no. 179. H. 45 cm, Dia. 13.3 cm. *Fig.14.*

**6** Mazer, maple wood with silver-gilt mounts, before 1437, given by Thomas Ballard to All Souls; on loan to the Ashmolean Museum: Marks & Williamson 2003, cat. no. 102.
H. 20.5 cm,
Dia. 18.5 cm.
*Fig.76.*

**7** Cup and Cover, silver-gilt, *c.*1480, called the Warden's Grace Cup, New College: Moffatt 1906, cat. no. XXXI; Oman 1979, pp. 295–6, pl. 69.
H. 40.3 cm,
Dia. (lid) 14.6 cm.
*Fig.82.*

**8** One of a pair of Ablution Basins, London 1493–4, mark of a horseshoe, Corpus Christi: Ellory *et al.* 1999, pp. 179–94; Marks & Williamson 2003, cat. no. 106.
Dia. 42 cm.

**9** One of a pair of Ablution Basins, London, 1514–15, mark of an orb and cross, Corpus Christi: Ellory *et al.* 1999 pp. 179–94; Marks & Williamson 2003, cat. no. 106.
Dia. 43 cm.
*Figs 37 & 38.*

**10** Crozier, silver-gilt, late 15th or early 16th century, given by Bishop Fox to Corpus Christi: Shaw 1836; Moffatt 1906, cat. no. LXIII: Ellory *et al.* 1999, pp. 51–73; Marks & Williamson 2003 cat. no. 104.
H. 181 cm.
*Figs 8 & 9.*

**11** Standing Salt and Cover, silver-gilt and red glass, *c.*1475–94, given by Warden Walter Hill to New College: Skelton 1823; Shaw 1836; Moffatt 1906, cat. no. XXXII: Oman 1979, p. 296, pl. 70: Marks & Willliamson 2003, cat. no. 181. H. 37 cm, Dia. 13.5 cm.
*Fig.71.*

**12** Pair of Chalices and Patens, silver-gilt, London 1498–9, Brasenose: Moffatt 1906, cat. no. LVI. Chalices H. 17.5 cm, Dia. 11.1 cm, Patens Dia. 15.7 cm.
*Fig.34.*

**13** Hexagonal Standing Salt and cover, silver-gilt with rock crystal, pearls and enamel, *c.*1494–1501, presumed given by Bishop Fox to Corpus Christi: Shaw 1836; Moffatt 1906, cat. no. LXV; Ellory *et al* 1999, pp. 130–73; Marks & Williamson 2003, cat. no. 108.
H. 29.8 cm, Dia. 10.8 cm. *Fig.73.*

**14** Coconut Cup with silver-gilt mounts, late 15th century, said to have been presented by Bishop John Carpenter to Oriel: Skelton 1823; Shaw 1836, pl. LXVIII; Moffatt 1906, cat. no. XIX; Jackson 1911, no. 73; Jones 1944, p. 2.
H. 22.3 cm, Dia. 10.5 cm.

**15** Coconut Cup with silver-gilt mounts, early 16th century, Exeter: Moffatt 1906, cat. no. XII.
H. 25 cm, Dia. 8 cm.
*Fig.79.*

**16** Coconut Cup with silver-gilt mounts, known as the 'Palisade Cup', late 15th century, New College: Moffatt 1906, cat. no. XXXV; Oman 1979, p. 296, pl. 71. H. 20.3 cm. *Fig.78.*

**17** Coconut Cup with silver-gilt mounts, known as the 'Ave Maria Cup', late 15th century, New College: Moffatt 1906, cat. no. XXXV; Oman 1979, pl. 72. H. 22.4 cm, Dia. 11.5 cm. *Figs 42 & 43.*

**18** Standing Salt, silver-gilt with garnets and bowl of rock crystal, known as the 'Ape Salt', early 16th century, New College: Moffatt 1906 cat. no. XXXIII; Oman 1979, p. 297, pl. 73: Marks & Williamson 2003, cat. no. 180. H. 25.8 cm. *Fig.73.*

**19** Flagon or Pot, silver-gilt, English early 16th century, Magdalen: Moffatt 1906, cat. no. XLIX: Jones 1940, p. 24, pl. 2 (centre). H. 35.7 cm, Dia. 14.9 cm. *Fig.83.*

**20** Celadon Bowl, Chinese c.1400–50 with silver-gilt mounts, English c.1500–30, given by William Warham to New College: Moffatt 1906 cat. no. XXXIV; Oman 1979, pp. 297–8; Marks & Williamson 2003, cat. no. 188. H. 12.1 cm. *Fig.18.*

**21** Chalice and Paten, gold, London 1507–8, mark fleur de lys beneath a crown, given by Bishop Fox to Corpus Christi: Moffatt cat. no. LXII; Shaw 1836; Ellory *et al* 1999, pp. 75–110; Marks & Williamson 2003, cat. no. 105. Chalice H. 15.2 cm, Paten Dia. 12.7 cm. *Fig.35.*

**22** Cup and Cover, known as the Founder's Cup, silver-gilt, London 1515–16, Corpus Christi: Moffatt 1906, cat. no. LXVIII; Ellory *et al.* 1999. H. 20.2 cm, Dia. 14 cm. *Fig.10.*

**23** Pax, silver and gilt, c.1520, unmarked, New College: Oman 1979, pl. 74; Marks & Williamson 2003, cat. no. 305. H. 14 cm, W. 10.2 cm. *Fig.39.*

**24** Chalice and Paten, silver-gilt, London 1527–8, Magdalen: Chalice H. 14.5 cm, Paten Dia. 10.5 cm. *Fig.36.*

**25** Chalice, silver-gilt, London 1527–8, mark a saint's head in a shield, given by Sir Thomas Pope the Founder to Trinity: Skelton 1823; Shaw 1836; Moffatt 1906, cat. no. LXXV. Chalice H. 19.8 cm, Dia. 15 cm, Paten Dia. 15.8 cm. *(back cover).*

**26** Standing Mazer, maple wood with silver-gilt mounts, London 1529–30, given by Warden Hovenden to All Souls; on loan to the Ashmolean Museum: Moffatt 1906, cat. no. XLVII. H. 14.5 cm. *Fig.77.*

**27** Cup and Cover, silver-gilt, London 1533–4, mark illegible, given by President Robert Morwent to Corpus Christi, Oxford: Moffatt 1906, cat. no. LXIX; Ellory *et al* 1999, pl. XIV p.273. H. 18.3 cm, Dia (base). 8.9 cm. *Fig.68.*

**28** Drum Salt and cover, silver-gilt, London 1554–5, mark TL in monogram, given by President Robert Morwent to Corpus Christi: Moffatt 1906, cat. no. LXX; Ellory *et al* 1999, pl. XIX, p. 273. H. 21.6 cm, Dia. 10.2 cm. *Fig.75.*

**29** Standing Salt and cover, silver-gilt and rock crystal, London 1549–50, Trinity. H. 19.6 cm. *Fig.74.*

**30** Communion Cup and Paten, silver-gilt, London 1564–5, maker's mark illegible, All Souls: Moffatt 1906, cat. no. XLII. Cup H. 24.1 cm, Dia. 11.5 cm, Paten Dia. 14 cm.

**31** Tankard, silver-gilt, London 1578–9 given by Sir Paul Pindar to Trinity: Moffatt 1906, cat. no. LXXVIII. H. 19.8 cm, Dia. 15 cm.

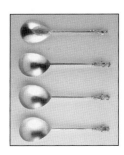

**32** Four Apostle Spoons, silver and silver-gilt, London 1595–6, with later engraving on bowl and stem, given by J.S. Crompton to Pembroke. L. 17.2–18.2 cm. *Fig.129.*

**33** Pair of Flagons, silver-gilt, London 1598–9, given by the Foundress Dorothy Wadham to Wadham: Moffatt 1906, cat. no. LXXXIX. H. 35.4 cm. *Fig.16.*

**34** German (Rhenish) stoneware tankard with silver-gilt mounts, Norwich, engraved 'DAS MAGADN VON ORLANS 1590' and 'HENRI-CUS IV NAV REX FRANCO 1590', given by A.T. Barton to Pembroke in 1885: H. 30 cm, Dia. 10.8 cm. *Fig.131.*

**35** Cup and Cover, silver-gilt, known as the 'Founder's Cup', London 1601–2, mark of an animal's head erased between W and I in a plain shield, with later 17th-century restorations, Magdalen: Moffatt 1906, cat. no. L. H. 41 cm, Dia. 13.8 cm. *Fig.15.*

**36** Standing Cup, silver-gilt, London 1603–4, mark a double-headed eagle displayed, the eagles' heads between the letters TS, in a shaped shield, given by President Ralph Kettel to Trinity: Moffatt 1906, cat. no. LXXVI. H. 26 cm, Dia. 12 cm.

**37** Rosewater Basin, silver-gilt, London 1605–6, maker's mark WI with an animal's head erased, Merton: Moffatt 1906 cat.no.VII; Jones 1938 (M) p. 26, pl. 2. H. 6.6 cm, Dia. 46.3 cm. *Fig.84.*

**38** Pair of Flagons, silver-gilt, London 1605–6, maker's mark LM and a harp, given by Roger Keblewhite and Richard Latewai in 1605 to St John's: Moffatt 1906, cat. no. LXXXI. H. 30.1 cm, Dia. 12.7 cm.

**39** Steeple Cup and Cover, silver-gilt, London 1610–11, given by John Radcliffe to Brasenose: Moffatt 1906, cat. no. LVIII. H. 39.4 cm, Dia. 11 cm. *Fig.19.*

**40** Ostrich Egg Cup, silver-gilt mounts, '1610' engraved on cover, Exeter: Moffatt 1906, cat. no. XIII. H. 54 cm, Dia (base). 13.6 cm. *Fig.80.*

**41** Communion Cup and Paten, silver-gilt, London 1612–13, given by the Foundress Dorothy Wadham to Wadham: Moffatt 1906 cat. no. LXXXIX. Cup H. 25.4 cm, Dia. 11 cm, Paten Dia. 13.3 cm. *Fig.40.*

**42** Communion Cup and Paten, silver, London probably 1614–15, maker's mark of a trefoil with a bordure in a plain shield given by Archdeacon Sanderson to Balliol: Moffat 1906, cat. no. IV. Cup H. 27.8 cm, Paten Dia. 20.7 cm.

**43** Recusant Chalice and two Patens, silver-gilt, London 1641–2, St John's: Moffatt 1906, cat. no. LXXXI. Chalice H. 23.3 cm. *Fig.44.*

**44** Oxford Crown, silver, Oxford 1644, Ashmolean Museum. Dia. 3.7 cm. *Fig.62.*

**45** Triple Unite, gold, Oxford 1643, Ashmolean Museum. Dia. 4.1 cm. *Fig.63.*

**46** Oxford Crown, silver, 1644, mounted as a table ornament, given by Charles Oman to St Peter's. H. 9 cm, W. 7 cm. *Fig.64.*

**47** Oxford Penny, silver 1643, given by Charles Oman to St Peter's. Dia. 3.6 cm. *Fig.65.*

**48** Oxford Penny, silver 1644, given by Charles Oman to St Peter's. Dia. 3.7 cm. *Fig.66.*

**49** Cup and Cover, silver-gilt, London 1660–1, known as the Cup of the Restored Fellows, Magdalen: Moffatt 1906, cat. no. LI: Jones 1940, p. 18, pl. 2, no. 3. H. 47 cm, Dia. 17.4 cm. *Fig.67.*

**50** Chapel Set given by Dean Fell:
Alms Dish, silver-gilt, London 1660–1, mark TC between three pellets above and below a circle, Dia. 48.3 cm.
Pair of Candlesticks, silver-gilt, London 1660–1, mark RA above a mullet and two pellets in a heart shaped shield. H. 42.2 cm, Dia. (base) 26 cm.
Pair of Communion Cups, Patens and Flagons silver-gilt, London 1661–2, mark PB between a crescent and two pellets above and below the letters in a escutcheon.
Moffatt 1906, cat. no. LXXI, LXXII.
Cups H. 23.5 cm, Patens Dia. 12.7 cm,
Flagons H. 30.5 cm, Dia. 23 cm.
Christ Church. *Fig.45.*

**51** Cup and Cover, 22ct gold, London 1661–2, mark of Richard Blackwell II, given by Bishop George Hall to Exeter: Moffatt 1906, cat. no. XIV. H. 14.6 cm, Dia. 16.3 cm. *Fig.21.*

**52** Ox-eye Cup, silver, London 1661–2, Merton. H. 13 cm, Dia. 17.2 cm. *Fig.90.*

**53** Trumpet, silver, given in 1666 by Sir Joseph Williamson to Queen's College: Moffatt 1906, cat. no. XXVII. L. 77 cm. *Fig.25.*

**54** Cup and Cover, silver, London 1666–7, mark a hound sejant, given by Edward Capel to Wadham: H. 185, Moffatt 1906, cat. no. XC. H. 22.3 cm, W. (across handles) 23.1 cm. *Fig.88.*

**55** Ox-eye, silver, London 1668–9, given by Cheeke, 1668 to Magdalen Hall, Hertford. H. 7.3 cm, W. 10.6 cm.

**56** Tankard, silver, London 1669–70, mark TI on tankard, GS for Gabriel Sleath on lid, known as 'The Man of Ross', given by John Kyrle to Balliol: Moffatt 1906, cat. no. V. H. 22 cm, W. 23.3 cm. *Figs 22 & 23.*

**57** Cup and Cover, silver, London 1672–3, mark TK with a mullet below in a plain shield, given by Sir John Barker to Merton: Moffatt 1906, cat. no. VIII: Jones 1938 (M) p. 10, pl. 4. H. 18 cm, W. 28.5 cm. *Fig.86.*

**58** Mug with two handles, silver, London 1677–8, mark TC, given by William Hooper to Exeter: H. 10.4 cm, W (incl. handles). 14.1 cm. *Fig.89.*

**59** One of eleven Ox-eye cups with circular ring handles, silver, London 1677–8, mark of IC, a star of six points below, engraved with the arms of the College, Queen's. H. 10.9 cm, Dia. 15.5 cm. *Fig.30.*

**60** Tankard, silver, London 1678–9, mark TC with a dolphin above and a fleur-de-lis in a lobed shield, given by Richard Wenman to Oriel: Jones 1944, p. 46, pl. 17. H. 27.5 cm, W. 30.5 cm. *Fig.91.*

**61** Cup and Cover, silver-gilt, London 1680–81, mark of Jacob Bodendeich, known as the Spanish Ambassador's Cup, New College: Moffatt 1906, cat. no. XXXVII; Oman 1979, pl. 75. H. 56 cm, Dia. 19.9 cm. *Fig.20.*

**62** Tumbler, silver, London 1681–2, mark of David Willaume, Merton. H. 6.5 cm, W. 7.7 cm. *Fig.87.*

**63** Mug with two handles, silver, London 1683–4, given by Sir Nicholas Stoughton to Exeter. H. 10.2 cm, W. 14.5 cm.

**64** Cup and Cover, silver, London 1684–5, mark RC three pellets above and below within a dotted circle, given by Thomas Mansell to Jesus: Moffatt 1906, cat. no. LXXXVIII (a). H. 29.6 cm, Dia. 39.5 cm.

**65** Ewer and Basin, silver, London 1685–86, mark of IR between a crown and four grouped pellets, engraved by Lemuel King, given by John Kent to St John's: Moffatt 1906, cat. no. LXXXIV. Ewer H. 21.8 cm, Basin (Dia). 20.5 cm. *Figs 111a & 111b.*

**66** Cup, silver, London 1685–6, engraved by Benjamin Rhodes, given by John Clarke to Magdalen. H. 18.5 cm, W. 24.5 cm. *Fig.106 & 113.*

**67** Porringer, silver-gilt, London 1689–70, engraved by Lemuel King, given by Sir John Pakington to St John's: Moffatt 1906, cat. no. LXXXV. H. 15.9 cm.

**68** The 'Halifax Bowl', silver-gilt and coins, South German *c.*1690, Corpus Christi. H. 9.2 cm, Dia. 20.9 cm.

**69** Ox-eye, silver, London 1690–91, one of three bearing mark JA conjoined in script, Queen's: Jones 1938 (Q), p. 75.

**70** Communion Cup and Paten, silver-gilt, London 1694–95, Brasenose: Moffatt 1906 cat. no. LVI. Cup H. 27.8 cm, Paten Dia. 20.7 cm.

**71** Oval filigree Box, silver, 17th century, bequeathed to the Library in 1686 by Dean Fell, Christ Church. H. 5.7 cm, L. 14 cm, W. 11.4 cm. *Fig.26.*

**72** Monteith, silver-gilt, London 1700–01, mark SM between a bird above and a pellet below, given by Sir John Harpur, Magdalen: Moffatt 1906, cat. no. LIII. H. 24 cm. Dia. 30.5 cm. *Fig.96.*

**73** Pair of Tankards, silver, London 1710–11, mark of David Willaume, given by George Watson to Merton. H. 24–2.45 cm, W. 23–23.4 cm. *Fig.92.*

**74** Ewer, silver, London 1713–14, mark VI, given by Frederick North and Basin, silver, London 1749–50, mark of William Peaston, given by William Legge to Trinity: Moffatt cat. no. LXXIX. Ewer H. 38.4 cm, Dia. 15 cm, Basin Dia. 46 cm.

**75** One of a pair of Tankards, silver, London 1720–21, mark of John Sanders, retailed by Timothy Dubber of Oxford, engraved by Benjamin Cole, and donated by Thomas Thornton in 1727 to Pembroke. H. 19 cm. *Fig.33.*

**76** Ox-eye, silver, London 1722–3, mark Augustine Courtauld, Queen's: Jones 1938 (Q), p. 12, plate 3. H. 10.9 cm.

**77** Tankard, silver, London 1723–4, mark of Humphry Payne, engraved by Benjamin Cole, donated by Thomas Northcliff in 1723 to Pembroke. H. 17.5 cm, W. 16.7 cm. *Fig.114.*

**78** Caster, silver, London 1724–25, maker's mark of Paul Crespin, given by J.S. Crompton to Pembroke in 1920. H. 22.5 cm, Dia. 8.7 cm. *Fig.130.*

**79** Punch Bowl and Ladle, silver-gilt, London 1726–7, mark John White, given by Sir Watkin Williams Wynn to Jesus: Moffatt 1906, cat. no. LXXXVIII (b). H. 30.5 cm, Dia. 50 cm. *Fig.27.*

**80** Punch Bowl, silver, London 1730–31, University. H. 18.6 cm, Dia. 26.4 cm.

**81** Ox-eye, silver, London 1735–6, mark of Edward Pocock, Queen's: Jones 1938 (Q), p. 12, pl. 3. H. 10.9 cm, Dia. 15.5 cm. *Fig.30.*

**82** Cup and Cover, silver, London 1742–3, mark of Charles Kandler, given by Phillip Wenman to Oriel: Jones 1944, p. 24. H. 36 cm, W. 34.5 cm.

**83** Tureen and Cover, silver, London 1750–51, mark of Paul de Lamerie, retailed by Wickes and Netherton in 1758, given by Gorges, Lloyd and Sneyd to Brasenose. H. 29.1 cm, W. 46 cm. *Fig.98.*

**84** Flagon, silver-gilt, London 1752–3, mark of John Swift, Wadham: Moffatt 1906, cat. no. XCIII. H. 17.6 cm. *Fig.118.*

**85** Cup and Cover, silver, London 1762–3, mark of Thomas Pitts, given by the Earl of Abingdon to Magdalen. H. 44 cm.

**86** Cup and Cover, silver, London 1763–4, mark of John Parker and Edward Wakelin, given by John Symmons to Jesus. H. 36.6 cm, W. 31 cm, D. 18.2 cm. *Fig.95.*

**87** Tureen, silver, London 1771–2, mark of Andrew Fogelberg (?), Oriel: Moffatt 1906, cat. no. XXI. H. 27 cm, L. 42 cm.

**88** Tea Urn and Two Vases, London 1776–7, mark of John Rowe, St John's: Moffatt 1906, cat. no. LXXXVI. Urn H. 56 cm, Dia. 27 cm, Vases H. 22.8 cm. *Fig.115.*

**89** Argyle, silver, London 1779–80, mark of John Wakelin and William Tayler, given by the Earl of Chesterfield to Queen's: Moffatt 1906, cat. no. XXVII; Jones 1938 (Q), p. 1, pl. 12. H. 34.5 cm. *Fig.28.*

**90** Serving spoon, Russian, St Petersburg, 1871, mark of Nicolls and Plinke, and Imperial Warrant mark, given by Henry Mayr-Harting on leaving his fellowship at St Peter's in 1997 to become Regius Professor of Ecclesiastical History & Lay Canon at Christ Church, St Peter's. L. 30.1 cm.

**91** Ox-eye, silver, London 1792–3, mark of Henry Chawner, given by Edward Stephenson to Queen's: Jones 1938, (Q), p. 13. H. 10.9 cm, Dia. 15.5 cm. *Fig.30.*

**92** Tureen, silver, London 1799–1800, given by William Coolidge to Balliol. H. 45 cm, W. 42 cm.

**93** Trafalgar Vase and Plinth, silver, designed by John Flaxman, supplied by Benjamin Scott and James Smith, London 1806–7, and awarded to Thomas Louis, Admiral of the White, victor off San Domingo, Balliol. H. 67.5 cm, Dia. 28.6 cm.

**94** Toasted Cheese Dish, silver, London 1815–6, maker's mark of Paul Storr, retailed by Rundell, Bridge and Rundell, given by William Ellis Gosling to Brasenose: Moffatt 1906 cat. no. LXI.
H. 11.4 cm,
L. 29.2 cm.
*Figs 99 & 100.*

**95** Sideboard Dish, silver-gilt, London 1820–1, mark of Phillip Rundell (for Rundell, Bridge and Rundell), presented by the Emperor Alexander I of Russia to Dr Routh, Magdalen: Jones 1940, p. 22, pl. 3 (centre). H. 3 cm, Dia. 54.9 cm.
*Fig.29.*

**96** Candelabrum, silver, London 1822–23, mark of Paul Storr, given by students from Oriel College to John Keble in 1823, Keble.
H. 64.8 cm,
W. (base). 29 cm.

**97** Viaticum Set, silver, London 1837, given by the Founder F.J. Chavasse, Bishop of Liverpool, to St Peter's.
H. 10 cm.

**98** Tea pot, silver, Calcutta 1837–8 and milk jug, Chester 1838–9, part of the 'Armenian Set', given in 1935 by Mrs A.G. Francis to St Hilda's. Teapot H. 21.8 cm, Jug H. 10.6 cm.

**99** Chalice, Paten & Flagon, silver-gilt, London 1856–7, designed by William Butterfield, mark of John Keith, Balliol. Chalice H. 23.7 cm, Paten Dia. 20.4 cm, Flagon H. 31 cm.
*Fig.48.*

**100** Decanter, silver, London 1867–8, mark for George Fox retailed by R. & S. Garrard, Brasenose.
H. 32.7 cm,
Dia. 17.4 cm.
*Fig.1.*

**101** Bible Cover (Old Testament), silver (and copper plaque), mounted by Barkentin & Krall, London 1867–8, Worcester.
H. 24 cm.
*Fig.49.*

**102** Bible Cover (New Testament), silver, Barkentin & Krall, London 1867–8, (incorporating a seventeenth-century Roman silver plaque), Worcester.
*Fig.50.*

**103** Ox-eye, silver, London 1877–8, mark of Rowell, given by Henry Mee to Queen's: Jones 1938 (Q), p. 14.
H. 10.9 cm,
Dia. 15.5 cm.

**104** Standing Cup and Cover, silver-gilt, London 1882–3, Queen's.
H. 55.8 cm, Dia. 22.8 cm.
*Figs 93 & 94.*

**105** Communion Cup and Paten, silver-gilt, London 1885–6, designed by C.E. Kempe for Pembroke. H. 24 cm, W. 17.9 cm.
*Fig.51.*

**106** Pair of Candlesticks, silver copies of the bronze candlesticks by Annibale Fontana in the Certosa di Pavia, donated in 1885 by A.T. Barton and Athelstan Riley, Pembroke.
H: 72.5 cm.

**107** Reproduction of the New College 'Palisade' Cup, silver gilt and coconut, 1903, lent by Payne & Son, Oxford.
H. 20 cm, Dia. 10 cm.
*Fig.127.*

**108** Drinking Horn, silver-gilt, London 1937–8, mark of Tessier, given by A.T.C. Carter to Queen's.
H. 45 cm, L. 49 cm, W. 25 cm.
*Fig.128.*

**109** Rose Bowl and Basin, silver, London 1902–3 and 1905–6, mark of Gilbert Marks, given by St Helier to Hertford.
Bowl. H. 21.3 cm, Dia. 22.7 cm, Basin Dia. 41 cm.
*Fig.132.*

**110** Communion Cup, silver, London 1931–2, mark of Charles Boyton, Exeter.
H. 30.8 cm.
*Fig.53.*

**111** Four piece tea and coffee service, comprising coffee pot, tea pot, sugar bowl, milk jug, W.N. Ltd Birmingham, 1936–7, St Anne's. Coffee pot H. 20 cm, Tea pot H. 14 cm, Jug H. 8.8 cm, Bowl. 7.4 cm.
*Fig.133.*

**112** Ox-eye, silver, London 1936–7, mark of Tessier, given by A.T.C. Carter to Queen's.
H. 10.9 cm, Dia. 15.5 cm.

**113** Claret Jug, silver mounts and glass, London 1938–9, mark of Omar Ramsden, Keble.
H. 29 cm, W. 26 cm.

**114** Cup and Cover, silver, London 1945–5, mark of the Guild of Handicraft, Brasenose. H. 24 cm, Dia. 12.6 cm.

**115** Communion Cup and Paten, silver, London 1945–6, mark of the Guild of Handicraft, St Edmund Hall. H. 17.8 cm. *Fig.52.*

**116** Salt and Pepper Pot, Silver 1945–46, Leslie Durbin, commissioned in 1946 from money donated by Sir Alan Barlow, Honorary Fellow, Corpus Christi. Salt H. 12.1 cm, Pepper Pot H. 15.9 cm.

**117** Eights Week Bowl, silver, London 1951–2, designed by Eric Clements, made by Wakely and Wheeler, Merton. H. 24.8 cm, W. 34.8 cm. *Fig.134.*

**118** Chapel Set, lavabo, wine and water cruets, flagon & wafer box, silver-gilt, London 1953, designed by Alex Styles, made by John Bartholomew of Wakely and Wheeler, retailed by Garrard, Corpus Christi. Lavabo, W. 20.7 cm, Cruets and Flagon H. 24.9 cm, Wafer Box. H. 3.4 cm. *Fig.54.*

**119** Ciborium, silver, London 1954–55, designed by Eric Clements, Lady Margaret Hall. H. 24 cm, W. (base). 14 cm. *Fig.55.*

**120** Rosewater Bowl, silver, London 1966–7, mark of Leslie Durbin, Lincoln. H. 4.6 cm, Dia. 44.5 cm.

**121** Communion Cup, silver, Birmingham 1966–7, designed by Cyril Shiner, Exeter. H. 26.6 cm. *Fig.56.*

**122** One of Three Casters, London 1968–9, mark of Gerald Benney, Trinity. H. 18.5 cm, Dia. 5 cm.

**123** Globe Salt, Pepper and Mustard, silver, Denmark 1965, designed by Anton Michelsen and given by Arne Jacobsen to St Catherine's. Salt H. 5.5 cm, Pepper H. 4.5 cm, Mustard H. 5.6 cm. *Fig.136.*

**124** Jug, silver and gilt handle, London 1973–4, mark Stuart Devlin, given by L.D. Hamilton to St Catherine's.
H. 28.5 cm,
W. 17 cm,
Dia. 8.2 cm.

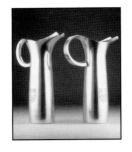

**125** Pair of Wine Jugs, silver, London 1974–5, designed by Alex Styles for Garrard, presented by Sir Ralph Vickers to Nuffield.
H. 30 cm.
*Fig.135.*

**126** Bowl, Candlestick & Jug, silver, London 1975–6, designed and made by Anthony Hawksley, Wolfson.
Bowl H. 5 cm,
Dia. 41 cm,
Candlestick H. 14 cm, Jug H. 8.3 cm.
*Fig.137.*

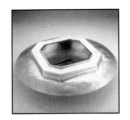

**127** Rosewater Bowl, silver, London, 1993, designed and made by Rod Kelly, Green.
H. 11 cm, Dia. 48.7 cm.

**128** Pepper Mill Salt, silver & blue glass, London 1979–80, designed and made by Rod Kelly, given by Mr and Mrs Hanson to Green.
Pepper H. 12.6 cm,
Dia. 5 cm,
Salt H. 3.4 cm,
Dia. 10 cm.
*Fig.140.*

**129** Lavabo, silver and gilt, London 1998–9, designed and made by Rod Kelly, commissioned with funds given to the Chapel to mark weddings held there, including two members of the family of John Ledingham, New College.
Dia. 30 cm.
*Fig.57.*

**130** Altar Cruet, silver and gilt, London 2003, designed and made by Rod Kelly, commissioned with funds given to the Chapel from an anonymous donor, New College.
H. 28 cm.
*Fig.58.*

**131** Millennium Bowl, Germanium silver, London, Millennium Mark for 2000, designed and made by Jenny Edge, commissioned by M.J.M Leask for St Catherine's.
H. 8 cm, L. 37 cm, Dia. 28 cm.
*Fig.141.*

**132** Pair of Candlesticks, silver, London, Millennium Mark for 2000, designed and made by the Guild of Handicraft, given by Professor and Mrs Stevens to Pembroke.
H. 18 cm,
Dia. 10 cm.

**133** Finger Bowl, silver with gilt interior, London 2002–3, designed and made by Peter Musson, New College.
H. 7 cm, W. 15 cm.
*Fig.144.*

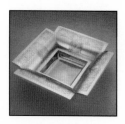

**134** Dish, silver, designed and made by Rod Kelly, 2004, St Cross. *Fig.143.*

**164 (135)** Design for a Dish, silver, designed and made by Rebecca de Quin, 2004, St Cross.

**164 (136)** Pembroke, double-Head of the River Trophy, silver, London 2004, designed and made by Peter Musson, engraved by John Harris. H. 37 cm.

**137** Altar Cruet, silver, in process of making by Rod Kelly, not yet hallmarked, commissioned with funds raised for the Chapel to celebrate the Amicabilis Concordia, New College. H. 27 cm.

## ELECTROTYPES

**138** Electrotype of the Standing Salt *c.*1400–1450 from All Souls College, late 19th century, Museum of Oxford on loan from the Victoria and Albert Museum. H. 44.5 cm D. *Fig.125.*

**139** Electrotype of the Founder's Cup, 1515–16 from Corpus Christi, late 19th century, Museum of Oxford on loan from the Victoria and Albert Museum. H. 20.5 cm, Dia. 15.5 cm. *Fig.125.*

**140** Electrotype of Warden Hill's Standing Salt *c.*1475–94 from New College, late 19th century, Museum of Oxford on loan from the Victoria and Albert Museum. H. 37 cm, Dia. 13.5 cm. *Fig.125.*

**141** Electrotype of the 1610–11 'TvL' cup in the Victoria and Albert Museum, London 1910, Wadham. H. 33.4 cm, W. 18.2 cm.

## WORKS ON PAPER

**143** Inventory of Goods belonging to a Warden of New College upon his resignation, 1396, New College. H. 23.8 cm, W. 38 cm.

**144** Bursar's Long Book showing inventory of 1631, New College. H. 40 cm, W. (open). 30.2 cm, (closed). 18 cm. *Fig.105.*

**145** Liber Magnus (Bursar's Long Book) 1622, Corpus Christi. H. 40 cm. *Fig.5.*

**146** Calculus (Bursar's Long Book) 1724, Lincoln. H. 40 cm. *Fig.4.*

**147** Bursar's Long Book, 1657–8, New College. H. 59.5 cm, W. (closed). 220 cm.

**148** Book of Benefactors from the Year 1642, Brasenose. H. 35.8 cm, W. (closed). 27.2 cm, (open). 56 cm.

**149**  Liber Albus Benefactorum, 1650–1815, Trinity. H. 44.2 cm, W. (closed). 34.4 cm, (open). 69.6 cm.

**150**  Album Benefactorum, with gold-tooled, red leather binding, 1664, Pembroke. H. 35 cm, W. (closed) 28 cm, (open) 56 cm. *Fig.33.*

**151**  Account Book for the colleges, 1885–1916, Payne & Son, Oxford. L. 37.6 cm, W. (closed) 25.5 cm, (open) 51.3 cm.

**152**  Bill from George Tonge to New College. H. 15.4 cm, W. 16.2 cm. *Fig.6.*

**153**  Bill from Rundell, Bridge & Rundell to New College. H. 16 cm, W. 19.8 cm.

**154**  Bill from George Wickes & Samuel Netherton to Brasenose, 1758. H. 38.2 cm, W. 23.4 cm. *Fig.97.*

**155**  Bill from R.& S. Garrard to Brasenose, 1838. H. 20.4 cm, W. 24.4 cm.

**156**  Bill from George Tonge to St John's, 1773–7 H. 60.7 cm, W. 38.9 cm. *Fig.116.*

**157**  Bill from Daniel Porter to New College, 1690. H. 20.7 cm, W. 16.5 cm.

**158**  Bill from Richard Dubber to New College, 1700. H. 23.8 cm, W. 13.8 cm.

**159**  Bill from John Wilkins to New College, 1712. H. 12.2 cm, W. 15.7 cm. *Fig.6.*

**160**  *Art Treasures of the United Kingdom*, 1858, chromolithographic book, Private Collection. H. 39.5 cm, W. 29.5 cm, D. 58 cm. *Fig.124.*

**161**  Designs by Rod Kelly for Salt and Pepper Mill, 1978 (**128**), Green. H. 29.5 cm, W. 41.5 cm.

**162**  Designs by Rod Kelly for Rose Bowl, 1998 (**127**), Green. H. 29.5, W. 41.5 cm.

**163**  Design by Rod Kelly for Bowl, 2003 (**134**), St Cross. H. 29.5 cm, W. 41.5 cm. *Fig.142.*

**164**  Designs by Rebecca de Quin for Bowl 2003, (**135**), St Cross. H. 29.5 cm, W: 41.5 cm.

**165**  Designs by Peter Musson for Double Head of the River Trophy, 2004 (**136**), Pembroke. H. 29.5 cm, W. 21.1 cm.

## PAINTINGS AND DRAWINGS

**166**  Portrait of William Hodges, College Servant, *c.*1768. Oil on Canvas, New College. H. 77 cm, W. 65 cm. *Fig.102.*

**167**  Portrait of William Palmer, Butler (1782–1824), by Stephen Taylor *c.*1824–5. Oil on Canvas. Oriel. H. 74.9 cm, W. 65 cm. *Fig.101.*

**168**  Portrait of Henry Bly, Senior Common Room Butler (1923–46), by R. Schwabe, 1946. Pencil on Paper. Hertford. H. 43 cm, W. 24 cm. *Fig.103.*

**169**  Photograph of the Merton Butler. Tollygraphics. *Fig.104.*

**170**  Portrait of a Scullion *c.*1680–90 by John Riley. Oil on canvas. 99.7 x 60.5 cm. Christ Church. *Fig.108.*

## MISCELLANEOUS

**142**  University Chest, iron-bound wood, 17th century, Corpus Christi, on loan to the Ashmolean Museum.

# GLOSSARY

**ALMS DISH**: A large plate on which money, collected in smaller plates, boxes or bags from the congregation, is assembled for presentation at the altar in Anglican churches.

**ARGYLE**: Also called 'Argyll', a gravy warmer made in various shapes and sizes but generally similar to a covered coffee-pot with a handle and a spout. The gravy is kept warm by means of hot water contained in a compartment created by a double wall, or a central vertical cylinder. Said to have been invented by the 3rd Duke of Argyll (1682–1761), and made in silver from the mid 1750s.

**BEDEL**: An archaic form of 'beadle'. The office of Bedel (there are four: for Divinity, Law, Medicine and the Arts) is one of the oldest in Oxford, going back to the thirteenth century, and requires the holder to attend upon the Vice-Chancellor on ceremonial occasions.

**BUTTERY**: A college store where wine, beer and other provisions are for sale to students.

**CHALICE**: Cup for wine at the Eucharist. The term 'chalice' is an anglicized form of the Latin *calix*, meaning cup.

**CHASUBLE**: A cloak of circular or oval shape worn by the priest at the Eucharist.

**CIBORIUM**: Covered cup fitted with a lid, containing the consecrated wafer bread.

**COLLEGE CUP**: See Ox-eye.

**COMMUNION**: The partaking of the consecrated elements at the Eucharist, whereby there is a communion or participation in Christ and in him with all members of the congregation.

**COMMUNION CUP**: Wine cup for the Eucharist, introduced by Protestants in the sixteenth century. It resembles a household cup to show that the wine is for the people as well as the priest.

**CORPORAS CASE**: Cloth used in the celebration of the Mass.

**CROZIER**: The pastoral staff with a curled top or crook, symbolic of the Good Shepherd of souls, which is carried by bishops of the Roman Catholic, Anglican and some Lutheran Churches as well as by abbots and abbesses. First adopted at the fourth Council of Toledo in 633.

**CRUETS**: Derived from the medieval French 'cruette', meaning 'little jug', a pair of such vessels are used to contain the wine and water used at the Eucharist.

**ELECTROTYPE**: The process creates an exact copy of a model by depositing a thin layer of silver or copper metal by means of an electrical current, a technique, developed in the 1840s by Elkington & Co. Birmingham, which involves first making a negative mould in Plaster of Paris, then casting a positive mould in a lightweight metal, silicon, gutta-percha, plastic or other material on which a coating of silver is deposited in thicknesses related to the duration of the current.

**EUCHARIST**: From the Greek word meaning 'thanksgiving'. The service which re-enacts the sharing of bread and wine at the Last Supper. Also known as the Mass, Holy Communion and the Lord's Supper.

**FILIGREE**: A delicate surface decoration using fine wire in an intricate foliate or geometric design often soldered to objects such as boxes, book covers, buttons and purses.

**GILDING**: The process of overlaying or covering an article with a thin layer of gold or gold alloy. Silver is gilded in two ways a) mercury gilding (fire gilding) by applying an amalgam of gold and mercury with a brush, then heating the object to cause the mercury to vaporise and leave a thin layer of gold b) electro-gilding introduced from the 1840s, by depositing a layer of gold by an electric current.

**MAGDALEN CUP**: A type of covered beaker, so-called in some mid-sixteenth century inventories because it is in the same form as the covered pot containing ointment that Mary Magdalen(e) is seen holding in certain paintings of the late fifteenth and early sixteenth centuries.

**MANCIPLE**: An officer or servant who buys provisions for a college.

**MATRICULATION:** From the Latin *matricula* (roll), matriculation is the ceremony by which an entrant to a college becomes a member of the University.

**MISSAL:** A service book, containing Masses for feast days and saints' days.

**MITRE:** The origin of the mitre is obscure, but by the eleventh century it emerged as the distinctive liturgical hat of bishops, although some abbots and cardinals have been granted the privilege of wearing one.

**MONSTRANCE:** A vessel designed for the purpose of showing the consecrated host to the people that came into use from the thirteenth century.

**OX-EYE:** A type of cup with a bulbous body, and slightly flaring mouth, and characteristically having two opposed ring-shaped vertical handles at the neck, that look like 'eyes' or 'ears', hence also eared cups.

**PARCEL GILT:** Partly gilded.

**PASTORAL STAFF:** See Crozier.

**PATEN:** A small flat plate for the consecrated bread at the Eucharist. After the English Reformation patens became shallow dishes with a stem and often served as a cover for the Communion cup.

**PAX:** Small tablet kissed in turn by the congregation at the Eucharist in the Middle Ages, as a subsitute for giving the kiss of peace to each other, as a sign of fellowship.

**PORRINGER:** A small, spoutless, two-handled cup used for drinking broth or soup; from the French word *potage*: soup.

**PYX:** A container for the consecrated wafer bread known as the Reserved Sacrament, for use by a priest when travelling outside the church ('viaticum').

**RECUSANTS:** English Roman Catholics in the sixteenth and seventeenth centuries, who refused to accept Protestantism or acknowledge the monarch as head of the Church of England.

**REFORMATION:** The break with the Church of Rome in the sixteenth century, by which Protestant Churches, including the Church of England, were set up.

**REREDOS:** In the later Middle Ages the intervening space between the east window and its sill, and the altar was filled in with a structure of wood or stone.

**THURIBLE:** Incense burner, usually swung on chains held in the hand, an alternative word for censer.

**TRENCHER:** Thick slices of bread set before each guest at the dining table to act as a plate, replaced in the sixteenth century at noble tables with square or round trenchers of wood.

**TURKEY WORK:** A carpet made in or imported from Turkey, or of a style in imitation of this, woven in one piece of richly coloured wools and having a deep pile, cut to resemble velvet.

**WHITE:** Silver without gilding.

**VIATICUM:** See Pyx.

# BIBLIOGRAPHY

Ackermann, R. *History of the University of Oxford: Its Colleges, Halls and Public Buildings*, 2 vols, Oxford 1814.

Alexander, J. & Binski, P. *The Age of Chivalry*, London 1987.

Aylmer, U. *Oxford Food An Anthology*, Oxford 1995.

Bede, C. *The Adventures of Verdant Green An Oxford Undergraduate* (1853–4), Oxford 1982.

Beeton, Mrs I.M. *Household Management*, 1859–61, London 1985.

Brears, P. 'Decorating the Tudor and Stuart Table' in C.A. Wilson 1991, pp. 56–97.

Brodrick, G.C. *Memorials of Merton College*, Oxford 1885.

Brown, P. 'Dining by Design', in Brown (ed) *British Cutlery. An illustrated history of design, evolution and use*, York 2001.

Buck, A. 'Silver by Leslie Durbin at New College, Oxford', *The Silver Society Journal*, Autumn 1998, pp. 103–5.

Bury, S. *Copy or Creation. Victorian Treasures from English Churches*, London 1967.

Butler, A.J. 'Brief notes on Brasenose plate', *Athenaeum*, November 25 & December 9, 1882.

Butler, A.J. 'The College Plate, with a complete list of donors', *Brasenose College Quatercentenary Monograph*, vol. 1, no. 5, Oxford Historical Society, Oxford 1909.

Buxton, J. & Williams, P. *New College Oxford 1379–1979*, Oxford 1979.

Campbell, M. 'Medieval Founders' Relics: Royal and Episcopal Patronage at Oxford and Cambridge Colleges', in D.Coss and M. Keen (eds) *Heraldry, Pageantry and Social Display in Medieval England*, Woodbridge 2000, pp. 125–142.

Carter, J. *Specimens of Ancient Sculpture and Painting*, vols. 1 & 2, Oxford 1780–94.

Clifford, H. 'The Silver at Brasenose College, Oxford: Patterns of Purchase and Patronage in the Eighteenth and Nineteenth Centuries', *Studies in the Decorative Arts*, vol. III, no. 1, Fall–Winter 1995–1996, pp. 2–28.

Clifford, H. 'Interpreting the New College Crozier', *Apollo*, vol. CXLV, no. 423 (new series), May 1997, pp. 48–50.

Clifford, H. 'Archbishop Matthew Parker's gifts of plate to Cambridge', *The Burlington Magazine*, vol. CXXXIX, no. 1126, January 1997, pp. 4–10.

Clifford, H. 'Corporate Dining' in P. Glanville and H. Young, *Elegant Eating. Four hundred years of dining in style*, London, 2002, pp. 132–135.

Clifford, H. 'Eric Clements', *Goldsmiths' Review*, 2000/2001, pp. 20–24.

Cluneglass-Davies, D. 'Coconut Cups' *Antiques Review*, June/August 1954, pp. 41–2.

Cobban, A.B. *The Medieval Universities: Oxford and Cambridge to 1500*, London 1988.

Cordeaux E.H. & Merry, D.H. *A bibliography of printed works relating to the University of Oxford*, Oxford 1968.

Crighton, R. *Cambridge Plate, An exhibition of silver, silver-gilt and gold plate arranged as part of the Cambridge Festival 1975 drawn from the holdings of the City of Cambridge, the University of Cambridge, the Colleges, the National Trust (Angelsey Abbey) and the Cambridge Beefsteak Club*, Cambridge 1975.

Cripps, W.J. *College and Corporation Plate: A Handbook to the Reproduction of Silver Plate in the South Kensington Museum from Celebrated English Collections*, London 1881.

Cross, L.B. 'The College Plate' *Jesus College Magazine*, vol. VI. June 1947, pp. 58–66.

Culme, J. *Nineteenth Century Silver*, London 1986.

Culme, J. 'Attitudes to Old Plate 1750–1900' in *The Directory of Gold & Silversmiths Jewellers & Allied Traders 1838–1914 from the London Assay Office Registers*, Woodbridge 1987, vol. 1, pp. xvi–xxxvi.

Dale, T.C. 'The Plate of Magdalen College', *Genealogy Magazine*, September 1928, vol. 4, no. 3, pp. 58–9.

Davies, J.G. (ed) *A Dictionary of Liturgy & Worship*, London 1972.

Denholm-Young, N. *Cartulary of the Medieval Archives of Christ Church*, Oxford 1931.

Dewey, J. & S. *Payne and Son Two Centuries of a Family Firm*, 1790–1990, Wallingford 1990.

Donohoe, T. 'A silver bottle shade', *The Silver Society Journal*, no. 15, 2002, pp. 126–7.

Duffy, E. *The Stripping of the Altars. Traditional Religion in England 1400–1580*, New Haven and London 1992.

Duncan, G.D. 'An Introduction to the Accounts of Corpus Christi College' in J. McConica (ed.), *The History of the University of Oxford*, vol. 2, Oxford 1986, pp. 574–596.

Ellis, M. (ed) *Eric Clements*, Birmingham Museum and Art Gallery, Birmingham 2002.

Ellory, C., Clifford, H. & Rogers, F. (eds) *Corpus Silver, Patronage and Plate at Corpus Christi College, Oxford*, Barton under Needwood 1999.

Emmerson, R. *Church Plate*, London 1991.

F.M. Powicke and A.B. Emden (eds). *The Universities of Europe in the Middle Ages*, vol. III, Oxford 1936.

Foster, E. & Atkinson, T.D. *Old Cambridge Plate*, Cambridge 1896.

Fowler, T. *The History of Corpus Christi College with Lists of its Members*, Oxford 1893.

Gilchrist, A. *Anglican Church Plate*, London 1967.

Glanville, P. *Silver in Tudor and Early Stuart England*, London 1990.

Graham, M. *Oxford City Apprentices 1697–1800*, Oxford 1987.

Green, V. *The Commonwealth of Lincoln College 1427–1971*, Oxford 1979.

Grimwade, A. 'Cardinal Wolsey's Plate', *The Silver Society Journal*, Autumn 1997, p. 573.

Groos, W. *The Diary of Baron Waldstein A Traveller in Elizabethan England*, London 1981.

Gutch, J. (ed) *History and Antiquities of the Colleges and Halls in the University of Oxford*, Oxford 1786.

Hammer, C.I. 'Oxford Town and Oxford University', in J.M. McConica, (ed), *The History of the University of Oxford*, vol. 3, Oxford 1986.

Hansen, A.N. *Oxford Goldsmiths Before 1800*, Columbus, Ohio 1996.

Hayward, J.F. 'Early Church Plate' *Country Life*, 6 January 1955, pp. 28–30.

Hayward, J.F. 'The Tudor Plate of Magdalen College, Oxford', *Burlington Magazine*, 125, May 1976, pp. 260–5.

Hayward, M. 'The storage and transport of Oxford silver', *The Silver Society Journal*, no. 11, Autumn 1999, pp. 245–251.

Hibbert, C. & Hibbert, E. (eds) *The Encyclopaedia of Oxford*, London 1988.

Highfield, J.R.L. (ed) *The Early Rolls of Merton College Oxford*, Oxford 1964.

Hill, R.H. 'The University plate in the 16th century', *Bodleian Quarterly Record*, 1924, vol. 4, pp. 141–4.

Hiscock, W.G. *A Christ Church Miscellany, new chapters on the architects, craftsmen, statuary, plate, bells, furniture, clocks, plays, the library and other buildings*, Oxford 1946, see esp. chapter XV 'The Plate and Some Oxford Goldsmiths', pp. 134–142.

Hope, W.H. St John 'Mazers at All Souls', *Archaeologia*, 1887, vol. 50, pp. 136–7, 150, 155, 162 & 166.

Hope, W.H. St John 'The Episcopal Ornaments of William Wykeham and William Waynflete, sometime Bishops of Winchester, and of certain Bishops of St Davids', *Archaeologia*, vol. 60, 1907, pp. 465–92.

Hughes, G.B. 'Oxford plate exhibited and the modern silver-smith', *Apollo*, 1928, vol. 8, pp. 335–40.

Hughes, G.B. 'Silver and the Oxford Colleges', *London Mercury*, vol. 19, 1928, pp. 60–8.

Hughes, G.B. 'Treasures of Oxford', *Country Life*, May 21, 1953, pp. 1610–1612.

Hughes, G.R. *The Worshipful Company of Goldsmiths as patrons of their craft 1919–53*, London 1965.

Impey, O. *Chinoiserie. The Impact of Oriental Styles on Western Art and Decoration*, New York 1977.

Ingram, J. *Memorials of Oxford*, 3 vols, Oxford 1832–7.

Jeffery, R.W. 'Church Plate & an inventory made in 1591 of goods in Brasenose College Chapel', *Proceedings of the Society of Antiquaries*, 1888, ser. 2, vol. 9, pp. 242–43.

Jeffery, R.W. 'A Common Room Account Book 1773–1841', *The Brasen Nose*, 1915, vol. 2, pp. 55–9. II (1904), pp. 82–128.

Jeffery R.W. 'A College Butler's [E. Shippary] notebook [1650–1706], *The Brasen Nose*, 1920, vol. 3, pp. 86–91.

Jones, E.A. 'The Silver Plate of Jesus College, Oxford', *Y Cymmrodor*, XVII (1904), pp. 82–128.

Jones, E.A. *The Old Plate of the Cambridge Colleges*, Cambridge 1910.

Jones, E.A. 'Three engravers of Heraldry on English Plate', *Apollo*, November 1935, pp. 268–72.

Jones, E.A. *The Silver of the Queen's College*, Oxford 1938.

Jones, E.A. *The Silver of Merton College*, Oxford 1938.

Jones, E.A. *The Plate of Magdalen College*, Oxford 1940.

Jones, E.A. 'An Oxford Goldsmith at St John's College', *Oxoniensia*, 1941, vol. 6, pp. 90–92.

Jones, E.A. *The Silver of Oriel College*, Oxford 1944.

Lightbown, R.W. *Secular Goldsmiths' Work in Medieval France: A History*, London 1978.

Lytle, G.F. 'Patronage Patterns & Oxford Colleges c.1300–c.1530' in L. Stone (ed) *The University in Society*, Princeton & London, 1975.

Macleane, D. *A History of Pembroke College*, Oxford 1897.

McConica, J. (ed.) *The History of the University of Oxford*, Oxford 1986–9.

Macray, W.D. *A Register of the Members of St Mary Magdalen College, Oxford*, vol. 4, London 1904.

Madan, F. 'A short account of the Phoenix Common Room 1782–1900', in *Brasenose Quatercentenary Monographs*, vol. II, IX–XIV, Oxford 1909, pp. 93–135.

Marks, R. & Williamson, P. *Gothic. Art for England 1400–1547*, London 2003.

Martin, C.T. *Catalogue of the Archives of All Souls College*, 2 vols, Oxford 1877.

Mayhew, N. 'Currency and plate: some thoughts based on Oxford coinage and the Civil War', *The Silver Society Journal*, no. 11, Autumn 1999, pp. 236–239.

Mellor, M. *Pots and People that have shaped the heritage of medieval and later England*, Oxford 1997.

Moffatt, H.C. *Old Oxford Plate*, London 1906.

Montagu, Jeremy, 'The crozier of William of Wykeham', *Early Music*, November 2002, pp. 541–62.

Mordaunt Crook, J. (ed) *The Strange Genius of William Burges Art-Architect 1827–1881*, Cardiff 1981.

Mordaunt Crook, J. *John Carter and the Mind of the Gothic Revival*, London 1995.

Morris, J. *The Oxford Book of Oxford*, Oxford 1989.

Oman, C. 'Sir Joseph Williamson', *Apollo*, November 1953, pp. 125–27.

Oman, C. *English Church Plate 597–1830*, Oxford 1957.

Oman, C. 'The Winchester College Plate', *Connoisseur*, 149 (1962) pp. 24–33.

Oman, C. 'The College Plate', in Buxton & Williams 1979, pp. 293–305.

Oman, C. 'Plate from a lost Oxford College', *Archaeologia Cantiania*, XCV (1979), pp. 49–53.

Pantin, W.A. 'College Muniments: A Preliminary Note', *Oxoniensia*, I (1936), pp. 140–3.

Pantin, W.A. *Oxford Life in Oxford Archives*, Oxford 1971.

Pearson, D. 'Bookbinders and goldsmiths: their tools and trade in Oxford', *The Silver Society Journal*, no. 11, Autumn 1999, pp. 240–244.

Pinto, E.H. 'Mazers and their Wood', *The Connoisseur*, 123, March, pp. 33–6.

Rackham, O. *Treasures of Silver at Corpus Christi College, Cambridge*, Cambridge 2002.

Richard, G.L. & Salter, H.E. *The Dean's Register at Oriel 1446–1661*, Oxford 1926.

Riley, H.T. 'Inventory of goods belonging to a Warden of New College, Oxford 1396', *The Archaeological Journal*, vol. XXVIII, 1936, pp. 232–4.

Scarisbrick, D. 'Queen Mary and the New College Jewel' *Jewellery Studies*, vol. 4, 1990, p. 25.

Shaw, H. *Specimens of Ancient Furniture*, London 1837.

Skelton, J. *Oxonia Antiqua Restaurata*, London 1823.

Skerry, J.E. 'Ancient and Valuable Gifts' – The Evolving Role of Colonial Silver at Harvard College' Term Paper (type-script), American and New England Studies Program, Boston University, Spring 1992.

Smith, E.J.G. 'Richard Blackwell & Son', *The Silver Society Journal*, 2003, pp. 19–45.

Smith, H.C. 'A Catalogue of the Plate of University College' (typescript), 1943.

Smith, H.C. 'The Plate of University College', *Country Life*, 1 July 1949, vol. 106, pp. 42–3.

Smith, J.J. *Specimens of College Plate*, Cambridge 1845.

Southwick, L. 'The silver vases awarded by the Patriotic Fund', *The Silver Society Journal*, Winter 1990, pp. 27–46.

Steer, F.W. *The Archives of New College*, Oxford 1974.

Stevenson, W.H. & Salter H.E. *The Early History of St John's College*, London 1939.

Stovin, P. '19th Century Cambridge College Ceramics and a Comparison with Oxford Colleges', *Northern Ceramics Society Journal*, vol. 16, 1999, pp. 51–75.

Sweet, R. *Antiquaries. The discovery of the past in eighteenth-century Britain*, London and New York 2004.

Sylvester, R.S. & Harding, D.P. (eds) *Two Early Tudor Lives. The Life and Death of Cardinal Wolsey by George Cavendish The Life of Sir Thomas More by William Roper*, New Haven and London 1962.

Teasdale, D.W.S. 'Heirlooms of Tomorrow. Contemporary College, Corporation and Presentation Plate, *Antiques Review*, part 1, December 1953–February 1954, pp. 21–3, part 2, March/May 1954, pp. 25–27.

Thomson, E.C. 'The College Silver', *Jesus College Record*, 1965.

Thompson, P. *William Butterfield*, London 1971.

Truman, C. *Sotheby's Concise Encyclopedia of Silver*, London 1993.

Turner, E. 'Post-war Silver' in Truman, C. 1993, pp. 175–185.

Turner, W.H. *Selections from the Records of the City of Oxford 1509–85*, Oxford 1880.

Varley, F.J. 'Oriel College Plate', *Oriel Record*, vol. 3, 1920, pp. 170–2.

Varley, F.J. *The Siege of Oxford*, Oxford 1932.

Wainwright, C. *The Romantic Interior. The British collector at home 1750–1850*, London and New Haven 1993.

Wallis, R.R. *Treasures of the 20th Century. Silver, jewellery and art medals from the 20th century collection of the Worshipful Company of Goldsmiths*, London 2000.

Wardle, P. *Victorian Silver and Silver-Plate*, London 1963.

Watts, W.W. *Catalogue of Pastoral Staves*, London 1924.

Watts, W.W. *Catalogue of a loan exhibition of silver plate belonging to the Colleges of the University of Oxford*, Oxford 1928.

Watts, W.W. 'An exhibition of silver belonging to the colleges of Oxford', *Burlington Magazine*, 1928, vol. 53, pp. 220–6.

Willis-Bund, F.L.M. 'The College Silver' in H.W.C. Davis, *A History of Balliol College*, Oxford 1963, Appendix II, pp. 285–300.

Wilson, B. 'A Gentle History of the Silver collection [at Pembroke College]', [typescript] 2004.

Wilson, C.A. '*The Appetite and the Eye' Visual aspects of food and its presentation within their historic context*, Edinburgh 1991.

Wilson, T. 'Spoons with a taste of history', *The British Museum Society Bulletin*, no. 46, July 1984, pp. 24–26.

Wood, A. *Historia et Antiquitates Universitatis Oxoniensis*, 2 vols, Oxford 1674.

Woodforde, J. *The Diary of a Country Parson 1758–1802*, Oxford 1978.

# NOTES

1 Catalogue of the Exhibition at the University Office Oxford, 10 January–28 February 1977.

2 Oxford University Archives, Bodleian Library, Liber Computi, WB/21/4, Vice Chancellor 1547–1666.

3 Crighton 1975.

4 For example see Clifford 1997, pp. 4–10.

5 See Campbell 2002, p. 141, Appendix I 'Exhibitions and Studies of College Collections'.

6 Followed by Jones 1910.

7 Watts 1928, and reviews: A. Shirley 'Oxford College Silver: the exhibition at the Ashmolean', *Country Life*, vol. 64, 1928, pp. 573–6; Watts 1928.

8 Christ Church College Archives, Disbursements, p. 91.

9 *Walpole Society*, vol. XXX, 1955, p. 85.

10 Gervase Jackson-Stops, 'The Building of the Medieval College', in Buxton & Williams 1979, pp. 180–2.

11 Martin 1877, p. 1.

12 Jesus College Archives, Foundation Register, 1602–24, 1625.

13 St John's College Archives, ACC VI.A.Z/F3.17.

14 St John's College Archives, ACC.VI.A.1.

15 Quoted in W.A. Young *The Siver and Sheffield Plate Collector. A Guide to English Domesic Metal Work in Old Silver and Old Sheffield Plate*, London, n.d., p. 55.

16 Merton College Archives, Subwarden's Rolls, 1277, 3964a.

17 Queen's College Archives, Compoti 1340, 453/1 (index).

18 Lincoln College Archives, Compoti 1456, SR.1.

19 Magdalen College Archives, Engrossed Accounts, 1481, LCD/1.

20 Corpus Christi College Archives C/1/1/1 (begins 1521) to C/1/1/20 (ends 1866). Duncan 1986, pp. 574–596.

21 Magdalen College Archives, CP2/28 p.bv.

22 St John's College Archives, ACC.VI.A.1.

23 New College Archives, Long Book, p. 1, 4219.

24 New College Archives, Vouchers, 11,405 (1807–1808).

25 Campbell 2000, p. 125.

26 Sylvester & Harding 1962, p. 21.

27 E.G.W. Bill, *A Catalogue of Treasury Books*, 1955, and Dpiv.b.2.

28 My thanks to Timothy Schroder for information about Katherine's personal emblem.

29 Groos 1981, p. 135.

30 Oriel College Archives, Transcript of the 1596 Inventory, ETC A8/12.

31 Campbell. 2000, p. 179.

32 Corpus Christi College Archives, Tower Book, C/7/2.

33 Alexander & Binski, 1987, no.640, and Scarisbrick 1990.

34 Lowth p. 256.

35 Impey 1977, p. 54.

36 Campbell in Marks & Williamson 2003, p. 318.

37 Christ Church Archives, Bursar's Book, 1601–2.

38 New College Archives, ref 5526.

39 I am extremely grateful to Brian Wilson for finding this reference in the Pembroke Archives, 47/1/2b, listed against 'Pagget' in an 'Old List (Chandler)' written in ink, and with a remark in pencil 'The list seems to be about 1716 from Dr Hall's papers in the Library cupboard' which I found in the 'Pembroke College Plate List 1873'.

40 Staffordshire Record Office, D603/K/3/4.

41 Lincoln College Archives, 10/22.

42 Hiscock 1946, p. 139, fig.52.

43 Glanville 1990, p. 111.

44 Jones 1904, p. 94.

45 Aylmer 1995, p. 69 quoting from J.H. Hakewill, *The Builder*, vol. 38, 1880, being his father's memoranda of 1814.

46 From the first *Report of the Committee for Managing the Patriotic Fund*, London, 1 March 1804, p. 1, quoted in Southwick 1990, p. 27.

47 'Inventories from the Old Plate Book', *Brasenose Quatercentenary Monographs*, Appendix V.

48 Hertford College Archives, 4/1/1, letter undated, early 19th century.

49 Oriel College Archives, SMH 2 E1.

50 Exeter College Archives, Folio: Silver 1954–1967, correspondence.

51 Balliol College Archives, Plate Record 2, p. 11.

52 Quoted by Brian Wilson in 'A Gentle History of the Silver Collection [at Pembroke College], ms, 2003.

53 St John's College Archives, XC,1, p. 116.

54 Morris 1989, p. 95.

55 St John's College Archives, 'Plate Acct about 1623', XC.9.

56 Balliol College Archives, Plate Record 2.

57 New College Archives, 1954, six inventories, this one headed 'plate wantinge'.

58 Balliol College Archives Plate 1, 'Plate 14 Nov: 1598', F.12.28.

59 Balliol College Archives, Plate 1, 'Given to the King in the Year 1642, F.12.28.

60 New College Archives, 4212, 'A Note of Plate delivered to the Butlers Jan: 13, 1657'.

61 Brasenose College Archives, B1d.3.

62 Brasenose College Archives, Receipts, 49, 1737–8.

63 Morris 1989, p. 165.

64 Queen's College Liber Albus Benefactorum begun 1650; Jesus College Benefaction Book 1650–1758 (B.7.13); Corpus Christi Benefactors Book 1660–1805 (B/1/11); New College Liber Benefactorum begun 1679 (3531); Pembroke College Liber Benefactorum 1694–1807 (39/1/1); University College Benefactors Book begun 1694; Trinity Catalogus Benefactorum begun 1698 (A3); Oriel College 1764–1813 [St MaryHall] 1775 (SMH I A1); Exeter College Benefactor's Book begun early 18th c. (C.II.1). At New College John Field's account survives for 'Writing New College Benefaction Book for the Year 1719 For one Large Benefaction 3s, For Six small ones 3s'. Oriel College paid Robert Stratford, on 16 October 1775 for 'entering 58 benefactions at 2s each-£7 5s' and '5 ditto with large Initial Letters & Decorations at 3s each-15s'.

65 Lincoln College Archives, Calculus 1676.

66 Exeter College Archives, Computus A.III.2

67 Corpus Christi College Archives, B11./1.1. Benefactors Book 1660–1805.

68 Queen's College Archives, Library Accounts, rebound 1828.

69 University of Oxford Archives, HYP/B/.11–13/D–F.

70 University of Oxford Archives, HYP/B/10/38.

71 University of Oxford Archives, HYPB/20.

72 University of Oxford Archives, HYP/B/11/Br–C.

73 C.W. Boase, *Registrum Collegii Exoniensis*, 1894, p. xlii.

74 University of Oxford Archives, University Chest, Plate Pledged, 1557–1576, WPA10/3/, 2&3.

75 University of Oxford Archives, WPA10(3),p. 6.

76 Bede 1982, p. 18 & p. 61, p. 65.

77 Aylmer 1995, p. 14 quoting from L. Crosby, F. Aydelotte & A.C. Valentine, *Oxford of Today. A Manual for Prospective Rhodes Scholars*, Oxford 1927.

78 Campbell 2000, p. 129.

79 Green 1979, p. 24.

80 New College Archives, 16; 12,429, Reg. Evident, 1, p. 186, in Latin.

81 Campbell in Marks & Williamson 2003, p. 242.

82 Schroder in Marks & Williamson 2003, cat.no.106, pp. 242–3.

83 Stevenson & Salter 1939, see appendix XXVII.

84 Hibbert & Hibbert. 1992, p. 13.

85 Trinity College Archives, 'Grant of Chapel Plate from the Founder', vellum sheet with seal), C/1.

86 Trinity College Archives, 'An Indenture declaring plate and stuff of the founder the second tyme January 20, 1557', C/3 .

87 Gilchrist 1967, p. 19.

88 Wood 1674, p. 98.

89 Francis Peck, *Desiderata Curiosa*, London 1735, vol. 11, p. 33.

90 Fowler 1893, p. 111.

91 Exeter College Archives, 'Ex Fundatore Colegi Exoniensis', C.II.1, Edmund Strafford.

92 Queen's College Archives, Library Account, p. 237, 23 December 1637.

93 Exeter College Archives, Liber Implementorum, 1623, C.II.4.

94 Magdalen College Archives, 14 January 1659, CP2/32.

95 Davies 1972, p. 112.

96 St John's College Archives, XC.6 1759.

97 'The Cathedral Plate', *The Friends of Christ Church Cathedral*, September 1966, p. 9.

98 New College Archives, 11,380 (1740–41).

99 Quoted in Gilchrist 1967, pp. 77–8.

100 Bury 1967, including the chalice at St George's Cathedral Suffolk (1847), St Michael, Withyham, Sussex (1849) and another now in the Victoria and Albert Museum of the same date for St Barnabas, Pimlico (1850).

101 Bury 1967, catalogue no. B5. The St George's chalice appears in the Hardman ledger, entry dated June 30, 1848. The chalice and matching paten cost £35 12s. The purchaser was the Reverend Thomas Doyle, who was largely responsible for seeing through Pugin's designs for the building of St George's (1839–1848).

102 I am grateful to Ian Miller for sharing his research on Barkentin & Krall with me, and look forward to his forthcoming publication on them in the *Silver Society Journal*, part of a proposed post-graduate research project.

103 Peter Doll, 'The [Pembroke College] Chapel Fabric' [type-script], kindly lent to me by Ian Miller.

104 Mordaunt Crook 1981, p. 17, cat.no.A.5.

105 Trinity College Archives, Benefaction Book, 1890, p. 20 lists an altar cross, 1890, 'executed by Messrs Barkentin & Krall of London was presented to the College Chapel by the folowing members of College' and therefollows a list of 89 names.

106 New College Archives, 9032, Statement of Repairs, 27 June 1907, see further Clifford, 1997, p. 49.

107 College Inventory, 351, see Macleane, *A History of Pembroke College*, Oxford 1897.

108 From *Manchester College, Oxford Proceedings and Addresses on the occasion of the Opening of the College Buildings and Dedication of the Chapel, 18–19 October 1893*, London 1894.

109 From *Manchester College A Short History 1786–1990*, Oxford 1989.

110 See further D.W. Jackson, *Balliol College Record*, 1980, pp. 74–8.

111 Lincoln Cathedral Treasury, which opened in 1960 was the first open treasury ever to be provided in an English cathedral church, it was designed by the architect goldsmiths Louuis Osman in 1960.

112 Lady Margaret Hall Archives, Gift Book 1878. p. 9.

113 See Clifford 2000/2001, pp. 20–24.

114 Smith 1949.

115 From *The Faber Book of English History*, 1989, p. 173.

116 Glanville 1990, p. 125.

117 Mayhew 1999, p. 236.

118 Hiscock 1946, pp. 137–8.

119 Morris 1989, p. 85.

120 *Brasenose Quatercentenary Monograph*, vol. 5, 1909, p. 7.

121 Jesus College Archives, B:3:Pl, a loose sheet from the Foundation Register.

122 Mayhew 1999, p. 236.

123 Exeter College Archives, a small leather bound book, entitled 'College Plate', C.II.9.

124 Glanville. 1990.

125 Corpus Christi Archives, B/4/3/2 Register, p. 70, memorandum 21 October 1653.

126 With thanks to Brian Wilson for this information, from his then unpublished 'A Gentle History of the Silver Collection', [typescript].

127 Jesus College Cambridge Archives, Treasury Book, AC.6.3, memorandum 'that these peeces of Plate following were taken up out of the masters Orchyard where they were hid', includes a pair of flagons, an 'Elimosinary Dish', a chalice and cup, gilt, a two eared pot, two stoops, two bowls, three cans, four more stoops, a pot, four flat wine bowls, two dozen of 'cutt' spoons, a salt, two trencher salts and 'one bigge salt without a name'.

128 New College Archives, 4219, Long Book 1664.

129 St John's College Archives, XC.9.30.

130 Corpus Christi College Cambridge Archives, MS 624 A.

131 Hayward 1976.

132 Hayward 1976.

133 Jesus College Oxford, Computus, 1643, p. 134.

134 New College Archives, 5526, f.9.

135 Macray 1904, vol. IV, p. 20, noe of 22 January 1663.

136 Brasenose College Archives, B.53.14.

137 Green 1979, pp. 230–1.

138 Brears in Wilson 1991, p. 74, quoting from Caxton, *Eneydos*, 1490, 'made trenchers of brede for to putte theyr mete upon'. Wooden trenchers were already in use on the Earl of Northumberland's table in 1512, while Sir William Petre purchased three dozen for 18d for Ingatestone Hall in Essex in 1561.

139 Stovin 1999, p. 51.

140 Aylmer 1995, p. 25 quoting G.J. Cowley-Brown, 'Christ Church, Oxford, Sixty Years Ago', *Oxford Magazine*, 1915.

141 Morris 1989, p. 66.

142 Morris 1989, p. 66–7, quoting Nicholas Fitzherbert, *Oxoniensis in Anglia Academia Desccriptio*, 1602.

143 St John's College Archives, XC.9.30.

144 Aylmer 1995, p. 50 quoting from Sir William Hayter, *Spooner A Biography*, 1977.

145 Lincoln College Archives, Bursar's Day Book.

146 Brasenose College Archives, B1d1, 'An Account of Plate belonging to Brazen Nose College 1761'.

147 Madan 1909, p. III.

148 Lincoln College Archvies, Calculus 1784–5.

149 *Jackson's Oxford Journal*, 1780, Thursday 27 January, 1397, iii.

150 Brasenose College Archives, B.53.14.

151 Queen's College Archives, Library Accounts, re-bound 1828.

152 Brasenose College Archives, B.1.d.2, An Account of Plate belonging to Brasen Nose Coll.', 1809 with later amendments.

153 Pembroke College Archives, 4/5/1 'An Account of Money Received for Plate, 1759–1772', p. 61.

154 Hibbert and Hibbert, 1992, p. 72, at Pembroke in 1772 caution money was fixed as follows: gentlemen-commoners £24, commoners £12, scholars 10, battlers £6, servitors £4.

155 Magdalen College Archives, Bursar's Day Book, B.I.16, 1623.

156 Christ Church Archives, College Plate Book 1679, xlv.b.1a

157 Glanville 1988, p. 3.

158 Highfield 1964, p. 61.

159 Tim Schroder kindly mentioned this aspect of the history of the salt which he is currently working on.

160 Glanville. 1990, p. 29.

161 Hunt, *Exemplars of Tudor Architecture adapted to modern habitation with illustrative details selected from Ancient Edifices*, London 1830, p. 132.

162 New College Archives, Bursar's Accounts, 4194 (1619).

163 A similar salt of the same date, with a figure of Lucretia was sold in 1945, see *Antiques Review*, XI, December 1952–February 1953, p. 15.

164 E.A. Alcorn, *English Silver in the Museum of Fine Arts, Boston, vol. 1, Silver before 1697*, Boston, 1993, cat.no.10, pp. 58–60.

165 Magdalen College Archives, Estates Papers 144/39, Letter from Dale to Yerbury concerning attempts to replace pawned plate'.

166 Magdalen College Archives, 'A note of all the Plate, 1580 with later additions, CS/1/1.

167 Oriel College Archives, transcription of 1596 inventory, ETC A8/12.

168 Green 1979, p. 26, Wynslaw the pewterer mended it in 1506, again in 1517, and a new one was purchased in 1525.

169 G. Bernard Hughes, 'Old Pewter Spoons, *Country Life*, 26 November 1953, p. 1728.

170 David Mitchell, 'The Clerk's View', in P. Brown, 2001, p. 25.

171 St John's College Archives, 'Money, Plate and Muniments taken out of the Tower 1562–1648', ACC VI A 1.

172 Magdalen College Archives, Libri Computi, p. 74, LCD/2 1582–1614.

173 Christ Church Archives, Disbursements, p. 91 xii.b.1.

174 Hope. 1887.

175 Magdalen College Archives, CP2/27.

176 Marks & Williamson, 2003, p. 236, cat.no.102.

177 N. Pevsner, *Buildings of England, Oxfordshire*, London 1959, p. 138.

178 Jesus College Archives, Shelf 18, Foundation Register 1602–24, p. 25, no.47.

179 Lightbown 1978, pp. 63–4, and plate LIV.

180 Campbell 2003, p. 239, cat.no.101.

181 I would like to thank Timothy Schroder for this reference.

182 Mellor 1997.

183 Quoted in G. Bernard Hughes, 'The Brilliance of Tigerware', *Country Life*, 23 October 1969, p. 1049.

184 Quoted in G. Bernard Hughes, 'Old English Silver Beakers', *Country Life*, 9 August 1956, p. 293.

185 University College Archives. 'Indenture made xxvii day of November Nicholas Metcalfe Clarke Master of the College', [1525] D.57.158

186 Hayward 1983, pl. 6 and 7, quoted in Glanville 1987, p. 47.

187 St John's College Archives, XC.9.30.

188 Jesus College Archives, Shelf 17.

189 Magdalen College Archives, 'A full and perfect inventorie of all manner of moveable utensills, furnitures of tooes and other particulars of household stuff in the President's Lodgings Octob.16 1667', CP2/37.

190 Brown 2001, p. 46.

191 Green 1979, pp. 218–9.

192 G. Bernard Hughes, 'Silver Tumblers and travelling Sets', *Country Life*, 10 November 1955, p. 1084.

193 Wadham College Archives, 'Wadham College Plate Dec 6 1790', 13A/2.

194 Oriel College Archives, [Inventory taken by the Bursars] John Horne & Charles Tooker 1623.

195 Jones 1944, p. 46, pl.17.

196 Aylmer 1995, p. 81.

197 Lincoln College Archives, Bursars Day Book 1778–9.

198 Brasenose College Archives, B.53.14.

199 Oriel College Archives, SMH, Catalogue of Plate.

200 St John's College Archives, Accounts, ACC.V.B.

201 Now in the possession of the Walker Art Gallery, Liverpool.

202 Corpus Christi College Archives, 'An Account ot the College Goods in the Presidents Lodgings 1720', H3/1/4.

203 Donohoe 2002, p. 126–7.

204 Aylmer 1995, p. 29.

205 Brasenose College Archives, PCR 114 B.1.b.

206 Macleane 1897, p. 486 with thanks to Brian Wilson for drawing my attention to this.

207 *Brasenose Quatercentary Monographs*, Monograph V, 'Inventories from the Old Plate Book', p. 15.

208 *Brasenose Quatercentary Monographs*, Monograph V, 'Inventories from the Old Plate Book', p. 19, 1594.

209 Christ Church Archives, indenture 1849, Ms Estate 125.5, item 15.

210 Brasenose College Archives, 'An Account of Plate belonging to Brasen Nose College', B1d5.

211 See Wilson 2004, [typescript].

212 I would like to thank Prof. Toby Barnard for drawing my attention to 'Henry Bly SCR Butler, Hertford College', *The Isis*, 27 November 1946.

213 New College Archives, 5526, p. 35.

214 Silver was measured from 1527 in troy weight, and when in 1878 Avoirdupois was introduced, Troy remained for silver.

215 Trinity College Archives, Plate 2, begins 1778 and checked to 1818.

216 New College Archives, 5526.

217 Brasenose College Archives, A.2.46, p. 8.

218 New College Archives 4260, Long Book 1720.

219 Lincoln College Archives, Calculus 1675.

220 Lincoln College Archives, Calculus 1696.

221 Magdalen College Archives, MS904 c. 1947.

222 Jesus College Archives, Shelf 18, Foundation Register 1602–24, p. 26.

223 Corpus Christi College Archives, h3/1/3.

224 Exeter College Archives, B.I.16 Bursars's Day Book 1613–1630.

225 1980, p. 175.

226 Matthew Boulton Papers, Birmingham City Archives, MBP 140, Letter book G, p. 830, 15 February 1777.

227 Beeton (1859–61), 1985 p. 995.

228 Christ Church Archives, Ch.CH.MS.xii.b.2a.

229 Brasenose College Archives, Receipts, 1829, 657.

230 New College Archives, Vouchers 11, 408.

231 New College Archives, 2440, 12 December 1660.

232 Jones 1944, p. 24.

233 New College Archives, Vouchers 3312.

234 Wadham College Archives, 13/A/2.

235 *Brasenose Quatercentenary Monographs*, Monograph V, p. 21, Mrs Joyce Frankland was the widowed daughter of Robert Trappes, late of the City of London goldsmith and the gift of William Saxye her son by her last will and testament.

236 Christ Church Archives, MS.xii.b.74, 1630–31.

237 Magdalen College Archives, Libri Computi, LCD/4 1648–97.

238 New College Archives, Long Book 1702, 4241.

239 New College Archives, Long Book 1715, 4255.

240 Lincoln Colllege Archives, Computus, 1644.

241 St Edmund Hall Archives, Green Folder of Correspondence, p. 337.

242 Pembroke College Archives 1805–1863, p. 93v.

243 Balliol College Archives, Plate Record 23a.

244 Balliol College Archives, Plate Record 12, p. 4.

245 Balliol College Archives, Plate Record 23

246 If we look at the College account books however, the sum was in fact £150.

247 Oman, 1979, p. 45.

248 Pembroke College Archives, Bursar's Accounts, p. 69, 4/3/3.

249 Pembroke College Archives, Bursar's Accounts, p. 109, 4/3/3/.

250 Brasenose College Archives, Receipt 63.

251 Woodforde 1978, p. 446.

252 New College Archives, Vouchers, 11,402 (1798–1800).

253 Jesus College Archives, Bursar's Books. 1738–9 'To Mr Vertue for engraving a Plate from Dr Hugh Price's Picture £21'.

254 See further Culme 1987, vol. 1, pp. xvi–xxxvi.

255 Wainwright 1989, p. 270.

256 Clifford 1997, p. 48.

257 Carter 1780–94, vol. 1, p. 24.

258 Watts 1924, p. 15, see also Watts's notes New College Archvies, 2835–2839.

259 Exeter College Archives, Computus Rectoris, A.II.12.

260 Exeter College Archives, Computus Rectoris A.II.12.

261 Charles Nash, *The Goodrich Court Guide*, 1845, quoted by Wainwright 1989, p. 268.

262 Jones 1945, addendum added by F.J. Varley, pp. 95 'the Founder's Cup was made by a London goldsmith to the order of the College in or about 1493 and was paid for out of corporate funds', abjuring 'the French heresy' followed by Cripps and others. Eric Smith, is at this moment researching the Cup.

263 Bede 1982, p. 203.

264 Victoria and Albert Museum Registry Papers, Elkington & Co., Minute Paper, T.19579/06.

265 Stone 1961, p. 145.

266 Culme 1987, p. xxxi.

267 Wadham College Archives, 13A/7.

268 Jones 1938, p. 73.

269 New College Archives, 'Account of Restoration of Wykeham's Staff', June 27, 1907, 9032.

270 Hope 1907, pp. 465–92.

271 Clifford Smith 1949, pp. 42–44

272 Letter from Canon Peter Hawker, 9 November 1994.

273 Wallis 2000, p. 31.

274 Hughes 1965, p. 3.

275 I am greatly indebted to Brian Wilson for the following facts on Crompton, a fascinating character who deserves further research.

276 Wilson 2003, ms, p. 11.

277 *Catalogue of the Exhibition of Oxford University Regalia* organized by the University Marshall, 10 January–28 February 1977, section 8.

278 Magdalen College Archives, loose sheet, CP2/34.

279 Balliol College Archives, Plate 23a, 1940–48.

280 Turner in Truman 1993, p. 180.

281 Hughes 1953, p. 1610.

282 Borthwick Institute, York, Halifax A4.410.1/74, May 1953 'notes made for GR Hughes from Speech at opening of Oxford exhibition'.

283 Buck 1998, pp. 103–5.

284 See further *Retrospective Alex Styles*, Goldsmiths' Company Exhibition catalogue, 1987.

285 Pevsner 1975, p. 240.

# INDEX

# LIST OF LENDERS

Warden and Fellows of All Souls College, Oxford 4–6, 26, 30

Balliol College, Oxford 42, 56, 92, 93, 99

On loan by kind permission of the Principal and Scholars of the King's Hall and College of Brasenose, Oxford 12, 39, 83, 94, 100, 114, 148

Dean and Canons of Christ Church, Oxford 50

Governing Body of Christ Church, Oxford 71, 170

By permission of the President and Fellows of Corpus Christi College, Oxford 8–10, 13, 21–2, 27–8, 68, 116, 118, 142, 145

On loan from Exeter College, Oxford 15, 40, 51, 58, 63, 110, 121

Courtesy of Green College, Oxford 127–8

Principal and Fellows of Hertford College, Oxford 55, 109, 168

Principal and Fellows of Jesus College, Oxford 64, 79, 86

Warden and Scholars of Keble College, Oxford 96, 113

On loan from Rod Kelly M.A. (RCA), Goldsmith Silversmith 161–2

Lady Margaret Hall 119

By permission of the Rector and Fellows of Lincoln College, Oxford 120, 146

The President and Fellows of Magdalen College, Oxford 19, 24, 35, 49, 66, 72, 85, 95

Merton College, Oxford 37, 52, 57, 62, 73, 117

Courtesy of the Victoria and Albert Museum and the Museum of Oxford 138–40

With permission of the Warden and Scholars of New College, Oxford 3, 7, 11, 16–18, 20, 23, 61, 129–30, 133, 137, 140, 143–4, 147, 152–3, 157–9, 166

Nuffield College, Oxford 125

Oriel College, Oxford 2, 14, 60, 82, 167

Lent by Payne and Son, Oxford 107, 151

Master and Fellows of Pembroke College, Oxford 32, 34, 75, 77–8, 105–6, 132, 136, 150, 165

The Provost and Scholars, the Queen's College, Oxford 1, 53, 59, 69, 76, 81, 89, 91, 103–4, 108, 112

By kind permission of St Anne's College, Oxford 111

The Master and Fellows of St Catherine's College, Oxford 123–4, 131

By kind permission of the Master and Fellows of St Cross College, Oxford 134–5, 163–4

St Edmund Hall, Oxford 115

St Hilda's College, Oxford 98

St John's College, Oxford 38, 43, 65, 88, 156

St Peter's College, Oxford 46–8, 90, 97

By kind permission of the President and Fellows of Trinity College, Oxford 25, 29, 31, 74, 122, 149

University College, Oxford 80

Loan by Wadham College, Oxford 33, 41, 54, 84, 141

Private Collection 160

Wolfson College, Oxford 126

The Provost and Fellows of Worcester College, Oxford 101–2